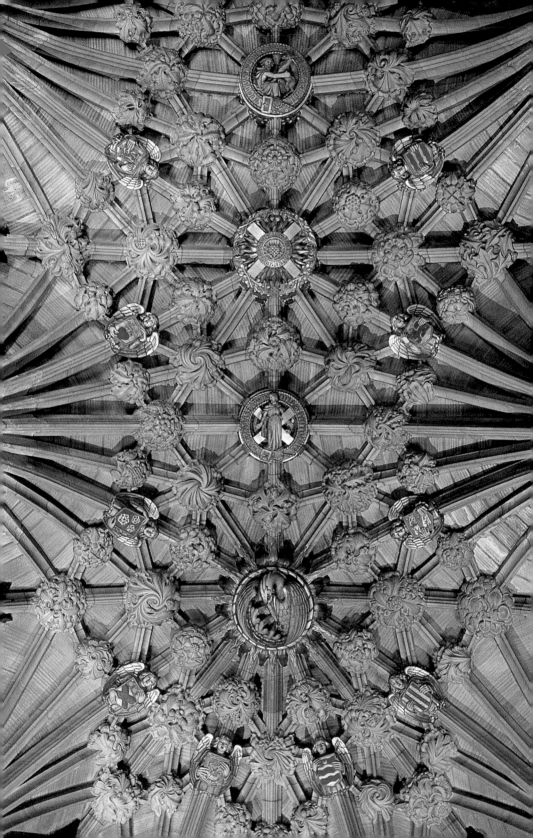

INSIGHT GUIDES

The world's largest collection of visual travel guides

EDINBURGH

Edited and Produced by Brian Bell
Photography by Douglas Corrance
Editorial Director: Brian Bell

Discovery CHANNEL

APA PUBLICATIONS
Part of the Langenscheidt Publishing Group
L

INSIGHT GUIDES
EDINBURGH

CONTACTING THE EDITORS: Although every effort is made to provide accurate information in this publication, we live in a fast-changing world and would appreciate it if readers would call our attention to any errors or outdated information that may occur by writing to us at Apa Publications,
P.O. Box 7910, London SE1 8ZB, England.
Fax: (44) 171-620-1074.
e-mail: insight@apaguide.demon.co.uk.

First Edition 1993
Second Edition (updated) 1999

Distributed in the United States by
Langenscheidt Publishers Inc.
46–35 54th Road
Maspeth, NY 11378
Fax: (718) 784 0640

Distributed in the UK & Ireland by
GeoCenter International Ltd
The Viables Centre, Harrow Way
Basingstoke, Hampshire RG22 4BJ
Fax: (44) 1256-817988

Distributed in Australia & New Zealand by
Hema Maps Pty. Ltd
24 Allgas Street, Slacks Creek 4127
Brisbane, Australia
Tel: (61) 7 3290 0322
Fax: (61) 7 3290 0478

Worldwide distribution enquiries:
APA Publications GmbH & Co. Verlag KG
(Singapore branch)
38 Joo Koon Road, Singapore 628990
Tel: 65-8651600
Fax: 65-8616438

Printed in Singapore by
Insight Print Services (Pte) Ltd
38 Joo Koon Road
Singapore 628990
Fax: 65-8616438

This guidebook combines the interests and enthusiasms of two of the world's best known information providers: Insight Guides, whose range of titles has set the standard for visual travel guides since 1970, and Discovery Channel, the world's premier source of nonfiction television programming.

The editors of Insight Guides provide both practical advice and general understanding about a destination's history, culture, institutions and people. Discovery Channel and its Web site, www.discovery.com, help millions of viewers explore their world from the comfort of their own home and also encourage them to explore it firsthand.

The structure of this book was planned in the Old Bailey, London's Central Criminal Court. In the visitors' cafeteria, project editor **Brian Bell**, who was standing by to serve as a juror, occupied his time by sketching out a synopsis for *Edinburgh*, his sixth guidebook for Apa. As a London-based journalist with wide experience in newspapers and magazines, Bell was first attracted by Apa's approach to travel guides because it combined detailed reporting about what makes a place tick with a bold, photo-journalistic style of illustration. In a crowded publishing market, he believes, too many guidebooks content themselves with anodyne prose and picture-postcard photography; yet a city's warts can often be as interesting as its beauty spots. It would be an incurious tourist indeed, for instance, who wouldn't be fascinated to learn why a prim place such as Edinburgh has the highest incidence of Aids *per capita* of any city in Europe.

Fortunately, it was a slow week at the Old Bailey and, Bell's services not being needed by the judicial process, he begin seeking out writers and photographers who would turn his ideas into a book. Having edited *Insight Guide: Scotland*, his first call was on three stalwarts of that guide, Julie Davidson, George Rosie and Douglas Corrance.

Julie Davidson, who wrote half of the "Places" section, contributes to *The Scotsman*, Britain's national newspapers and magazines

Bell

Davidson

Massie

and frequently analyses the nation's media for the television programme *What the Papers Say*. She finds it hard to imagine living anywhere other than in Edinburgh ("well, perhaps, France or Italy for four months of the year"). She has mixed feelings about the impact tourism has made on Scotland generally and the manner in which it can falsify the country's history into easily digestible myths.

George Rosie, who wrote the remainder of the "Places" section, is another of Scotland's leading journalists. Like more than one critic, Rosie regards the fable of *Dr Jekyll and Mr Hyde* – whose author, Robert Louis Stevenson, was an Edinburgh man – as a handy metaphor for the city. "Behind the amiable and rational intelligence of Dr Henry Jekyll," he says, "stands the cold glare of Edward Hyde. Yet for all its shy duality and shifty ways, Edinburgh remains one of the most beautiful and amenable cities in Europe."

Douglas Corrance started his career on a local Inverness paper and has since built up an international reputation as one of Scotland's top photographers. Wherever his assignment, he enjoys coming back to Edinburgh because it's such a restful place. Unlike most cities, it has retained a large amount of residential accommodation in its centre, and unlike most tourist destinations, it has coped well with its visiting hordes. "People become part of this city very easily," says Corrance. "Although I live close to the city centre, I never feel oppressed by tourists, the way I do in Paris or London. And the constantly changing light is very attractive to a photographer. Although I have photographed the same places many times, they are always different. The weather is an unavoidable issue: when it's bad it's really bad, and when it's good it's great."

W. Gordon Smith, whose contributions include a report on the city's world-famous festival, is a writer, photographer, playwright and songwriter. Being born in Edinburgh, he thinks, is a curse and an affliction because it spoils you for most other places. Indeed it has only two mild disadvantages: "first, you

Morrice

Corrance

Brooke

Smth

couldn't commit adultery here without being found out because you can never walk more than 100 yards without meeting someone you know, and secondly, the east wind makes even the warmest day seem that much colder – you notice people leaning into the wind as they walk, as if they were fishermen."

The wind is also cited as a disadvantage by **Allan Massie**, who wrote the history chapters. He sees Edinburgh as "a city where people tend to live in professional compartments so that university people socialise with university people and lawyers socialise with lawyers. That's why it has been called a city of cliques. It is much maligned – by people who don't live there. The city it most reminds me of is Florence – it has the same kind of feeling that the rest of the world doesn't quite measure up."

Julie Morrice compiled the "Travel Tips" for the first edition. Since moving to Edinburgh from her native Aberdeen, she discovered both the city's faults – "it is two-faced, cautious and indefensibly proud" – and its virtues: "its spiritual shortcomings are compensated for by its sudden beauty on the rare days when the sun shines and by the few remaining pubs which offer good beer and no frills."

Four more Scotsmen complete the line-up. A full low-down on Edinburgh's pubs and the music performed in them was provided by **Alastair Clark**, who has written a music column for *The Scotsman* for more than 20 years. **Conrad Wilson**, who also contributes to *The Scotsman*, is author of the panel on Scottish food. **Brian Morton**, author of the "Literary Edinburgh" chapter and the panel on Sir Walter Scott, is a Scot who moved to London to become literary editor of *The Times Higher Education Supplement*.

Marcus Brooke, a Scot who has spent many years travelling the world with typewriter and camera, thoroughly revised the book for the second edition and **Jane Ladle**, a resident of Edinburgh, provided new information for the "Travel Tips" section at the back of this updated edition.

CONTENTS

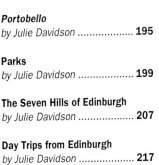

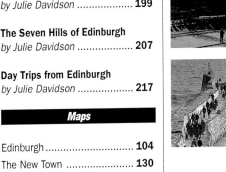

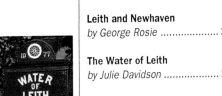

TRAVEL TIPS

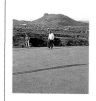

It's been said before, but it's worth repeating: not for nothing was that great parable of the divided self *Dr Jekyll and Mr Hyde* written by an Edinburgh man. Robert Louis Stevenson may have set the story in London, but the character was conjured out of the life of one of Edinburgh's more notorious 18th-century denizens, William Brodie, Deacon of Wrights and Masons.

Like Dr Jekyll, William Brodie was a pillar of society during the day; like Mr Hyde, he was a ruthless villain at night. He ended his days dancing on the end of the Edinburgh hangman's rope, suspended from an "improved" gallows which he himself had designed and built.

Pride and paradoxes: Many have seen Stevenson's famous tale as a handy metaphor for Edinburgh itself: something at once universal and characteristically Scots. Where else does a semi-ramshackle, late-medieval town glower down on such Georgian elegance? What other British city combines such civic pride with intractable drug problems? Which European city (except London) juggles so many billions of pounds, dollars, Deutschmarks and yen, but never has quite enough to keep the streets clean?

Could any other city in Europe stage the world's biggest festival of music and drama for 47 years while refusing to build a decent opera house or even a new theatre? (The gap was finally filled in 1994 with the opening of a magnificent, multipurpose Playhouse.) Edinburgh may be one of Europe's urban jewels, but its setting is some of the bleakest housing estates in the whole of Britain. Yet southern liberals, expecting to find Edinburgh a bastion of Calvinism, are startled that most pubs are open all day, and often into the early hours of the morning.

All of which makes for a kind of psychic confusion in both citizens and visitors. Somehow Edinburgh has acquired a reputation which has little to do with the facts. On the world stage, it is a medium-sized city inhabited with variations on the theme of Muriel Spark's novel *The Prime of Miss Jean Brodie*. A sniffish, cold-hearted kind of place, full of petit bourgeois pretension and intolerance, totally lacking Glasgow's proletarian warmth and urban raffishness. A town of chilly streets stalked by flinty lawyers and hard-eyed ac-

countants. To Glaswegians especially, Edinburgh is a "west endy, east windy" kind of place, "all fur coats and nae drawers (*no underwear*)" as the old jibe goes. "A toon (town) wi' ideas above its station" in the words of one West of Scotland businessman.

None of which Edinburgh folk recognise. In fact, it is hard to trace where the notion of Edinburgh's extreme respectability originated. Possibly it is to do with the fact that Edinburgh houses Scotland's largest middle-class population. Maybe the impression grew out of the 19th-century boom in middle-ranking clerical jobs in banking, insur-

Preceding pages: Edinburgh Castle; St Giles' Kirk; the city by night; Linlithgow Palace; festival frolics; the castle from the air; lamp-maker; swimming the Forth; students. <u>Left</u>, double trouble in George Street. <u>Right</u>, military tradition.

ance and government. Or perhaps, as many Edinburgh people claim, it is simply provincial sour grapes on the part of Glaswegians, Aberdonians, and the rest of Scotland.

But whatever the reasons for Edinburgh's prim reputation, it has not prevented the city racing up the "quality of life" charts. According to one report by a team of academic geographers and market researchers, Edinburgh is *the* best city in Britain in which to live, bar none. Edinburgh, said the report, has more of the good things of life – space, culture, good food, hospitals – than anywhere else. Which came as no surprise to the citizens but was a nasty shock to Glasgow

with Newcastle or Bristol and not nearly as important as Manchester or Birmingham. Edinburgh was a stateless capital, a city with a hole where its Parliament used to be, the pseudo-metropolis of a nearly country.

Much of that dissatisfaction may disappear when the new Scottish Assembly opens for business in the year 2000, giving the Scots a significant degree of authority, including tax-varying powers, over their own affairs. In addition, of course, Edinburgh will remain the focal point of the Scottish legal system, home to the General Assembly (the annual parliament of the Church of Scotland) and Britain's second-biggest fi-

which was placed 25th in the ranking (though that was still nine places ahead of London). The message was clear: Glasgow may be "miles better", as its civic slogan confidently claimed, but it still has a long way to go – especially to catch up with Edinburgh.

But for all that, Edinburgh has been in many ways a vaguely unsatisfactory place, one of Europe's more baffling cities. Until now, it has had the trappings of a capital city without any of the political and constitutional clout. It may have been the centre of things to the Scots, but to the English it was just another middle-ranking provincial centre, on a par

nancial centre. It will certainly wield more power than any British city outside London.

Anyone in Scotland wishing to consult the official records – land titles, government archives, records of births, marriages and deaths – has to come to Edinburgh. Not much relating to Scotland is held in London; Edinburgh has most of it. And the Edinbourgeois are touchy about their role as the guardians of Scotland's historic capital. English incomers looking for a quiet provincial life are often taken aback with the ferocity with which many Scots defend Edinburgh's status. The idea of Edinburgh as a "real" capital like London or Paris or Washington strikes them as remote, even absurd. But Edinburgh is just enough of a capital to give itself a sense of its own importance.

This air of unfulfilled potential which haunts Edinburgh infuriates many, among them the poet Hugh MacDiarmid who wrote: "There is no one really alive in Edinburgh yet/ They are all living at the tiniest fraction of the life they could easily have." MacDiarmid saw the citizens as people living in great houses "who prefer to live in their cellar and keep all the rest sealed up." The Marxist writer Tom Nairn sees Edinburgh's soul as "bible-black, pickled in boredom by centu-

Edward Topham thought that only 18th-century Madrid rivalled Edinburgh for sheer squalor. As late as 1944 the Chinese writer and traveller Chiang Yee found the inhabitants of Edinburgh sociable and garrulous to the point of being alarming. (They kept trying to force whisky down his throat.) For centuries the Edinburgh mob was notorious for its violence and unpredictability. It did, after all, lay down the law to the City Magistrates, and it did once hunt down the Captain of the City Guard (the equivalent of the Chief Constable) and lynch him from a barber's pole in the Grassmarket. While this kind of turbulence no longer plagues Edin-

ries of sermons, swaddled in the shabby gentility of the Kirk (church)."

This notion of Edinburgh as a nirvana of the pious and the genteel is a fairly modern one. The 17th-century English traveller Sir William Brereton found Edinburgh folk a "most sluttish, nasty and slothful people". Daniel Defoe said that "the nastiness of this place" could not be denied. Edward Burt asked providence "for which of my Sins I have been sent to this country". Captain

burgh, the city still has two of the busiest police stations in Britain (Drylaw and Craigmillar) and late-night discos and pubs have a way of erupting into the kind of aggravation that takes dozens of police and dogs to quell.

This undertow of Edinburgh nastiness was well captured by the poet and playwright Donald Campbell who wrote: "In the Morningside chippie/ I was confrontit by nae feugher than ten/ o the reuchest and the teuchest/ o yer haurdest-haurd men/and (O Gode!) How I wished I was in Glasgow".

Even the archetypal Miss Jean Brodie has been much misrepresented. Muriel Spark

Left, formality in the Assembly Rooms. **Above**, informality on the streets.

makes it plain that Miss Brodie and her ilk were ladies of some complexity. "There were legions of her kind during the 1930s," she wrote, "women from the age of thirty and upward, who crowded their war-bereaved spinsterhood with voyages of 'discovery' into new ideas and energetic practices in art, social welfare, education or religion." And Italian Fascism, Miss Brodie's predilection, was just one such "new idea".

Edinburgh has, of course, produced more than its share of great philosophers, writers, doctors, lawyers and divines. But for a city which is so supposedly straight-laced it has also given the world some colourful talent;

the TV comedian Ronnie Corbett, the film actor Alistair Sim, the former world lightweight boxing champion Ken Buchanan, TV presenter Magnus Magnusson, the Incredible String band, the Bay City Rollers, and one of Britain's few "bankable" superstars, Sean Connery (one of whose early jobs was driving a horse and cart around the Fountainbridge area for the St Cuthbert's Cooperative Society).

Like most European cities, Edinburgh's texture has been much enriched and enlivened by immigration. Edinburgh is no cultural monolith. There is an intricate overlay of "ethnic" groups throughout Edinburgh, some of whom have been in the city for generations. The biggest is the Irish (who flooded into Edinburgh in the 19th century in the wake of the Great Famine), but there are also lively communities of Poles, Ukranians, Chinese, Norwegians, Sikhs, Jews, Pakistanis and Italians – and, of course, English.

Many of these individuals have made a powerful impact on Edinburgh. The historian David Daiches is Jewish, as is the former Tory Cabinet minister Malcolm Rifkind. Nobody has done more to brighten up Edinburgh's artistic life than the engaging entrepreneur Richard Demarco, whose Italian family came to Scotland to make ice-cream. The Edinburgh Labour Party seems to be run almost entirely by people with Irish names like Milligan and Mulvey.

The truth is that the character of Edinburgh, like that of other European cities, is a bewildering tapestry of subcultures, interests and traditions. Many – perhaps most – have little in common. Where's the community of interest between a Gorgie slaughterhouse worker and a Court of Session judge? Or a Charlotte Square money-shuffler and a Fountainbridge brewery hand? Or a West End management consultant and the deckhand on the Forth Port Authority's sewage barge *Gardyloo*? Or the man who spends his free time playing the bodhran in Sandy Bell's pub, and the Queen's Counsel whispering legal tactics in the New Club? Other than the fact that they both spend their lives on the south bank of the Firth of Forth, what does the financier who spent £500,000 buying a neo-classical palace in the New Town have in common with the drug-wrecked youth in a hovel on a peripheral housing estate?

Edinburgh's capacity to tolerate such contrasts has always shocked visitors. But respectable Edinburgh has long since learned to contemplate the other Edinburgh with the equanimity of Henry Jekyll seeing the face of Edward Hyde in the mirror for the first time. "I was conscious of no repugnance," Dr Jekyll says, "rather of a leap of welcome. This, too, was myself."

Left, a colourful piper at the Castle. **Right**, an antique shop in St Stephen Street.

Robertus dei gracia Rex Scottorum Omnibus probis hominibus totius terre sue ...

... firmasse burgensibus burgi nostri de Edinburgh predictum Burgum sirui de ...

... ganssibus et eorum successoribus de nobis et heredibus nostris libere quiete plenarie et honorifice ...

... Burgum iuste prestare consuebant tempore bone memorie Regis Alexandri predecessoris ...

... foris Quinquaginta duas marcas sterlingorum ad duos terminos Pentecostes et ...

... tenemus apud ... Testibus Valtero de Twynham Cancellario nostro ...

... Gilberto de Haya Constabulario nostro, Roberto de Keth marescallo nostro Scocie ...

... dat̄ vos de Mis ... concessisse et de fac[t]o firmit͛ dimisisse p[er] hac p[re]sentem c[art]am nr̄am con ...

... cont̄ di Petri de Rusi molend[inis] et t̄e[r]ris p[er]tinenc[ijs] suis. Tenend̄ et h[ab]end̄ eisdem bur ...

... p[er] om[n]es Pa[r]tes Mundi et t̄utile suas cū ep̄s t̄ b. f[ir]madic[i]b[us] d[e]b[iti]s a eisdem t[er]ris p[ro] eis dn[ijs] ...

... dn̄o defunct. Et t[en]end̄ ṁ nob̄ et h[er]edib[us] v[r]is B[er]nardin[o] dn̄i Dnrge[n]sis [et] ... dn[ijs] ...

... m[art]ini in h[y]ema p[ro] equal[i] pontc[i]o[n]. In aī v[e]l testimonium p[re]sent[ium] et me d̄ no sigillū apēn p[ro] ...

... Com[ite]s Bordue dn̄o vaillie ... et w[i]ll[el]mo copans n[ost]ri Jacobo dn̄o de Douglas ...

... dn̄ m[ore] militi[bus]. Apud Castres Daffno octauo die m[a]ij L ... o regni n[ost]ri ... G[e]n[er]osno q[ui]b[us]no ...

Robert Bruce sends a defiance to Edward III.

Two early chroniclers of Scottish history, John Stow and Andrew of Wyntoun, asserted that Edinburgh had been established in 989 BC when a mystical (if reputedly much-married) King Ebrauke built a "Mayden Castel" on its famous rock. The first true historical reference to the city comes more than 1,000 years later, in Ptolemy's *Geography* (AD 160); he wrote that the Votadini (Goddodin) inhabited a town called Dunedin in the Forth Valley.

This reference disproves the later claim that the city takes its name from Edwin, King of Northumbria, who conquered the Lothians in AD 638. The resemblance of Edwin's burgh to Edinburgh is mere coincidence, Edinburgh being in reality the anglicised version of the Celtic *Dunedin*.

At that time and for centuries later, the kings of the Scots held their courts further north. It would be premature to talk of a "capital" of their kingdom, but even in the 11th and 12th centuries they were more likely to be found across the Firth of Forth in Dunfermline than in Edinburgh.

However, Malcolm III (known as "Canmore"), who reigned from 1057 to 1093, built a castle in Edinburgh to serve principally as a hunting lodge, and his English wife Margaret (later St Margaret) built the chapel within the castle walls which still bears her name and which is almost certainly the oldest building in the city. It was in the castle that Margaret received news that her husband and eldest son had been killed in battle at Alnwick, and it was there that she herself died three days later.

Her youngest son, David I, king from 1124 until 1153, who "*illumynyd in his dayis/His landys with kirkis and abbayis*", built the Abbey of the Holy Rood (Holy Cross) below Arthur's Seat, the city's volcanic hill supposedly named after the legendary King Arthur; and the Royal Mile is the name still

Preceding pages: the Bruce Charter. **Left,** King Edward III is defied by Robert the Bruce. **Above,** memorial in Edinburgh Castle to William Wallace.

given to the street that runs from the Castle to the Palace later built beside David's abbey. The charter he granted the abbey makes it clear that Edinburgh was already a town sufficiently important to pay tax.

The monks were also granted permission to build another town between the abbey and Edinburgh; and the road linking the two became known as the Canongate. So, from early times, medieval Edinburgh was held between the two poles of Castle and Abbey,

the stronghold and the civilising church.

The Castle, dominating Lothian and commanding the Forth estuary, inevitably came under attack during the English invasions of Scotland. During the Wars of Independence it was held by them from 1295 until it was recaptured in 1314 by Thomas Randolph, Earl of Moray, who scaled the rock in a daring night assault. Randolph was the nephew of Robert the Bruce, whose successful struggle to reach Scotland's throne is remembered in the tale of his inspiration from observing the persistence of a spider weaving a web in a cave on Rathlin Island, off the coast of Ireland, where Bruce was exiled for a year.

When in power, Bruce was so impressed by the ease with which the English could advance on Edinburgh and then dominate the country from the castle, that he demolished it, except for St Margaret's little chapel. Perhaps by way of compensation, he granted Edinburgh a Royal Charter, so that its history as a royal burgh dates from 1329, the last year of the great king's life.

England's aims: By the end of the century the castle had been re-built, though it is one of the curiosities of history that much of its fortification was the work of English armies. They always found the castle more useful as a means of controlling the Lothians than the Scots found it an effective defence.

Enlargement of the enclosed area was made by the English king Edward III. He had previously embarked on great building works at Windsor Castle, near London, and the fortification of Edinburgh imitated Windsor in several respects. Meanwhile, in the late 14th century, after the English had withdrawn, Robert II of Scotland gave the Edinburgh burghers permission to build houses within the castle walls and to pass freely in and out without paying toll.

The castle was never to be a regular royal residence. It was an armoury and a stronghold; the Parliament met there and courts of justice were held in its great hall, but it was not adapted for even that modest degree of domestic comfort: the room where Mary Queen of Scots gave birth to her son James in 1566 is scarcely more than a cupboard. When in Edinburgh, kings generally preferred to reside at the Abbey of the Holy Rood.

Nevertheless, the castle was the setting of one of the nastiest political murders in Scottish history. In 1439 the young William, sixth Earl of Douglas, and his brother David were lured there under promise of safe conduct, seized and summarily beheaded without a trial. This deed was known as the Black Dinner because the signal of the brothers' fate was reputedly given by the bringing in of a black bull's head to the dinner table.

Right, King David II shakes hands with England's Edward III while held captive in the English court.

By the beginning of the 16th century, Edinburgh was established as the capital of Scotland, and the Old Town had assumed its present shape. The Flodden Wall was constructed to defend the city, begun in the alarm that followed the disastrous battle of that name in 1513. It was, however, still unfinished half a century later, and now only a few stretches remain; the best preserved tower is at the Vennel in the West Port above the Grassmarket.

Edinburgh and the Canongate were still separate burghs. St Giles was the High Kirk of the City, a parish church which only became a Cathedral at the order of Charles I in 1633. Though the Royal Mile is properly four streets – Castle Hill, Lawnmarket, High Street and Canongate – it has always impressed people as a unity. In 1636 an English traveller, Sir William Brereton, found it "the glory and beauty of this city...and the longest street that ever I have seen."

It was, however, in a state of continuous change and redevelopment throughout these centuries. Among the oldest buildings in the High Street are John Knox's house, Moubray House and Tweeddale House; they have, of course, been altered over the years, yet all retain their air of antiquity.

So does Moray House in the Canongate, built about 1630 for Mary, Dowager Countess of Home. It was in its Garden Pavilion that the Treaty of Union between Scotland and England was signed in 1707.

Many of the Scots nobility had their houses in the Canongate; others favoured the Cowgate, which runs parallel to the Royal Mile but at a lower level. Cardinal Beaton had his palace there, long since demolished, on the corner with Blackfriar's Wynd, while the Regent Morton's House can still be found, greatly altered, in Blackfriars Street.

Both Cardinal and Regent met violent deaths in the turbulent – indeed revolutionary – 16th century. That century was the last

in which Edinburgh had a resident monarch, even though other royal palaces, Linlithgow and Falkland, might be more favoured. Much of the drama of the brief reign of Mary Queen of Scots was concentrated in Edinburgh.

It was in Holyrood that she argued with the Protestant leader John Knox for her right to practise her own Roman Catholic religion, and it was in Holyrood that she was compelled to witness, while pregnant, the brutal murder of her Italian secretary and confi-

dant, David Rizzio. It was in the castle that her son was born, and in the Provost's house of Kirk o'Field on the outskirts of the city that her second husband, Darnley, was murdered. Within a week, a placard was nailed to the door of the Tolbooth in the High Street, naming the Earl of Bothwell as his murderer, and it was in Edinburgh that he was acquitted of the charge by a court influenced by the armed retainers he had brought with him.

It was, finally, to Edinburgh that Mary returned captive, after her disastrous marriage to Bothwell and the evaporation of their army at Carberry Hill outside Mussel-

Left, memorial to John Knox. **Right,** the death mask of Mary Queen of Scots at Linlithgow.

burgh, to encounter an angry mob shrieking "Burn the hoor (*whore*)". Nothing in Edinburgh's history is quite so moving as its association with the unfortunate queen.

Two thrones: Holyrood saw yet more drama during the reign of her son, James VI: he was besieged there by his mad and dangerous cousin, Francis Stewart, Earl of Bothwell, who was a nephew of Mary's husband. But it was also there that he was awakened on the night of 27 March 1603 by the Englishman Sir Robert Carey who had galloped north from Elizabeth of England's deathbed to hail James as "King of Great Britain, Ireland and France".

Charles I to impose a uniformity of religion on his two kingdoms which aroused fury in Scotland and precipitated the civil wars that provided Edinburgh with some of its most dramatic moments.

In 1633 Charles visited his Scottish capital, bringing with him his new Archbishop of Canterbury, William Laud. They ordered that a new prayer book be used in Scottish churches. This provoked a riot in Edinburgh, set off when one Jenny Geddes threw a stool at the preacher. Subsequently the mob tried to lynch the city's Bishop.

Resistance to the king's innovations grew fiercer, and in 1638 the National Covenant,

The throne of England was a prize which James had long coveted and which he knew could be his because Elizabeth, the Virgin Queen, had no heir. Nine days later he left Edinburgh to take possession of his new inheritance, and neither Scotland nor Edinburgh was ever the same thereafter.

Yet though the kingdoms were united under one man, they remained two independent sovereign states, and Parliament continued to function in Edinburgh. More important still, the city was the regular meeting-place of the General Assembly of the Church of Scotland. It was the attempt by James's son

binding its signatories to defend the Scots form of worship "against all sorts of persons whatsoever", was drawn up; the people flocked to Greyfriars Churchyard to sign it. This led to the Bishop's Wars which secured the independence of the Scots kirk.

In 1641 Charles, alarmed by the opposition now aroused in England also, returned to Edinburgh to attempt to reconcile his native land. It was while playing golf on Leith Links that he received news of the Irish Rebellion; this precipitated the Civil War in England and Scotland which ended in his defeat and execution.

Edinburgh was spared fighting. But in 1650, the year after the king's death, the city was the setting for one of the most memorable and dramatic scenes in Scottish history.

The central figure was the great Marquess of Montrose. He had been one of the first signatories of the Covenant, and prominent in the Bishops' War. But, believing that these wars had secured the liberties of Scotland, and suspicious of the ambitions of the Marquess of Argyll and some of the other Covenanting leaders, he had taken the king's side in the subsequent civil war.

In 1644–45 he had conducted a remarkable campaign which had terrified his Covenanting enemies and made him for a few weeks master of Scotland, until his little army was defeated in Philiphaugh. Five years later he returned to try to win support for Charles II; but he failed in the attempt, and was captured and brought to Edinburgh for execution.

His entry to the city was made by the Watwergait, at the foot of the Canongate. "The street," in the words of his best biographer, John Buchan, "was lined by a great crowd – the dregs of the Edinburgh slums, the retainers of the Covenanting lords, ministers from far and near – all the elements most hostile to the prisoner. But to the amazement of the organisers of the spectacle there was no sign of popular wrath. Rather there was silence, a tense air of sympathy and pity and startled admiration."

As they passed Moray House, Argyll, who was attending a wedding there, looked out, caught Montrose's eye, and turned away. An English soldier cried that "it was no wonder they started aside at his look, for they durst not look him in the face these seven years".

Montrose was taken to the Tolbooth, now a museum, and three days later, was hanged at the Mercat Cross, which stood between the Tolbooth and the Iron Kirk. His body was dismembered and the trunk buried beside the public gallows on the Boroughmuir, on a spot later occupied by the printing-works of the publishers Thomas Nelson & Sons. His head was placed on a spike protruding from the west front of the Tolbooth.

Eleven years later, after the monarchy was restored under Charles II, Montrose's head was replaced by Argyll's. Montrose's remains were then collected to lie in state in the

Left, Robert Herdman's portrait of the execution of Mary Queen of Scots. **Above**, Sir George Harvey's portrait of the Covenanters preaching.

Abbey Kirk of Holyrood, before being interred in St Giles. There are now monuments to both great marquesses there.

Charles II's reign was notable for the reconstruction of Holyrood House, undertaken in 1672 according to the design of Sir William Bruce and carried out by Robert Mylne, the king's master mason. The palace, as it now stands, is their work.

It was occupied for two years by Charles's brother, James, Duke of York (the future James VII of Scotland and II of England), who was sent to govern Scotland during the last Covenanting rebellion of 1679-80. Unfortunate Covenanting prisoners were held

for weeks, in miserable conditions, in the Churchyard of Greyfriars, awaiting transportation to the West Indies.

James also converted the Abbey Church at Holyrood into a chapel for the Knights of the Thistle. This displaced congregation was handsomely housed in the new Canongate Church, designed by James Smith in 1688.

In 1707, after the increasingly stressful experience of the Dual Monarchy, the Scots Parliament was persuaded, with the help of bribes, to vote itself out of existence, and accept the Treaty of Union with England. This was "the end of auld sang (*old song*)".

A new role: Parliament House, which had been built between 1632 and 1639 to serve the double purpose of a Parliament and High Court of Justiciary, was now abandoned to the lawyers alone. The handsome building, as seen today, is the result of extensive remodelling in the early 19th century, which aroused the ire of that lover of old Edinburgh, Lord Cockburn; he wrote that "no one who remembers the old exterior can see the new one without sorrow and indignation". Some of the interiors – in particular Parliament Hall, and the Laigh Hall beneath – retain the original features.

The Union marked the end of one Edinburgh, and the age which succeeded saw the development of a new, richer and more splendid city. There are, however, three interludes in its development which seem properly to belong to the old city, and which therefore deserve a brief mention here.

The first was the Porteous Riot of 1737, a spontaneous and yet disciplined outburst of popular and national feeling. This shook the Government in London, which demolished the Nether Bow Port to make it easier for its troops to enter the city in the event of future rebellions. The best account of the episode is in the opening chapters of Sir Walter Scott's finest novel, *The Heart of Midlothian.*

Eight years later Holyrood House became for a few weeks again a royal palace. Its occupant was Prince Charles Edward, the grandson of James VII and the champion of the exiled line of native kings. He seized the city (but not the castle) with his Highland army, which was quartered in the Queen's Park outside the palace. It was from there that he marched out to defeat the Hanoverian army under Sir John Cope at Prestonpans.

Finally, during the Napoleonic Wars, when many French prisoners were held in the castle, Holyrood was the refuge of the claimant to the French throne, the future Louis XVIII, and his brother the Comte d'Artois; the latter returned there for 18 months in 1830, when as Charles X, he had been driven from his throne by the July Revolution.

<u>Left</u>, today's queen of England (and Scotland) at the Thistle Ceremony. <u>Right</u>, Covenanters being taken to execution during "the killing times".

The 18th century was Edinburgh's Golden Age, when it came to be called "the Athens of the North". It had ceased to be a political capital; instead it became a cultural and intellectual centre of unprecedented influence. It was said that a man could stand by the Mercat Cross and "in a few minutes take 50 men of genius by the hand". The observation was testimony both to the cultural riches of the city and its small size.

Until the middle of the century it was still confined within its late medieval limits – to the Royal Mile, the Cowgate, the Grassmarket, and the closes and wynds running off these streets. In the words of Daniel Defoe, the author of *Robinson Crusoe* and a Government spy who left a full account of the city just before the Union, it stood "on the narrow ridge of a long ascending mountain".

It was a filthy city, for the inhabitants of the tall tenements were accustomed to tip their refuse and filth from their windows, crying "Gardyloo" (a corruption of the French *gardez-vous*) to warn anyone unfortunate enough to be below. But, by its nature, it was also a city still ignorant of the segregation of classes: tradesmen, lords, lawyers, merchants, clerks and labourers might all inhabit the same tenement.

Great expansion: At first, people were most aware of what they had lost by the Union: it was hard to make their grievances heard effectively when the reins of power were held 400 miles away in London. But the benefits of the Union were soon to be experienced in an expanding economy and a new prosperity. Edinburgh at last broke the bounds of the medieval city.

It spread first to the south of the city with the building in 1763–64 of George Square (where Walter Scott would live as a child) and of Buccleuch Place from 1772. Only the west side of the square now survives of the

Preceding pages: a City Halberdier. Left, Raeburn's famous portrayal of the Rev. Robert Walker skating on Duddingston Loch. Right, Charlotte Square.

original design, the other three sides having been barbarously re-developed by the University in the 1960s.

From the middle of the 18th century, the city grew steadily to the south. Among the notable buildings of this period is the Old College of the University, designed by Robert Adam in 1789. Only the street frontage on South Bridge is his work, the single court within having been designed by William Playfair and completed in 1834.

More audacious, however, was the decision taken by the Town Council, at the instigation of Lord Provost Drummond, to build a completely New Town on the north side of the loch. The loch then lay below the castle, and has since been replaced by the railway line and Princes Street Gardens.

A competition for its design was won by a 22-year-old architect, James Craig. His plan was for single-sided terraces facing over gardens to the south and north: Princes Street and Queen Street respectively. Between them ran a street of unprecedented breadth, George Street, completed at either end by an expansive square, St Andrew's Square and Charlotte Square. Other streets ran north and south on a grid pattern and between the main thoroughfares were two narrow service streets. The original design provided for a great circus in the middle of George Street, but this was never built.

Early in the 19th century, further expansion to the north would take place below Queen Street Gardens, and most of what is now the residential area of the New Town should properly be termed the Second New Town. The building of the New Town was an expression of the intellectual and economic confidence characteristic of 18th-century Edinburgh. It was a consequence of the Scottish Enlightenment, two of whose luminaries, David Hume, philosopher and historian, and Adam Smith, philosopher of the new economics, lived in the Old Town.

The history of Walter Scott's dwelling-places in Edinburgh may be taken as an illustration of how the city was changing. He was born in the dark and squalid College Wynd in the Old Town, lived as a child in George Square, moved after marriage to Castle Street in the New Town, and then, after his financial crash in 1826, to lodgings in Walker Street, then recently built to the west of Charlotte Square. It had been open country when he was a young man.

Family links: For most of the 18th century, though, social life was concentrated in the taverns of the Old Town. Claret was the favoured drink there, for Scotland had kept its links with France sufficiently for gentlemen to continue to favour Bordeaux wine rather than the coarse port which was the usual drink of English gentry. It was a small society where anonymity was impossible. Everyone in 18th-century Scotland enjoyed an extensive cousinage; pride of family was powerful, and secrecy impossible.

In this atmosphere it was no wonder that ideas were stimulatingly exchanged. Everyone knew that knowledge was being rapidly expanded, and both in the taverns and through the agency of learned societies, people came to realise that they were living in an age of improvement.

In the second half of the century, the University – though the youngest in Scotland,

having been founded only in 1582 – began to acquire a reputation as the most progressive school of learning in Britain (despite the fact that Hume had earlier been denied a Chair on account of his reputed atheism). But it was less formal bodies such as *The Honourable Society for Improvement in the Knowledge of Agriculture* and *The Select Society* – founded by Hume, Allan Ramsay and Adam Smith, among others, to discuss general moral and political questions and the improvement of Scottish society – which represented the focal points of the city's intellectual life.

Such developments were common, both in Europe and America; similar clubs were

found in, for example, Dijon, Bordeaux, Boston and Philadelphia. The Scottish clubs, however, felt a special urgency: they were aware of how Scotland had lost its historic identity as a sovereign state, and they sought a new understanding which would validate their new condition.

One consequence was that intellectuals came to be regarded as natural leaders of society. Contemporaries frequently commented on the high status they enjoyed, and it was generally recognised that Edinburgh's reputation rested on its contribution to philosophy, history, art and science.

Nevertheless it was still an aristocratic city. The greatest nobles might have followed Court and Parliament to London, but many landed families maintained a house or flat in Edinburgh.

There was little in the way of formal administration of Scotland by the Government: when a Scottish secretary was appointed in 1762, for instance, he found that there were no papers relating to Scottish business, but the members of the Faculty of Advocates managed what there was of public business; for more than a century and a half the Lord Advocate was, in effect, the Government's man in Scotland.

there for 40 years, this acquired a reputation which attracted students from other parts of Britain and even from the Continent; in the 20th century the attraction has been worldwide. Not even the scandalous involvement of the Professor of Anatomy, Robert Knox, with the bodysnatchers and murderers Burke and Hare in the 1820s seriously checked the growing reputation of Edinburgh medicine.

Law lords: Edinburgh's reputation as an intellectual and cultural centre was reinforced when *The Edinburgh Review* was established in 1802. Its founders were three advocates: Francis Jeffrey, Henry Brougham and Francis Horner, and a Church of Eng-

Meanwhile, other Edinburgh lawyers, the Writers to the Signet, achieved a dominant position as men of business for the Scottish nobility. By the end of the century Edinburgh was on the way to becoming a city dominated by the professions, especially law and medicine.

The Royal College of Physicians had been founded in 1681, and the Edinburgh Medical School about the same time. Under Alexander Monro (1697–1767) who taught anatomy

land clergyman Sydney Smith, who was then resident in the city. The fact that the first three were advocates provides further evidence of the importance of the legal profession in Scottish cultural history; Jeffrey eventually became Lord Advocate and Brougham Lord Chancellor of England in the Whig Ministry of 1832.

The *Review* was published by Archibald Constable, to whom Lord Cockburn (another advocate and later a judge) said: "the literature of Scotland has been more indebted than any other of his vocation". It quickly established itself as the leading peri-

Left, Ramsay's portrait of David Hume. **Above**, the Royal Company of Archers.

odical of its day. Within five years its circulation was 7,000; by 1818 it had monthly sales of over 18,000. It decreed the canons of taste – not only in Scotland but throughout Britain – for the expanding middle-class, but its politics were Whig. It soon had a Tory rival in *Blackwood's Magazine*.

The first three decades of the century were the age of Sir Walter Scott. First as a poet, then as the author of the Waverley novels, he presented a new and Romantic picture of Scotland to the world. His influence was profound, extending far beyond literature: he organised the visit of George IV to Scotland in 1822, the first by a reigning monarch

be taken as marking the decline of the Scottish Enlightenment. It was significant that Carlyle could not find sufficient intellectual sustenance in Edinburgh.

Cockburn was to declare that "the 18th century had been the last purely Scotch age. Everything that came after was English". There was some truth in this judgement, though it was grossly exaggerated. Scotland had achieved a new confidence as part of the United Kingdom.

The strength of Britishness had been strengthened by the experience of the wars against Napoleon. Significantly, the eastward continuation of Princes Street was called

since Charles I had come north in 1641. For that visit, Scott put half of Edinburgh into tartan, the fashion for which soon extended to Paris. The influence of Scott's medieval novels, and of the code of chivalry they revived, was so great that Mark Twain held him responsible for the American Civil War.

End of Enlightenment: The reviews remained influential throughout the 19th century, but their great days were over by the end of the 1830s. Scott himself died in 1832, the same year that Thomas Carlyle, the outstanding figure in the next generation of writers, settled in London. That date may conveniently

Waterloo Place, and a fine equestrian statue of the Duke of Wellington was erected outside Robert Adam's Register House. Some, however, may discern a darker, but more accurate, symbol of the relation between Scotland and the rest of the UK in the National Monument to commemorate Waterloo built on the Calton Hill; it was left unfinished due to a lack of funds.

Above, an artist's portrayal of the possibly apochrypal meeting between Robert Burns and the young Walter Scott. **Right**, Sir Walter Scott's monument in Princes Street.

THE LIFE AND TIMES OF SIR WALTER SCOTT

Although he wrote surprisingly little about the city of his birth, Walter Scott haunts Edinburgh. In a very real sense, he can be said to have invented it. Visitors arrive at Waverley Station – named in honour of his great sequence of novels – and almost the first sight to greet them is George Meikle Kemp's enormous Gothic monument to Scott on the south side of Princes Street.

The old Tollbooth is gone, but a stone outline in the High Street pavement marks the Heart of Midlothian, where one of his most powerfully evocative scenes took place. "Scott country" begins 25 miles to the south, in the environs of Abbotsford, the "castle" to which he moved in 1812. Nevertheless, it's impossible to escape his presence in the capital.

He was born in 1771 and was soon ailing from a bout of polio that left him with a lifelong limp. His father was a Writer to the Signet, an important law officer, and as a child Scott imbibed a strong sense of Scotland's independent culture – Scots law had not been affected by the Union with England in 1707 – and the fund of stories, both romantic and tragic, of which Scottish history consisted. Apprenticed to his father's office, he quickly learned the workings of that law and history and rose to be one of the clerks of Session and, later, Sheriff of Selkirkshire, the county where Abbotsford was located and which is now part of Borders Region.

Scott was not the recklessly spontaneous artist demanded by romantic tastes. His first literary interests were mainly scholarly, collecting Border songs and legends. These were published in *The Minstrelsy of the Scottish Borders*, whose success prompted Scott to develop a growing poetic bent. His "first" literary career was as the author of a series of long poems – *The Lay of the Last Minstrel* (1805), *Marmion* (1808), *The Lady of the Lake* (1810) – which were very popular.

Scott was, though, still very much an amateur writer. The economic success of his long poems was almost incidental and most of his energies went into his legal and publishing interests. The

work for which he is best known is the product of an accident. Like Mark Twain later in the United States, Scott had been quick to see the commercial potential of new printing techniques and had plunged a great deal of his inherited wealth into the Edinburgh publishing and printing company of Ballantyne. But in 1813 and then, more disastrously, in 1826 the company suffered massive financial collapses.

Scott was shattered but refused the coward's way out of bankruptcy, preferring to accept full liability for all his debts. His remaining years, until he died, a broken man, in 1832, are a story of extraordinary perseverance.

By 1812, Scott had realised that the vogue for his poems was over. Byron was the new, racier hero. In 1814, he published anonymously what has been claimed to be the first historical novel in English, *Waverley*. It was a remarkable success and began a long stream of works – including *The Antiquary* and *Old Mortality* (both 1816), *The Heart of Midlothian* (1818), *Redgauntlet* (1824), and a stream of novels on medieval and foreign themes – all ascribed to "The Author of Waverley".

Scott was, and remains, "The Great Unknown". There is something almost symbolic in the way the grisly Gothic spire of the Scott monument – known to Edinburghers as the "Gothic Rocket" – almost obscures the statue of the novelist beneath, sitting quietly with his favourite dog. Scott's heroism was of a specialised sort, prompting one critic to dub him a "bourgeois saint".

It has long been critically unfashionable for a writer to be too successful and Scott's willingness to regard fiction-writing as a trade – rather than as an art – has denied him a certain snob appeal. Certainly, he is the least read of the great 19th-century writers. Yet most of our suppositions about the Middle Ages come from Scott. So, too, does the whole myth and culture of tartanry, the result of Scott's remarkable stage-managing of King George IV's visit to Scotland in 1822.

Scott was a man of his time and very close to the heart of its most important movements. It's rare for a writer to wield such influence but it's altogether typical that we should never have forgiven him for it. ∎

A TIME OF TURMOIL

The Victorian Age, which may be considered in this context as lasting till the outbreak of World War I, was a period of paradox in Edinburgh's history. On the one hand, the city's expansion continued; on the other, it declined from occupying the position of an intellectual metropolis to the condition of a provincial capital.

It grew vastly – though far more slowly than did Glasgow or many English provincial cities. The area north of the Meadows was covered with lofty stone terraces, and, in Grange and Morningside, with substantial villas; the city now extended almost to the base of the Pentland Hills. To the west it stretched out to include the once rural village of Corstophine. Working-class tenements covered Gorgie and Dalry, and the fringes of Leith Walk and Broughton.

Unlike Glasgow, however, the city had very little heavy industry. There was shipbuilding in Leith, still a separate burgh, but Edinburgh was predominantly a commercial and professional city, not an industrial one. Brewing and printing were the main industries. The *Encyclopaedia Britannica* was first published here, as was *Chamber's Encyclopaedia* and maps, including *The Times Atlas*.

Era of the train: Edinburgh handled the printing for most London publishers, sheets being carried on the steam packets that now ran between Leith and London. The railway arrived in the 1840s, drawing Scotland and England more closely together. Rival companies established their own stations. Princes Street at the east end and Waverley at the west end of the city's main thoroughfare, and in the first decade of the 20th century, the two great railway hotels, the Caledonian and the North British, were built to serve the customers of the respective companies.

The city's growth hastened the decline of the Old Town, which soon became a territory

of insalubrious slums. In 1851 half the population, about 30,000 people, still lived there, crammed into tenement blocks which lacked any kind of sanitation. The old social homogeneity had gone. In his essay, *Edinburgh: Picturesque Notes*, Robert Louis Stevenson remarked that "to look over the South bridge and see the Cowgate below full of crying hawkers is to view one rank of society from another in the twinkling of an eye."

Probably this loss of homogeneity was

inevitable. It affected most great cities in the 19th century, which saw a sharp delineation taking place between the districts inhabited by a growing, ever more prosperous bourgeoisie, and the expanding working-class.

There were, of course, distinctions within this class, too: between the respectable and regular wage-earners, who mostly inhabited the rows of new tenements, and the indigent poor, many only working at casual trades, who thronged the slums of the Old Town. As a city with a high proportion of the middle class, Edinburgh also housed huge numbers of domestic servants; according to the 1881

Preceding pages: North Bridge memorial to the city's regiments who helped build the British Empire. Left, Libberton's Wynd. Right, military glory remembered in the Castle Museum.

THE DISRUPTION

At the east end of George Street in Edinburgh is a cool, elegant, neo-classical church, built in 1783 by David Kay and now known as St Andrew's & St George's. In the porch there is a modest sign which explains that, on 18 May 1843, this building was the scene of one of the most dramatic events in 19th-century Scottish history – the "Disruption" of the Church of Scotland. On that day almost 500 ministers startled Britain by turning their backs on salaries, homes, careers and social standing and walked into the wilderness to set up the Free Church of Scotland.

This was no obscure falling-out among theologians over the exact date of Creation. The Disruption was the culmination of decades of bruising, politically-charged argument which split Scotland's established church down the middle and led some of the most law-abiding men in Britain to mount a fierce (and successful) challenge to the power of the British government and aristocracy. In fact, it has been argued that the Disruption of 1843 was the only rebellion in 19th-century Britain that succeeded.

These turbulent events projected on to the international stage Presbyterian divines like Thomas Chalmers (whose statue stands at the crossroads of George Street and Castle Street) and Thomas Guthrie (whose image graces the west end of Princes Street Gardens). And the church they created did much to underpin the essential differences between Scottish and English societies.

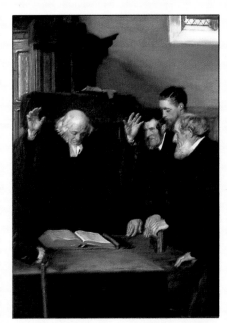

It all began with a thoroughly bad piece of legislation. This was the Patronage Act of 1712, a notorious piece of Jacobite-inspired law-making which gave the Scottish gentry the right to appoint (or "intrude") clergymen of their own choosing on Church of Scotland congregations – a right the English gentry had enjoyed for hundreds of years. The Scots were outraged. Ever since John Knox's Reformation of 1560 Scottish congregations had elected their own ministers. The process lay at the heart of Presbyterian church government, and the Patronage Act was a flagrant violation of treaties with England. But the English-dominated parliament could see nothing wrong with bringing Scotland into line with England.

In the late 18th century the General Assembly of the church became dominated by the "moderate" party, most of whom were appointees of the gentry. But eventually the "moderates" gave way to the "evangelical" party led by Dr Thomas Chalmers, who was a brilliant theologian, mathematician and orator.

After 10 years of unsuccessful political and legal battles with the British establishment, Chalmers and about 500 "evangelical" ministers walked out of the General Assembly of the Church of Scotland on 18 May 1843 to set up the Free Church of Scotland. The walk-out took Britain completely by surprise. But it was no romantic gesture. Chalmers and his colleagues were brilliant organisers and tireless money raisers. A well-oiled machine was set in motion, money and support came pouring in, and within a very few years the Free Church had built hundreds of new churches, manses (that is, clergy homes) and schools, plus three substantial theological colleges.

Not that Chalmers and company had it all their own way. In many parts of Scotland, and particularly in the Highlands, the lairds refused to give (or sell) the Free Church any land on which to build churches. Like their 17th-century ancestors, many adherents were forced to hold their services on open hillsides, woods, beaches and gravel pits, often in the foulest of weather and usually harried by the laird's men.

Eventually, after much publicity, parliament set up an inquiry in 1847 into why so many of Queen Victoria's most pious subjects were being denied the right to worship, and the aristocracy were embarrassed into dropping their resistance. One of the last things Thomas Chalmers did was give evidence to the committee. He died a few weeks later. But by then the future of the Free Church was secure.

In 1874 the Patronage Act was scrapped, and in 1929 most of the Free Church congregations returned to the established Church of Scotland. But not everybody accepted the new order: a minority, particularly in the Highlands, clung to their independence and remain the democratic (if somewhat stern) Free Church of Scotland. ∎

census they amounted to more than 20 percent of the population.

It was a city of churches. The great event of the mid-century was the Disruption of the Kirk in 1843. This split in the Church of Scotland was brought about by a quarrel over patronage (the right to appoint the minister of a parish).

The seceders were led by Dr Thomas Chalmers, Professor of Theology at Edinburgh, and the most famous Churchman of the day. He led some 470 ministers, 40 percent of the whole number, out of the General Assembly meeting in George Street, down Hanover Street to Canonmills, where

Members of Parliament. He was a Gladstonian Liberal, and also the brother-in-law of the great English Liberal advocate of Free Trade and pacifism John Bright. The Liberals dominated Edinburgh, as indeed they did the whole of Scotland.

McLaren favoured the extension of the franchise to most householders, free trade, and legislation to control the sale of alcohol (the great cause of vice, as they thought, among the Scottish working-class). He was a Free Kirk man and suspicious of trade unionism. In 1873 he was described by the Trades Council of Edinburgh as "a traitor to the working-class interest" because of his

in a hall they proclaimed themselves The Free Church of Scotland. The great number of Churches in Edinburgh, many now converted to other uses, was the consequence of this secession, for the Free Kirk at once embarked on a policy of church-building, duplicating the existing parish churches.

The great political figure of mid-19th century Edinburgh was Duncan McLaren, several times Lord Provost and one of the city's

Left, a detail from Lorimer's classic painting *Ordination of the Elders*. **Above**, Victorian family life in Edinburgh is recreated for the camera.

part in the Criminal Law Amendment Act which had outlawed picketing; a great demonstration against him and his policies was held in the Queen's Park outside Holyrood.

This was evidence of the divisions within the city. There was a moral division too, so sharp that it may be called a duality. Towards the end of the century seven percent of the births in virtuous God-fearing Edinburgh were illegitimate.

The city was abundant in brothels. In 1842 Dr William Tait claimed that there were 200 in Edinburgh; it was said that those in Rose Street enjoyed their best trade during the week of the General Assembly of the Church. In 1862 an Act of Parliament empowered the police to close brothels and drive prostitutes from the streets. Even so, in 1901, Edinburgh police reported 424 known prostitutes and 45 brothels in the capital.

No-one was more conscious of the two faces of Edinburgh than the writer Robert Louis Stevenson. Though his masterpiece of duality, *The Strange Case of Dr Jekyll and Mr Hyde*, is set in London, no one has doubted that its inspiration came from Edinburgh. As a young man, Stevenson himself had frequented the brothels and disreputable taverns of Leith Walk and had fallen in love

with a prostitute, Kate Drummond.

The social stratification of the city was evident in its schools. Scotland has always boasted a democratic tradition of education, and certainly it was easier for a poor boy to get an education in Scotland than in England. Nevertheless, social distinction between different schools became more marked in Victorian Edinburgh (*see page 140*).

The Royal High School, where Scott and Cockburn had been educated, moved from the Old Town to a noble building, modelled on the Temple of Theseus in Athens, and situated on the Calton Hill. (In the 1960s the school would move again to the middle-class suburb of Barnton, while a decade later, the old building was prepared for the Scottish Assembly, remaining empty after the failure of the Referendum of March 1979.)

Dissatisfaction with the High School had led, in 1824, to the creation of The Edinburgh Academy, the great school for the sons of the professional classes. The schools owned by the Edinburgh Merchant Company also became more socially exclusive, and three public schools on the English model, Loretto, Merchiston and Fettes, were in being by 1870.

Sporting life: It was in these schools that rugby was first played, to become the team game favoured by the middle classes. The working-class game, Association Football, came into being a little later, as a result of greater leisure and the realisation on the part of employers that sport provided a valuable recreation and diversion for their workers: the two great Edinburgh clubs, Heart of Midlothian and Hibernian, were formed before the end of the century.

The name of the latter calls attention to the Irish Catholic immigration which had taken place. Although sectarian passions did not run as high in Edinburgh as in Glasgow, partly because Irish immigration was proportionally lower, Hearts were the Protestant club and Hibs the Catholic club; in time, the distinction between them would dwindle to a geographical one, Hearts representing the west side of the city and Hibs the east.

Edinburgh University flourished throughout the century, particularly in law, philosophy, history, medicine and natural science. Its greatest alumnus was James Clerk Maxwell, the outstanding theoretical scientist of the century; but, though born and wholly educated in Edinburgh, he never held a chair at the University.

The greatest figure in medicine was Sir James Young Simpson, Professor of Midwifery, and promoter of anaesthetics. He discovered the efficacy of chloroform in his house in Queen Street, which now bears a plaque recording the event.

Left, Princes Street flourishing in 1879, then as now the place to meet people.

"THE BEST CITY IN THE WORLD IN WHICH TO BE ILL"

It would be a travesty if Edinburgh's medical reputation was founded on the grisly stories of Burke and Hare, the body-snatching "resurrectionists" who sold their hellish parcels to surgeons for anatomical dissection. They are, of course, shivery footnotes to medical history and, if one strays up the dank alleys of the Old Town, it is easy to understand why they persist.

Ever since King James IV of Scotland, himself "weill learnit in the art of mediecein", granted his charter to the Guild of Surgeons and Barbers at Edinburgh in 1506, the city has made much more respectable claims to be one of the world's most important centres of medical science.

As the study and practice of medicine evolved down the centuries Edinburgh made conspicuous contributions to the understanding of anatomy, obstetrics, nervous diseases, midwifery, gynaecology, tuberculosis, diphtheria, forensic medicine and public health. In modern times important discoveries and techniques in neurosurgery, organ transplants, ophthalmic surgery and genetics have kept the city in the front line of the battle to cure disease and to alleviate human suffering.

One way and another, the existence of a medical school at Edinburgh since the 17th century led to the foundation of – among other things – modern chemistry, modern dermatology, modern military medicine, the invention of the Davy Lamp and the respirator, and the first British use of a hypodermic syringe.

To earn the right to put M.B.Ch.B(Ed) after one's name still lures students from all over the globe. Even in the middle of the 18th century many came from America and the West Indian colonies. The influence of Edinburgh on the wellbeing of the world is incalculable.

Long before Britain's National Health Service came into being, a caring profession looked after the burghers in an Infirmary which grew from six huts to a network of teaching hospitals served by the University's Faculty of Medicine and the Royal Colleges of Surgeons and Physicians. Not that

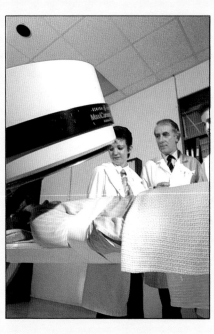

every student graduated – the standards have always been notorious for their severity – and not every graduate achieved the distinction of the man who was physician to Catherine the Great for 20 years, or the doctor who escorted Louis XVI to the guillotine, or the chief medical officer to the Jacobites at the Battle of Culloden.

Some achieved fame outside medicine: Conan Doyle and his mentor Joseph Bell whose diagnostic teaching techniques gave Doyle the model for Sherlock Holmes; Samuel Smiles and his Victorian Self-Help philosophy; Dr Hastings Banda, president of Malawi; Oliver Goldsmith; a Prime Minister of Canada; Roget with his thesaurus; the man who expurgated Shakespeare and Gibbon to make them fit for all the family; and Dr Allinson (1858–1918) whose recipe for healthy living is only now getting the response it deserved, who believed in wholemeal so earnestly that he milled it himself and the flour is named after him.

But then the gardenia, wisteria and poinsettia are named after Dr Alexander Garden, Dr Casper Wistar and Joel R. Poinsett, all of whom studied medicine in Edinburgh at a time when medicine and botany were inextricably interwoven.

Greatness there was in abundance in the 17th and 18th centuries. In the kirkyard of Greyfriars lie the remains of the Monros, *primus et secundus*, giants in anatomical research and scientific adventure who straddled the subject from 1697 to 1817 (Monro *tertius* was so feeble by comparison that students paid other lecturers to supplement his teaching). There, too, lie the remains of Pitcairne, Hope, Black, and Whytt whose work is the stuff of history.

The story of Edinburgh's medical past is not only a significant scientific archive but folklore and legend as well: the great Dr Gregory whose mixture of rhubarb, magnesia and ginger was, until very recently, the world's most frequently prescribed medication; Syme, described in his day as the Napoleon of surgery; Bright, of Bright's disease; Sophia Jex-Blake pioneering the rights of women doctors; Elsie Inglis doing the same for women patients.

One thing has always been certain, then and now, and a constant comfort if you live here: there is no better city in the world in which to be ill. ∎

The Great War took its toll on Edinburgh as on the rest of the country. The record of the city's contribution can be read in the lists of the dead in the Scottish War Memorial in the castle. The Memorial itself was the masterpiece of Sir Robert Lorimer, one of the two greatest Scottish architects of his generation, and himself the son of the University's Professor of International Law.

Throughout the period between the wars the suburbs continued to sprawl towards the Forth Rail bridge, out the Glasgow Road, and up the lower slopes of the Pentlands. The social stratification became still more marked, as the first attempts to renovate the Old Town resulted in the decanting of many of the poor to bleak housing estates on the city's periphery, a process that was to accelerate, even more dolefully, after 1945.

Filthy slum: Much of the Old Town remained *terra incognita* to the respectable middle class. David Daiches, literary critic and historian, then a schoolboy at George Watson's College, remembered the Grassmarket and Cowgate as "filthy slum with children with rickets and bare feet running around in obvious poverty, and ill-nourished, women with threadbare shawls coming out of the jug and bottle entrance of a pub, trying to drown their sorrows in gin."

It was middle-class Edinburgh, however, which presented its face to the world. This was the city of villas and terraces, hotels and great department stores (Jenner's and Forsyth's pre-eminent on Princes Street, Patrick Thomson's on North Bridge), of electric tramcars and a suburban railway, and, most of all, of tea-rooms. The sight of fur-coated ladies in extraordinary hats taking afternoon tea in McVitie's was one of the most characteristic of Edinburgh scenes.

The most important event between the wars was the re-establishment of the Scottish Of-

fice in Edinburgh. The Office had been created in 1885, but was then based in London. In 1936 Walter Elliot, the most imaginative of all Secretaries of State for Scotland, initiated its transfer to Edinburgh. This was, wrote historian Michael Fry, "more than administrative reform. It had immense symbolic value, making Edinburgh once again a seat of government, truly a capital rather than just the headquarters of the Church and the judiciary."

The city's prestige received another lift

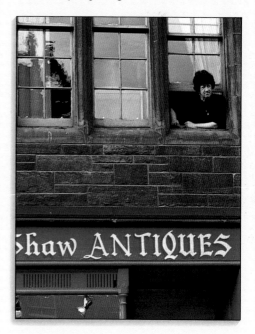

after World War II with the creation of the Edinburgh International Festival. Three men were responsible: Harvey Wood, Scottish director of the British Council, Rudolf Bing, general manager of Glyndebourne Opera, and Sir John Falconer, Lord Provost of Edinburgh. Sir John's involvement represented the first imaginative act performed by the Edinburgh City Council since the creation of the new Town almost 200 years before.

Unhappily, his example was not followed. The City Fathers' commitment to the Festival has hardly been more than lukewarm. Though it soon established itself as one of the greatest,

Preceding pages: working-class loyalty to trade unionism celebrated in a parade. **Left**, middle-class living in Ann Street. **Right**, city-centre tenement block.

and certainly the most comprehensive, among the world's art festival, the city's financial contribution has been consistently grudging and inadequate. Most notably, although the need for an opera house comparable to those habitually found in other European cities was evident from the first, none has been built.

Nevertheless the establishment of the Festival, and the growth of the Fringe around it, made modern Edinburgh; they helped also to make the city a mecca for tourists. They helped to reveal its beauties and individuality to the world.

In other respects, the first two decades after the war were unhappy. The city failed to come to terms with the problem which the motor car presents to all historic towns; the closure of the suburban railway was a prime example of myopic folly. Worse still, Edinburgh was careless of its architectural heritage: Princes Street was debased by new development; the University, to its enduring shame, was permitted to destroy George Square and its environs; even the New Town came under threat.

The Old Town was subject to redevelopment, benign in that it saved the fabric of the Canongate, reprehensible in that it resulted in the expulsion of its traditional inhabitants. Meanwhile, the Council built peripheral housing schemes which would have attracted still more well-deserved obloquy, if Glasgow had not built even worse ones.

Fortunately, there was a reaction. The New Town Conservation Committee was formed in 1970, after an International Conference – surely one of the few examples of such Conferences leading to practical benefit. The despoliation of the New Town was halted, even reversed. Soon afterwards, the idea of conservation and renovation was carried over to the Old Town. Evidence of the rehabilitation of historic Edinburgh is now apparent.

Why Aids took hold: In the late 1980s, Edinburgh was dubbed the Aids capital of Europe

– an incongruous accolade for such a seemingly prim place. The level of infection in Lothian Region – Edinburgh's home "state" – was as high as that in New York State, with an estimated 1 percent of males between the ages of 15 and 45 HIV-positive. Nearly all were or had been intravenous drugs users.

At one time, it was easier to buy "smack" on the streets of Edinburgh than in London. That traffic was brought under control – but the users turned to other drugs. Its legacy, however, was a frightening Aids problem.

All intravenous drugs users, when desperate, will neglect the protection of sterile needles and use dirty ones. But in Edinburgh the practice of needle-sharing became built into the social culture of drug abuse. It began because needles were in short supply. Encouraged by the Scottish Office, Lothian and Borders Police seriously discouraged chemists from selling needles and doctors from distributing them. This was a policy which seems to have been largely ignored by Strathclyde Police who, in any case, didn't face the same heroin problem.

Needle-sharing soon became part of the "sociability" of heroin abuse. As others pass the port or offer cigarettes, so the Edinburgh addict passed the needle during mainlining

Lothian Regional Council, and demoted the City of Edinburgh to the status of a mere District, it remains the seat of Scottish administration and, as a result of a referendum in 1997, will boast a new building to accommodate the pomp of a Scottish Parliament.

More importantly, it has established itself as an important financial centre, controlling more funds than any European city except London and Zurich. It is the headquarters of two of the three Scottish banks. It remains the headquarters of the Scottish legal system. It has three universities since Heriot Watt Technical College and Napier College were elevated to that status. It is pre-eminently the

sessions. This was the custom which gave Edinburgh its peculiarly virulent Aids problem. The provision of clean needles, although a controversial policy, did much to control the spread of the epidemic.

New optimism: Edinburgh faces the 21st century with a confidence which few would have predicted even 20 years ago. Though the city lost its full self-government status in 1975, when the re-organisation of local government transferred important functions to

Two aspects of Edinburgh culture: a National Gallery gathering (left) and the Festival Fringe.

city of the professions. It houses the national Galleries of Scotland, and has a rich artistic life. The 1990s have seen a renaissance of building activity.

Though it has many problems, though it is frequently jealous of the renaissance of Glasgow, and though it suffers from an unimaginative council, Auld Reekie remains a city which appeals to the imagination and which is one of the glories of European civilisation. Not for nothing have both the Old Town and the New Town, as well as other nooks and crannies, been designated by UNESCO as a World Heritage Site.

"If Edinburgh has not given the creative spirit due place," wrote the poet Hugh MacDiarmid, "the creative spirit has not been deluded as to Edinburgh's false position. It is a significant fact that, with all the romance attached to it, it has never been made the subject of any good, let alone any great, poem. It could not have failed to inspire the poets if there had not all along been something wrong with its pretensions – some essential falsity the instincts of their genius could never be deluded by."

Edinburgh has somehow always managed to resist the literary imagination. For MacDiarmid, writing about the city in 1934, the reason was plain: give the imagination short shrift in your civic culture, as Edinburgh had consistently done, and the imagination will quickly pack its bags and move elsewhere. He could never forgive Edinburgh its delusionary "pretensions", nor the fact that the university in Scotland's capital city had never troubled to found a professorial chair in Scottish literature. (It still hasn't.)

Rival city: Even Glasgow – which in the unwritten national epic plays a dark, commercial Sparta to Edinburgh's enlightened Athens – had enjoyed its share of literary limelight, even if only as "The City of Dreadful Night" in James Thompson's sombre verses or the no less gloomy cityscape of Alexander Smith's tribute. It's interesting that Smith, one of the short-lived "Spasmodic" school that briefly flourished in Scotland in the late 19th century, began a similar poem dedicated to the capital, but never managed to finish it before he died.

If Edinburgh really was one of the great cultural capitals of Europe – as its inhabitants and distinguished visitors insistently maintained – where was the modern masterpiece that would do for it what James Joyce's *Ulysses* had done for Dublin? Where was its Dickens? Why did its most famous sons – Walter Scott, Robert Louis Stevenson – prefer to retreat into

the fantasy-worlds of the Middle Ages or the South Seas?

Those who look closely at these things say that Stevenson never managed to shake the dust of Heriot Row from his feet; even when his neighbours were bare-breasted Samoan girls, his models of behaviour were "douce" Edinburgh ladies; equally, the nightmarish London that forms the backdrop to the decline and fall of the good Dr Jekyll – a man without a fault except that he thought too well of

himself and understood too little of the power of the imagination – was Edinburgh unmistakably.

MacDiarmid, in that sour essay in Scottish Scene, laid the blame for Edinburgh's literary shortcomings at the same door. A city that thought too well of itself was prey to the "hopeless preconceptions which vitiate almost all impressions of it: all the guide-book chatter, all the 'intellectual rabbit's food of historical tittle-tattle and miscellaneous facts."

Edinburgh's great literati were philosophers and historians like David Hume and William Robertson, economists like Adam

Preceding pages: contemporary calls for Home Rule. <u>Left</u>, Burns Memorial, Abbotsford. <u>Right</u>, Hugh MacDiarmid's portrait by William Menzies.

Smith. They dealt in hard, unromantic facts and appearances. The city's glamour, in the same way, was a matter of glorious architectural frontages and historical anecdotes. What lay behind?

The point about Glasgow is that its "dark side" lies on the surface. It takes an effort of imagination to find the "dear green place" – Gles Chu – and the warm heart under the toughened exterior. By legend, Edinburgh's heart is cold, but with the coldness of reason and intellect rather than cruelty.

MacDiarmid is too pessimistic, expects too much of a place he never really came to understand, even when they did begin to put

the novel's other great "moment", Jeanie Deans's desperate journey to London, should once again underline the post-1707 dependence on Union that had begun the dismantlement of a separate Scottish culture (and that had been the main cause of the Porteous disturbances).

By and large, though, history in Edinburgh has remained in the physical environment, rarely seeping through into the kind of imaginative writing the city has inspired. Largely, that has been private and intense, rather than public and expansive. That, of course, has not been how the city likes to see itself, or how visitors have liked to present it. Joan Lingard's

his poems on the literature curriculum and to offer him honorary degrees. The fact is that Edinburgh has always occupied a very special and complex place in the national literary imagination. Almost always, the theme which it suggests is that old philosophic interplay between imagination and reality, the suffering, passion and violence that underlie the reasonable surface.

Perhaps the greatest set-piece, and the one that most closely engages with Scottish history, is the reconstruction of the notorious 1736 Porteous Riots in Scott's *The Heart of Midlothian* (1818), though it's significant that

1964 novel *The Prevailing Wind* offers an Edinburgh devoid of irony, almost the kind of novel that could have been written by the City Fathers to sustain their own sense of well-being.

The feeling wasn't new to Miss Lingard or even to this century. When the "heaven-taught ploughman" Robert Burns sought literary fame, it seemed inevitable that he should come to his nation's capital: "At Edinburgh I was in a new world," he wrote, "I mingled among many classes of men, but all of them new to me; and I was all attention 'to catch the manners living as they rise'." Sadly, Edinburgh also persuaded Burns that the only poetic manner that mattered was the pompous solemnity of his *Address* to the capital, an inexcusable piece of drivel and thoroughly untypical of his greatest work.

Burns was lionised in the drawing rooms and salons of the New Town. A bare half mile away, across the Castle Moat and around the spine of rock that supports the High Street – the Royal Mile – a different reality awaited, one that had marked out the life and passing of the one Scottish poet that Burns wholeheartedly admired. Robert Fergusson died in the Edinburgh Bedlam in 1774, aged barely 24. His great poem *Auld Reikie* – which just about

answers MacDiarmid's accusation – is an astonishing blend of the simple vernacular that Burns was to make his own, with an equally astonishing learning, acquired at the university.

The "Blest place!" he celebrated, though, was also the site of some of Europe's worst slums and Fergusson's life was one of bizarre contrast, ranged between the convivial company of his intellectual peers in taverns and debating rooms, and the grinding poverty and

Left, the 1736 Porteous Riots. **Above**, Robert Burns, who was lionised in Edinburgh society.

privation which eventually led to his tragically premature death.

Another writer to perceive the astonishing contrasts of Edinburgh was the "Ettrick Shepherd", James Hogg, a self-taught poet who produced one of the most remarkable novels written in any language, *Private Memoirs and Confessions of a Justified Sinner*. Published in 1824, at a time when religious and political controversy were at their peak in Scotland, it is one of the greatest explorations of the unconscious mind and anticipates many themes in Stevenson's *Dr Jekyll and Mr Hyde*.

It concerns a pious young man haunted by a mysterious "twin" who goads him to the murder of his brother. Its most famous passages take place in the nightmare slums of the Old Town – alleys Fergusson knew only too well – and, unforgettably, on Arthur's Seat, where George is confronted with the mysterious mountain phenomenon known as "broken spectre", rationally the projection of a human shadow onto cloud below, but which became in Hogg's account a monstrous threat.

Such a threat also haunts the world of Edinburgh's most famous heroine, Miss Jean Brodie, and her "prime". It is as well to remember that the doctrine Miss Brodie preaches to her "girls" at Marcia Blaine School – in reality, James Gillespie's – is Mussolini's Fascism. *The Prime of Miss Jean Brodie* (1961) is Muriel Spark's most popular novel; it is also an almost archetypally "Edinburgh" work, the story of a "justified sinner", convinced of her rightness and reinforced in her conviction by the city in which she lives and works.

It's as well to be reminded, too, that at least one of "Miss Brodie's girls" goes off to her death. The strain of belonging to "*la crème de la crème*" is often fatal.

There is a sombre side to Edinburgh that is every bit as important to its reality as the orderly Athenian skyline. Like every town whose streets and public buildings exude history, its back alleys and the imaginations of its best writers hide human tragedies and dark questions. In recent years no-one has expressed these more poignantly than Irvine Welsh, best known for his novel *Trainspotting*, a horrifying look at Edinburgh's drug scene which inspired a celebrated film.

PUBS AND PERFORMERS

As recently as the 1960s, you could wander into just about any public house in central Edinburgh and find yourself in an environment that had hardly changed since Victorian times. It was all there: the solid oak bar, often built in circular island form; the high gantry, decorated with the twists and turns of a caring carpenter; the tobacco-stained ceiling; the non-existent view to the outside world – in order to prevent passers-by from viewing the dark secrets of every drinking den, windows had to be boarded up to above head height.

You would have found, too, that many pubs, while unable legally to banish women to the bleak little back room, ludicrously known as "the lounge", at least actively discouraged them from joining the men at the bar. And if you had asked for a glass of wine, the chances are that you would have brought a smirk to the barman's face and the riposte: "Nae wine. There's cider."

There was no music, either. In theory, a publican wishing to provide music simply had to apply for a special entertainment licence. But, like a visa from the Iraqi Government, it was granted only rarely. Without the special licence, even sing-songs were against the rules.

Some of the rules still persist, in spite of the sweeping changes that were introduced by the Licensing (Scotland) Act of 1976. Unlike their counterparts south of the border, pubs in Scotland are not permitted to serve beer in a used glass. The law harks back to the quaint Scots tradition of emptying some of the contents of the "slop" tray into every beer poured from the tap. The tray gathers the overflow that drips over the rim of the glass. The theory was that, if the glass was clean, the slops in the tray would be hygienically OK. It was all perfectly legal, but no barman would dare to do it now.

Perhaps some veterans of the Edinburgh drinking scene look back with misty affec-

tion at the days of slops and whiskies. And they will recall that Edinburgh's pubs, especially the string of splendid establishments that ran from one end of Rose Street to the other, were, in the pre-television, pre-jukebox era, important forums for debate among the "bonny fechters" of the city's animated cultural life.

At one time, during the 1950s, three pubs in particular were the honey-pots that attracted the biggest artistic bees: the Abbots-

ford and Paddy's Bar, both in Rose Street, and Milne's Bar, just round the corner. It was there that writers like Hugh MacDiarmid and Norman MacCaig and jazz musicians like Sandy Brown held court.

The pubs are still there, and at least one of them, the Abbotsford, is physically much the same as it always was, but today's literati seem to prefer an evening at home with their word processors. Perhaps they are simply confused at the changes that have taken place in the city's pub life since the 1960s.

Most of the independently-owned "free houses" have been bought up by the big

Preceding pages: Bennett's pub. **Left**, welcoming pub window. **Right**, Deacon Brodie's Tavern.

SCOTCH WHISKY

The variety of malt whiskies on sale in Edinburgh astounds visitors familiar with only a few heavily marketed brands such as Glenfiddich and The Macallan. But is the diversity an illusion fostered by advertising? Isn't the liquid behind the labels pretty much the same?

Certainly not, the experienced Scotch drinker will argue. The practised tongue can easily differentiate between Highland malts, Lowland malts, Campeltown malts and Islay malts, and there's no mistaking the bouquet of a drink such as Laphroaig, which is often described as tasting of iodine or seaweed. So which is best? Whole evenings can be whiled away debating and researching the question, with no very firm conclusions being reached. It all comes down to individual taste.

The one point of agreement is that a whisky made from a good single malt (the product of one distillery) should not be drunk with a mixer such as soda or lemonade, which would destroy the subtle flavour – though ice and water *can* be added. After dinner, malts are best drunk neat, as a liqueur. But blended whisky can be refreshing in hot weather when mixed with soda. The well-known brands of blends (such as Bell's, Teacher's, Dewar's and Johnnie Walker) contain tiny amounts of as many as 30 or 40 malts mixed with grain whisky containing unmalted barley and maize. A typical blend for a popular brand is 60 percent grain whisky to 40 percent malt.

In contrast with the upmarket images conferred on Scotch today, the drink's origins were lowly. The first written record dates back to 1494. In the 18th century it was drunk as freely as the spring water from which it was made, by peasants and aristocrats alike. It was said that a spoonful was given to new-born babies in the Highlands, and even respectable gentlewomen might start the day with "a wee dram".

The poorest crofter could offer his guest a drink, thanks to the ubiquity of home-made stills which manufactured millions of gallons of "mountain dew" in the remote glens of the Highlands. In Edinburgh, no-one needed to go thirsty: excise

Yet something as easy to make cannot be made authentically outside Scotland. Many have tried, and the Japanese in particular have thrown the most modern technology at the problem; but the combination of damp climate and soft water flowing through the peat cannot be replicated elsewhere. Indeed, no-one – not even the most experienced professional taster – can agree on what elements create the best whiskies. Is the water better if it runs off granite through peat, or if it runs through peat on to granite. Does the secret lie in the peat used to dry the malt in a distillery's kiln? Or in the soft air that permeates the wooden casks of whisky as the liquid matures for anything from three to 10 years? The arguments are endless, but the prize to Scotland is an annual export business approaching £2 billion.

So automated are Scotland's 100 or so distilleries that visitors are left with only the haziest idea of what goes on inside the beautifully proportioned onion-shaped copper stills. What happens is this. To make malt whisky, plump and dry barley (which, unlike the water, doesn't have to be local) is soaked in large tanks of water for two or three days.

It is then spread out on a concrete floor or placed in large cylindrical drums and allowed to germinate for between eight and 12 days. Next it is dried in a kiln, ideally heated by a peat fire. The dried malt is ground and mixed with hot water in a huge circular vat called a mash tun. A sugary liquid, "wort", is drawn off from the porridge-like result, leaving the remaining solids to be sold as cattle food. The wort is fed into massive vessels containing up to 45,000 litres of liquid, where living yeast is stirred in to convert the sugar in the wort into crude alcohol. It's a bit like mixing cement.

After 48 hours, the "wash" (a clear liquid containing weak alcohol) is transferred to the copper stills and heated to the point where alcohol turns to vapour. This vapour rises up the still to be condensed by a cooling plant into distilled alcohol which is then passed through a second still. The trick is to know precisely when it has distilled enough. It is then poured into porous oak casks and left to mellow for at least three years. ∎

brewery companies, who are locked in intense competition with their rivals and have adapted the public houses in order to reach specified market targets – mainly the young, of course. Some have been preserved, but many have had their beautiful bar fittings replaced with modern units.

Gone, too, is the gnarled old barman, breaking through the gentle murmur of voices with his crusty banter: in his place: blank-eyed young men and women who pull pints in a silent trance, rocking gently to the latest single by Madonna that blares from the jukebox in ear-clanging counterpoint to the soundtrack of the video that's being shown on the

Dancing in pubs! What next? Well, there are one or two unashamedly gay bars, and indeed Edinburgh's pubs now offer something for everybody. The safest way to find the bar that best fits your requirements is to jump into a taxi and let the driver know what you're looking for.

The new look: Some of the grimmer aspects of Victorian drinking, including the sodden sawdust that covered many a bar-room floor, have been swept away for good. Edinburgh's pubs are airier and brighter – some even have windows you can look out of – and there are perhaps just enough of the traditional pubs to keep the aficionados happy.

television set.

These bars are largely frequented by young drinkers. The lunchtime go-go dancers, ready to reveal just about all, bring in their fair quota of sheepish-looking middle-aged men from the insurance offices, but generally the generations tend to mix only in the more traditional pubs. In one of the latter, the White Horse in the Royal Mile, a notice reads: "Come along on a Saturday night and have a dance."

Above, essential supplies arrive at the Waverly Bar, off the Royal Mile.

The city has seen a flowering of café-bars, where you can eat pretty good food, drink wine, enjoy the company of your children, and order coffee without driving the proprietor and his staff to apoplexy.

The Edinburgh Wine Bar, in Hanover Street, established the trend years ago with its resolutely French ambience, and it has spawned many imitators. Near the top of Leith Walk, what used to be one of Edinburgh's most unsavoury pubs, the Black Bull, whose clientèle was said to be divided between those who had just come out of Saughton Prison and those who were on their way there, has re-emerged as a beacon of good taste and good service under its trendy new banner of The St James Oyster Bar. Yes, they do serve oysters.

All of the these changes in the Edinburgh way of drinking are directly related to the 1976 reforms. From being one of the most difficult places in Britain to find a drink, Edinburgh became one of the easiest. Bars were allowed to stay open all day if they chose, and, instead of the miserable 10pm closing time, they could carry on serving into the "wee sma' hours". Pubs were also able to open on Sundays, a privilege previously accorded only to hotel bars.

large number of amateur and semi-professional jazz musicians.

The early Edinburgh connection with jazz partly came from the Art College, where young painters, perhaps inspired by the fashionable Parisian jazz scene, were especially eager to pick up trumpets, clarinets and trombone in the pre-Presley years to produce a robust musical alternative to the sickly popular music that they heard around them.

Many of the early jazz innovators left Edinburgh to find fame, if not fortune, in London. But their disciples clung on tenaciously at a time when there were few outlets for their music. Today, the jazz scene in

Part of the reasoning behind it all was that the pressure of trying to cram too much booze into too little boozing time was itself causing a lot of drunkenness. Since the introduction of the new drinking hours, there have been conflicting reports on whether Scotland as a whole is less drunken that it was before, but the consensus seems to be that drinking is at least more civilised.

That's jazz: Along with the freeing of the hours, there came a more sympathetic attitude towards music. In this respect, Edinburgh has definitely led the way. Since the 1950s, the city had nurtured a surprisingly

Edinburgh is jumpin' – thanks in no small part to the willingness of publicans to feature jazz bands.

Mike Hart, director of the highly successful annual Edinburgh Jazz Festival – which is held in August to coincide with the big Edinburgh International Festival – reckons that something like 40 jazz sessions can be tracked down every week in a variety of pubs. For the jazz fans, there is no entry or cover charge. The jazz is predominantly in the New Orleans or Dixieland style, but mainstream swing and modern jazz also find a platform.

Folk music, too, is a popular attraction at several Edinburgh pubs, even if some of the best local performers have now graduated to the lofty heights of the concert hall and the recording studio. And a number of bars have welcomed rock music and blues.

A good brew: Another change for the better in Edinburgh pubs has been a widespread improvement in the past 10 years in the quality of beer offered. As the small brewing companies were gobbled up by their big brothers in the 1950s and 1960s, so the beer range was cut to some half-dozen gassy, canister brands that were indistinguishable from one another.

Eddie Condon, the wisecracking American jazz guitarist, when asked what he made of the harmonic adventures of the young "bebop" players, replied: "We don't flatten our fifths. We drink 'em." Edinburgh drinks 'em, too, and visitors from south of the Border are often pleasantly surprised to find that the standard spirit measure is a fifth of a gill and not the paltry sixth that is served in England. Indeed, some pubs proudly advertise themselves as quarter-gill houses.

A final word of warning, though. Should you find yourself in the modern equivalent of the old spit-and-sawdust joint – plastic bar awash with beer, tin ashtrays, no ice, lots of

An ardent effort by the local Campaign for Real Ale team, led by a man who went on to set up his own brewery to show what could be done, has borne fruit: few self-respecting pubs can now afford not to install at least one reasonable, cask-conditioned ale. In a pub like the Malt Shovel, in Cockburn Street, the Edinburgh pub revolution all adds up. There's a jazz band. There's a folk group. There's food and coffee. And there's real ale – in many varieties.

Left, Mather's bar in Queensferry Street. Above, a musical evening during the Folk Festival.

twitchy little men with murder in their eyes, it's best to keep your mouth shut.

A BBC radio producer, so the story goes, was in a bar such as this one evening. All eyes were on the TV wildlife film about elephants. The BBC man turned to the stranger next to him and said: "Elephants are such graceful creatures, considering their size, aren't they?" The little man considered the proposition for a split second and then punched him in the face, ran outside, and threw a brick through the window.

Sometimes, making polite conversation simply isn't worth the risk.

The sheer audacity of Edinburgh's decision to launch an international festival of the arts in 1947 is, even in the rosy light of retrospect, breathtaking. It is the kind of chutzpah that Edinburgh folk would expect from Glasgow folk and deny in themselves.

The world was, after all, still reeling from the ravages of a terrible war. The nation was bankrupt. Rationing and the grey pall of austerity prevailed. Yet here was this chilly northern capital, with no reputation as a patron of the arts let alone a fountainhead of culture, blowing trumpets, flying banners, and setting itself up as a unique European platform for the great performers of the world. An international flamenco fiesta in Sheffield would not have seemed less appropriate.

Yet the Edinburgh Festival, marching bravely towards its half-century, established itself in its first year as one of the red-letter entries in the international calendar of artistic events, and in its scale and variety has still no rival anywhere in the world. Although the Festival occupies only three weeks of the city's time and energies every year, the consequences of that audacious gamble in 1947 have had a profound effect on the character of the capital and the lives of its citizens.

Luck courted the Edinburgh Festival from the beginning. By the happiest of chances the idea of such an event, mooted even in the dark days of war, brought the right people together in the right place at the right time.

Rudolf Bing, the general manager of Glyndebourne Opera who became one of the arts world's most influential administrators, had even expressed an interest in Edinburgh's potential as a British equivalent of Salzburg as far back as 1939. At a lunch in London in 1944 he told representatives of the British Council that the United Kingdom should give a lead to the rest of Europe by celebrating peace when it came with a major festival of music and opera.

H. Harvey Wood, the British Council's man in Edinburgh, reminded Bing of the capital's suitability: it was exactly the right size, it had adequate staging and accommodation facilities for performances and visitors, its scenic beauties and historic associations commanded the admiration of the world, and it was a place with enough pride in itself to welcome strangers. It seemed a compelling argument.

When, eventually, the idea was put to the

Lord Provost, Sir John Falconer, he committed Edinburgh up to the neck: "She will surrender herself to the visitors and hopes that they will find in all the performances a sense of peace and inspiration with which to refresh their souls and reaffirm their belief in things other than material."

Perhaps the first Festival's most extraordinary stroke of luck came from an unlikely source: three weeks of blazing sunshine. The city shimmered under high blue skies. Native reserve melted. Hospitality flowed generously and the city was baked so remorselessly that South American journalists wrote

Preceding pages: setting the Festival's tone in Holyrood Park. **Left** and **above**, street theatre flourishes during the Festival.

home and complained about the heat. Like their colleagues in a vast Press corps from all over the world, however, they applauded the Festival as an astonishing, heartwarming success.

Everything had not been offered up as a hostage to chance. The legendary maestro Bruno Walter was reunited with the Vienna Philharmonic Orchestra – a musical triumph and an emotional affirmation of the Festival's wider intentions. Four of the world's greatest virtuosi – Schnabel, Szigeti, Fournier and Primrose – came together as a quartet of stunning radiance.

And it was under Walter's baton that the

faith in uniting human values and virtues… This is now shining history."

It was – and remains – a hard act to follow. For a few years, as a shattered Europe began to put itself together again, Edinburgh had the stage to herself and would have been excused a certain amount of freewheeling until other festivals caught up. But Sir John Falconer had offered the world "all that is best, year after year" and, with an inspired administrator of Bing's calibre as the Festival's first director, that idealistic promise was in safe keeping.

Five decades and seven administrators later, the current director, Brian McMaster,

young former telephonist from Blackburn, Kathleen Ferrier – recognised even before her untimely death in 1953 as one of the greatest singers of the century – gave one of the most memorable of all Festival performances in Mahler's *Song of the Earth*.

The great Austrian pianist Artur Schnabel spoke for most of the world's artistic community when he wrote: "The 1947 Festival, given in a city with no international record for a display of that kind, shortly after years of what human beings themselves condemn as inhuman ferocity… appeared as an incredibly early demonstration of an unbroken

shows no signs of being daunted or intimidated by the past pursuit of excellence. The world's great orchestras, instrumentalists, conductors, opera and ballet companies – the list reads like a directory of the elite in western culture – have performed joyfully on Edinburgh's sometimes inadequate platforms. But, says McMaster, "elitist I'm certainly not. Having worked in opera, which suffers from that label, I've always had to break that down. And populist? If it means, patronising, then No."

Of course, the world has become a much more complicated place since 1947. Virtuoso performers have been elevated to expensive megastars. Their engagements are booked years in advance while festival budgets are often allocated only on a year-to-year basis. Moving an opera company – even one small enough to be accommodated in Edinburgh's biggest playhouse – can cost more than the gross takings of its Festival run. The failure rate of commissioned new drama remains too high and too costly for much hope of further adventure, and established companies with a national reputation seem reluctant to leave their bases.

There are problems, too, with the visual arts. After making no provision for them in

After that, the Festival had to learn to live in the real world. Private owners became reluctant to part with their masterpieces. The astronomical costs of insurance and security combined with the growing nervousness of other countries to risk the transit of their treasures in the interest of national prestige. The alternative lay in mixed exhibitions – some thematic, others linked with national cultures or artistic styles – and an increasing emphasis on contemporary painting and new work.

These shows have, by and large, maintained the exceptional standards of the first 25 years, and the Festival's abundant good-

1947 the Festival soon began to repair the omission with a series of exhibitions, some of which stand to be counted among its major triumphs. It is a sad fact that their like may never be seen again, anywhere in the world. Rembrandt, Cézanne, Monet, Gauguin, Degas, Renoir, Braque, Soutine, Modigliani, Delacroix, Corot, Rouault and Derain were all celebrated with significant collections of their work before the end of the 1960s.

Left, a concert at the Usher Hall. **Above**, one of the many theatres commandeered by the rapidly expanding Festival Fringe.

will could still coax a millionaire philanthropist like the late Armand Hammer to share his priceless collection with the rest of the world for three weeks in Edinburgh.

If you live, breathe, and have any kind of sensitivity being in Edinburgh, August is the month when the city vividly demonstrates why Stevenson used its essential duality as a model for Jekyll and Hyde. The transformation is as astonishing as Dr J's metamorphosis. Off comes the hodden grey, on goes the motley. The staid and sober becomes vulgar and blowsy. That damp hush, settled for centuries up the vennels and closes of the

Old Town, explodes into undergraduate babble. A medieval fair splashes over the urban tundra like spilt paint. Where the town gibbet stood, jazz ricochets off the cobbles. Chaste neo-classical terraces blush with bunting.

The threat of heavy fines is no deterrent to a legion of billposting hucksters. Importuning develops into a form of stylised street theatre. One wink of watery sunshine and frigid matrons turn into shameless strippers. Police are polite, traffic wardens indulgent. Purple rain would not seem remarkable.

Although the official Festival has lost some of its early stuffiness and generates its own quota of gaiety, it is the unofficial festival,

chief to the church halls and warehouses which they fitted up as makeshift theatres. If the spirit of the official Festival is the celebration of quintessential excellence in the arts, the spirit of the Fringe is fun, enterprise, improvisation, and sheer brass neck.

In 1959, Dudley Moore – a serious musician in those days – accompanied a baritone in afternoon concerts and played jazz with cutlery and crockery at night. The next year he was part of the Beyond the Fringe quartet which took the official Festival, London and Broadway by storm. In 1964 one future Goodie and three future Pythons played the Fringe in undergraduate revues.

the Fringe, which works the miracle. This impudent parasite, which has been riding piggy-back on the official leviathan for most of its life, is now so renowned in its own right that in Adelaide and San Francisco it is not uncommon to see "straight from the Edinburgh Festival Fringe" posted on a marquee – as if that accolade should be enough to make you part with your money.

From the beginning, the Fringe mixed its metaphors by letting its hair down. Word got about that Edinburgh was a good place to be young, and the footloose and fancy-free brought irreverence and anarchy and mis-

Two generations of new dramatists have used the Fringe as workshop, platform and shop window. Several plays have transferred straight to London's West End. Experiment is expected, innovation assumed. Many talents have sprouted in this fertile seedbed, and even if you are playing to an audience of only six, two are probably critics and the others are perhaps script editors and casting directors for television companies.

The Fringe has now expanded – with its own headquarters and sophisticated administration – to the extent that in any given year something like 600 companies will present

1,300 shows in 12,000 performances in 180 venues. The turnover is well over £1 million.

These figures bear interesting comparison with the official Festival's most recent statistics – a total of 95 performances with ticket sales totalling more than £2.2 million – but it would be foolish to make comparisons or use these statistics to stoke the tiresome argument that either festival is strong enough in its own right to survive without the other. Because they evolved together they continue to nourish each other and would be immeasurably poorer without each other.

To some extent this is also true of other festivals and events which have been spawned upstart noise, joyfully sponsored by brewers whose commodity has been known to lubricate most of the proceedings. The thirst of its dedicated aficionados is rivalled only by the traditional drouth of Tattoo pipers. Their music spills out into the streets, reverberates through bar windows against kirk walls, and adds to the gaiety of the nations.

The Film Festival, which began as an ambitious flicker in 1947, has developed into what professionals in the business regard as the best non-competitive film festival in the world. It champions new work, explores the significance of cinema styles and techniques, and examines the *oeuvres* of

over the years. The Military Tattoo, almost as old as the Festival itself, has been seen on television by billions all over the world and is perhaps the most enduring international image of Edinburgh *en fête*. These glittering pageants, searchlit in the noisy cockpit of the Castle esplanade, have become folk festivals in their own right. Bagpipes prevail in a tidal wave of tartan fervour, but Breton bombards and Arabian bugles are not unknown.

The Jazz Festival is a relatively recent

Left and **above**, visual spectacle plays a crucial part in Festival performances.

important directors in comprehensive retrospective appraisals.

After many years of barely surviving on a shoestring, the Film Festival is in good heart. Its rivals envy the existence of Filmhouse, the hub and heart of the festival, whose role as an art-cinema for the other 49 weeks of the year generates a committed core audience. The most recent festival cost £420,000 to stage. Grants from various sources totalled only £150,000.

The Television Festival is probably too crowded out by other events to reach its full potential in Edinburgh at this time. The issues it has raised and confronted so responsibly over the past few years suggest the need for a rather less clamorous forum, uncluttered by so much persuasive distraction, and with fewer lures beckoning its all too complaisant delegates.

Each August, Charlotte Square's green grass disappears under giant marquees which house the Book Festival. Established authors from throughout the English-speaking world take part in readings, panels and discussions.

Unlimited funds would solve the major problems of most Festivals. Edinburgh, in all its proliferation, is no exception. After that bravely unequivocal declaration of intent in

1947, the City Fathers have wavered more than once and, in their niggardly support grants, seemed intent on enhancing a reputation – justified or not – for civic parsimony. Neither that behaviour nor the constant carping of a voluble minority of the citizenry – who see their town turning into an autumnal haven for limp-wristed wimps, posturing pseuds, and the world's unwashed flotsam – has ever put the Festival at any real hazard. The idea of Edinburgh without its Festival is now, surely, unthinkable.

Two events in 1988 gave support to that belief. A significant shortfall of funds, re-vealed late in the day, meant that important contributions to the balanced official programme would have to be cancelled. After many minor blushes this was the Festival's most serious financial embarrassment. *The Scotsman* newspaper launched an appeal and a swift response from readers and businessmen saved the day. Within months of that alarm the District Council went quite a long way towards solving a perennial problem by giving the Festival the degree of financial assurance it needs if the director's future planning is to mean anything more than pie-in-the-sky.

Although the city has still to lay a significant brick in the name of the Festival – there are actually fewer formal performing spaces now than there were in 1947 – the effect of what Sir Thomas Beecham called "your northern jamboree" on the fabric and texture of Edinburgh life during the second half of this century is as incalculable as the millions of pounds it has poured into the pockets of city merchants.

Hotels and hostels increase their tariff during the Festival, and every pub, café, restaurant, gift shop, department store, newsvendor, taxi driver, hamburger joint, and pizza parlour within a mile of the Scott Monument gets a little richer in August. Their increased turnover is tangible.

Less tangible is the Festival's enrichment of the human spirit, the elevation of artistic standards, the exposure to new sights and sounds and ideas, frequent demonstrations of an allegedly frigid community's natural bonhomie, and – maybe more important than anything else in conservative Edinburgh – a diminishing tendency to make monuments out of parish pumps.

Festivals are about many things: about hosannas and hallelujahs, about artistic adventure and curiosity, and the constant reiteration of that which has been proved to be special. They are also about people, the linking together of lives and cultures, and they give us the chance to celebrate the best that the best of us can do.

Above, a firework display ends the Festival. **Right**, gallery owner and flamboyant arts impresario Riki Demarco.

As Scotland's capital, Edinburgh has the honour of housing the nation's art collections in three principal galleries: the National Gallery of Scotland, just off Princes Street at the Mound; the Scottish National Gallery of Modern Art in Belford Road; and the Scottish National Portrait Gallery in Queen Street.

In recent times the National Gallery's imposing Ionic temple, designed by Playfair and completed in 1858, has been extended and extensively refurbished. The Gallery of Modern Art is Britain's only national museum solely devoted to the 20th century. Its collection, founded in 1960 in a small Georgian house in the Royal Botanic Garden, moved in 1984 into five times the previously available exhibition space at the former John Watson's School, a fine neo-classical building in its own extensive grounds. In 1998, the adjacent Dean Centre, another splendid building in extensive grounds, opened as the Eduardo Paolozzi Gallery, housing works of the eponymous Edinburgh artist plus Dada and surrealist art.

The National Gallery houses an important collection of Italian, French and Dutch master paintings as well as a fine representation of British and, of course, Scottish works.

As one would expect, there are delights to be found in paintings by Avercamp, Bacchiacca and Corot, Delacroix and Van Dyck, Goya, Hals and Holbein, Raphael and Rubens, Tiepolo, Tintoretto and Titian, Vermeer and Watteau. Tastes vary, of course, but the following paintings might be worth serious contemplation.

An Old Woman Cooking Eggs by Velazquez (1599–1660) is so rich in painterly authority it is difficult to believe that the artist was only 19 and had just finished his apprenticeship when he posed these two Andalusian peasants. Compare the domestic tranquillity of the Velazquez with *Fábula*, an earlier work by El Greco

(1541–1614). This eerie study of a boy blowing on charcoal to light a candle is haunted by the grinning man and monkey.

For sheer sumptuous splendour Bassano (1510–92), in *The Adoration of the Kings*, sings out with all the clamour of a fairground calliope. The artist of *Madonna and Child with Two Angels* is unknown, but it is a luminous example of the 15th-century Ferrarese School, powerful and idiosyncratic in design. Of the world's many Madonnas

perhaps the *Madonna and Child* by Verrucchio (1435–88) is the most exquisitely tender and affecting in its serenity.

Gainsborough (1727–1788), one of the glories of English painting, is most readily associated with portraiture – and, indeed, *The Hon. Mrs Graham* in all her finery is a shimmering example – but his *Rocky Landscape* typifies the technical skills from which Constable learned so much.

Chardin (1699–1779) is represented by his exquisite *Vase of Flowers*, a renowned arrangement of sweet peas, carnations and tuberoses, harmonious and fragile.

Preceding pages: Elizabeth Blackadder paintings in the Museum of Modern Art. Left, El Greco's *Christ* at the National Gallery of Scotland. Right, private showing at a gallery.

Nothing becomes the collection so much as the paintings by Rembrandt (1606–69), especially the *Self-Portrait*, painted in his maturity and, like the others that charted the course of his life, ruthless in its self-examination. *Three Legends of Saint Nicholas*, by David (1460–1523), speaks of some of the miracles worked by the original of Santa Claus. All three panels display fastidious technique and an almost mischievous narrative charm.

Cézanne (1829–1906) painted *La Montagne Sainte-Victoire* many times and used its challenging planes as a model for the highly personal and innovative style which has inspired painters ever since.

Massys (1465–1530) addresses us personally, perhaps on a vexed point of law. The young man is earnest and, one feels, gently adamant. His *Self-Portrait* by Sarto (1486–1530) tells us, with persuasive Italian bravura, what a bluff and hearty fellow he was in his time. The collection has three paintings by Gauguin (1848–1903). *Vision of the Sermon* (Jacob Wrestling with the Angel), greatly daring in design and composition, is as Breton in its Old Testament torment as *Three Tahitians* speaks so eloquently of the enigmatic islanders.

Claude (1600–82), master of the romantic landscape and major influence of genera-

When Van Gogh (1853–90) left Paris for the Midi in 1888 the sun set his palette alight. He died two years and 600 canvases later. *Orchard in Blossom* was painted soon after he arrived, when spring snow melted and trees burst into flower. Vuillard (1868–1940) painted *The Candlestick* at the turn of the century, heavily influenced by Gauguin, masterly in its poise and balance.

To see *Interior of St Bavo's Church, Haarlem* by Saenredam (1597–1665) is to enter its vaulted magnificence. Three tiny figures give it scale. Nothing explains its awesome grandeur. *Portrait of a Notary* by

tions of painters, exemplifies classicism in *Landscape with Apollo, the Muses and a River God*.

Constable (1776–1837) was deeply affected by Claude's vision and discipline. His bosky *Vale of Dedham*—"one of my best"—showing his beloved River Stour, may have been inspired by the French master.

The gallery's major programme of refurbishment recently set aside a special salon for the *Seven Sacraments* by Poussin, a cycle of paintings that would be treasured by any gallery in the world. The room is an evocation of the Poussin interiors.

Turner (1775–1851) is celebrated most spectacularly in the Vaughan Bequest of his watercolours which are shown publicly only in the month of January, when the available light can do least harm, or privately on request. But two oils, *Rome from Mount Aventine* and *Modern Rome-Campo Vaccino*, demonstrate his ability to combine unique handling of pearly, translucent light with an almost elegiac treatment of townscape.

There are many examples of Impressionist art in the gallery but none so explicitly typical of that genre as *Kitchen Garden at the Hermitage* by Pissarro (1830–1903). Compare this airy work of 1874 with the impressive, but

ness captured with sun-drenched, dappled warmth. The only mystery is how the anonymous lender could bear to part with it.

Portrait of Diego Martelli by Degas (1834–1917) is a bold, and at the time, revolutionary composition. The artist's enduring fascination with ballet is charmingly realised in the small bronze, cast after his death, *Nude Study of a 14-year-old Dancer*.

Of the Scottish paintings – and this is, after all, a national collection – visitors might find special reward in the portraits of Raeburn (1756–1823), particularly *The Rev. Robert Walker* skating, it seems, into eternity and the hauntingly beautiful *Mrs Scott Moncrieff*; the

heavily-pigmented *The Marne at Chennevières* of 10 years earlier.

The same violent contrast is also apparent in the work of Monet (1840–1926), with the inky *Seascape: Shipping by Moonlight* seen in stark relief alongside *Haystacks, Snow Effect*, one of a brilliant series, and the almost diaphanous *Poplars on the Epte*.

Renoir (1841–1919) is honoured with one of his master works, *La Promenade* (The Walk), an animated moment of human happi-

Left, restorer at work on Scottish masterpieces.
Above, the National Gallery of Scotland.

characteristically lyrical portrait of children, *Music of the Woods* by Hornel (1864–1933); and, by contrast, the realistic boldness of *The Hind's Daughter*, a superb child study by Guthrie (1859–1930); one of the great Scottish portraits, *The Painter's Wife*—an act of tender homage by Ramsay (1713–84); *Spring* by McTaggart (1835–1910) for its sweet simplicity alongside the same important painter's *The Storm* for its uncanny representation of an angry sea; *The Vegetable Stall* by Macgregor, for its honest realism; the *Still-Life* by Warrender (1673–1713), which reveals a house-painter of rare gifts; and a famous animated example of genre painting, *Pitlessie Fair* by Wilkie (1785–1841).

The Gallery of Modern Art frequently houses special exhibitions as well as showing its own constantly growing collection. This now straddles the century, from the cool abstraction of an early Mondrian to the fibreglass illusionism of Hanson's archetypal American tourists, from Magritte's sinister surrealism in *Le Drapeau Noir* to Hockney's witty *Rocky Mountains and tired Indians*. Picasso, Léger, Soutine, Klee, Hepworth, Giacometti, Ernst, Dubuffet, Epstein, Moore, Derain, and Braque are represented as well as some good Scottish painters.

The National Portrait Gallery provides an extraordinary parade of Scottish lives and character over the centuries. From earlier times, inevitably, the emphasis is on Scottish kings and queens and noblemen and their ladies who could afford to have their persons recorded for posterity. But before long the scene gives way to more modern faces, ranging from David Hume to Muriel Spark.

Every summer the Royal Scottish Academy holds an exhibition in its own Doric temple at the Mound – the one fronting Princes Street and dominated by Queen Victoria looking wistfully, it is said, towards Balmoral. The RSA show is one of the social as well as artistic events of the year. During Edinburgh Festivals the gallery is the venue for the main celebration of the visual arts. At other times, it houses the annual exhibitions of the Society of Scottish Artists, the Royal Society of Painters in Watercolour, and the Scottish Society of Women Artists.

The lively City Art Centre and Fruitmarket Gallery face each other behind Waverley Station and mount new or touring exhibitions throughout the year. The University's Talbot Rice Gallery and Church of Scotland's Netherbow Arts Centre show new work in regular exhibitions. Throughout the city there are at least a score of commercial galleries, large and small, dedicated to selling the output of Scottish painters. And there is the ubiquitous Richard ("Riki") Demarco, who fits no known category but is an Edinburgh arts institution in himself.

Right, meeting of minds at a diploma show.

Where else does a slightly ramshackle medieval town glower down on such Georgian elegance? What other comparable urban centre contains such huge chunks of sheer wilderness within its boundaries? Does any other city in Europe have so many solid Victorian suburbs surrounded by such bleak housing estates? The Edinburgh author Robert Louis Stevenson, summed it up: "Few places, if any, offer a more barbaric display of contrasts to the eye."

The Old Town probably packs more historic buildings into a square mile or so than anywhere else in Britain. Its spine, the Royal Mile, is a wide thoroughfare which runs from the Castle to the Palace of Holyrood House. Thanks to Scotland's young upwardly-mobile professionals, who have discovered the convenience of living in the centre of a city, many of the old, run-down tenements are being given a much-needed facelift.

The New Town, one of Europe's urban success stories, won Edinburgh its sobriquet "Athens of the North". Some saw its urbane classicism as regimentation, but it remains a memorial to the genius of the Scottish Enlightenment. This fact was recognised internationally in 1995 when both the Old and New Towns, together with other nooks and crannies such as Dean Village, were awarded the rare honour of being declared a UNESCO World Heritage Site.

What helps make Edinburgh so civilised is the fact that its centre is not a business area that dies after the offices close. The tenemented inner suburbs, a fascinating urban landscape, enable many of its citizens to live right in the heart of the city. And when they feel the need to fill their lungs, it's a short journey to harbours such as Leith and Newhaven, to riverside walks by the Water of Leith, to the variety of parks within the city limits or to the top of one of the seven hills on which Edinburgh stands.

Such is the scale of Scotland that, using Edinburgh as a base, you can comfortably take day trips to such historically rich locations as Stirling, Prestonpans, Dirleton, Tantallon, Haddington, Jedburgh, Abbotsford, Dunfermline and Loch Leven Castle. And it's less than an hour by rail or road to Glasgow, Scotland's other great city, which is giving Edinburgh a run for its money in both the industrial and cultural arenas. Not that anyone in Edinburgh could imagine why you would possibly want to visit Glasgow. They're in no doubt at all that Edinburgh is the best place in the world – and, for much of the time, it's perfectly possible to agree with them.

Preceding pages: the view from Arthur's Seat; Charlotte Square; meeting of cultures; the Royal Mile. **Left,** Eglinton Crescent oval.

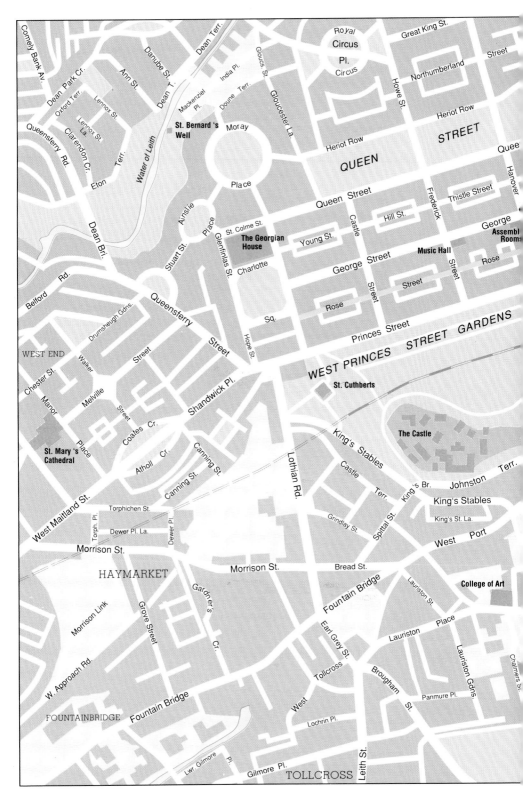

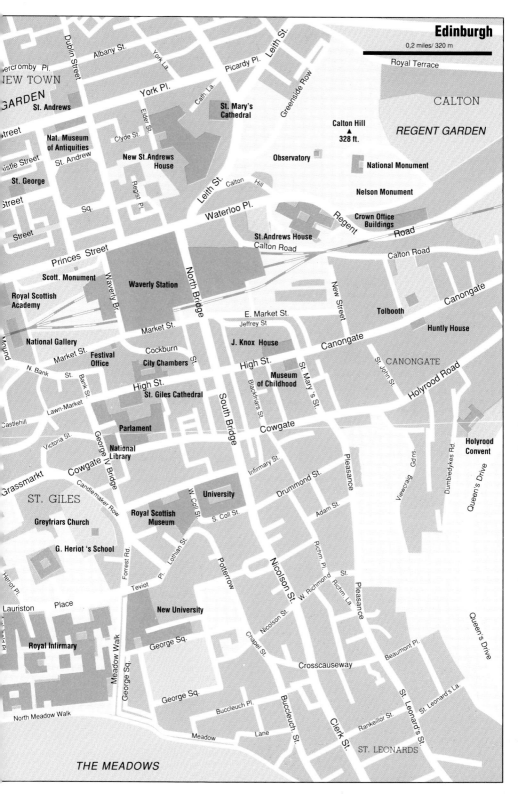

Edinburgh

0,2 miles/ 320 m

NEW TOWN

GARDEN

Abercromby Pl.

Dublin Street

Albany St.

York La.

Picardy Pl.

Leith St.

Royal Terrace

CALTON

St. Andrews

York Pl.

Cath. La.

St. Mary's Cathedral

Greenside Row

REGENT GARDEN

street

Nat. Museum of Antiquities

Clyde St.

Elder St.

Calton Hill ▲ 328 ft.

thistle Street

St. Andrew

New St.Andrews House

Observatory

National Monument

St. George

Regist Pl.

Nelson Monument

Street

Sq.

Leith St.

Calton Hill

Crown Office Buildings

Street

Waterloo Pl.

Regent

Road

Princes Street

St.Andrews House

Calton Road

Calton Road

Scott. Monument

Waverly Br.

Waverly Station

North Bridge

New Street

Canongate

Royal Scottish Academy

Tolbooth

Huntly House

Market St.

E. Market St.

Jeffrey St

J. Knox House

Canongate

National Gallery

Mound

N. Bank

Market St.

St.

Bank St.

Cockburn

City Chambers

St.

High St.

St. Mary's St.

CANONGATE

St. John St.

Holyrood Road

Festival Office

High St.

St. Giles Cathedral

Museum of Childhood

Blackfriars St.

Castlehill

Lawn-Market

Victoria St.

Parlament

South Bridge

Cowgate

Holyrood Convent

ST. GILES

Cowgate

George IV Bridge

National Library

Infirmary St.

Viewcraig Gdns

Dumbiedykes Rd.

Grassmarkt

Candlemaker Row

University

Drummond St.

Pleasance

Queen's Drive

Greyfriars Church

W. Coll St.

S. Coll St.

Adam St.

Royal Scottish Museum

Forrest Rd.

Lothian St.

Richm. Pl.

W. Richmond St.

Richm. La.

Pleasance

G. Heriot 's School

Heriot Pl.

Teviot

Pl.

Potterrow

Nicolson St.

Lauriston

Place

New University

Meadow Walk

George Sq.

Nicolson St.

Chapel St.

Beaumont Pl.

Queen's Drive

Royal Infirmary

George Sq.

George Sq.

Crosscauseway

St. Leonard's St.

St. Leonard's La.

North Meadow Walk

Buccleuch Pl.

Buccleuch St.

Clerk St.

Rankeillor St.

Meadow

Lane

ST. LEONARDS

THE MEADOWS

105

THE OLD TOWN

Not so long ago Tweeddale Court, at the bottom end of the High Street, was a dank ruin on the point of collapse. At one time it had been the Edinburgh home of a border aristocrat, the Earl of Tweeddale. Then it fell into the hands of the British Linen Bank; next it became the headquarters of a local publishing and printing firm, Oliver & Boyd; and eventually it was sold to Edinburgh Distict Council.

For years the courtyard lay derelict and unloved. Then the council sold the whole lot for the peppercorn sum of £1,000 to a 34-year old workaholic publisher, Robin Hodge. Hodge has managed to work a minor miracle. Tweeddale Court is now an amiable mix of flats and offices which house architects, music and book publishers, the Saltire Society and the well-stocked Scottish Poetry Library. Hodge has found enough space for a three-storey house for himself and offices for his events magazine, *The List*.

Fatal stabbing: The place is steeped in Edinburgh history. One side of the court is bounded by a fragment of the ancient "King's Wall", against which there is an old sedan-chair house. In 1806 a British Linen Bank messenger called William Begbie was knifed to death at the entrance to Tweeddale Court and robbed of more than £4,000, then a huge sum. Some of the money was recovered, but the killer was never caught.

"Which is all very historic," Hodge says wryly. "But, if I hadn't taken over when I did, Tweeddale Court would have fallen to the ground. The place was in an absolutely terrible state. I spent months up on the roof just trying to make the place windproof and trying to stop the rain getting in. Most of my friends thought I'd gone nuts."

This is the kind of energy and resourcefulness that the Old Town of Edinburgh has been starting to attract and which is gradually breathing life back into one of Europe's most ancient

cityscapes. Although the Old Town had been allowed over a long period to deteriorate disgracefully, it is now being revived. In 1977 it was declared a "Conservation Area of outstanding architectural and historic interest" and in 1985 the local authorities set up the "Old Town Committee" with a brief to spend modest sums of public money on the Old Town.

Now Scotland's young upwardly-mobile professionals have discovered the delights of city-centre living, and a handful of enterprising developers such as Robin Hodge have been restoring the 16th- and 17th-century tenements and 19th-century breweries to satisfy this enthusiasm. There is some irony in the fact that many of the young lawyers, medicos, stockbrokers and academics who have been snapping up Old Town flats are probably the descendants of the people who fled the Old Town in the late 18th and early 19th centuries.

Finest in the world: The "backbone" of the Old Town is the Royal Mile, a medieval thoroughfare just over a mile long

Left, the Heart of Midlothian. Right, hat trick in the Royal Mile.

which starts at Edinburgh Castle and runs down the hill to the Palace of Holyrood House. There are four separate sections: Castlehill (nearest the castle), the Lawnmarket, the High Street, and the Canongate (which was once an entirely separate burgh). The English author Daniel Defoe, writing in the 1720s, described the Royal Mile as "perhaps the largest, longest and finest street for buildings and number of inhabitants in the world."

But the Old Town is not what it was. Early maps reveal a truly astonishing labyrinth of streets, wynds, closes, courts and alleyways. A study dated 1724 calculated that there were no fewer than 337 closes and wynds in the Old Town, most of them absolutely teeming with people. In 1984 the "Edinburgh Old Town Study" worked out that only 110 remained, 18 of which were blocked off to the general public. The Old Town was fortunate, however, in that Edinburgh's 19th-century architects respected the ancient street patterns when they built the various Old Town "slum clearance" projects (al-though in the rebuilding of the Canongate 28 closes were wiped out).

The population of the Old Town reached a peak in 1851 when more than 40,000 people lived in the area. But in the next 130 years the people fled the Old Town whenever they could. The nadir was reached in 1981 when the population sank to less than 3,000. It now stands at around 5,000 and is climbing steadily.

At the end of the 18th century the Old Town was crammed with all kinds of merchants and manufacturers, from cape makers and bookbinders to brewers, goldsmiths, cabinet makers and brass founders. Today the Royal Mile and the surrounding streets rely heavily (too heavily) on tourism and the network of often tacky businesses that cater to them.

But even after two centuries of neglect the Old Town packs more historic buildings into a square mile or so than anywhere in Britain. Robert Louis Stevenson suggests the reason. "It [the Old Town] grew, under the law that regulates the growth of walled cities in precarious

A Royal Mile carving recalls the words of a survivor rescued from a collapsed house.

situation, not in extent, but in height and density. Public buildings were forced, whenever there was room for them, into the midst of thoroughfares; thoroughfares were diminished into lanes; houses sprang up storey after storey, neighbour mounting upon neighbour's shoulders, as in some Black Hole of Calcutta, until the population slept fourteen to fifteen deep in a vertical direction."

Sanitary arrangements were, of course, notorious. The most famous of Edinburgh street-cries was "gardyloo", a local version of the French "*gardez l'eau*" (look out for the water). This was yelled when the household "tub of nastiness" was emptied into the street from the window. "Haud yer hand!" the pedestrians shouted back as they scampered for safety. Traveller after traveller commented on the stench of the Edinburgh streets. But the slogan "Gardyloo" lives on; it is the name of the sludge boat which dumps sewage in the deep waters of the Firth of Forth.

The highly-stacked tenements (or "lands") were also prone to disastrous fire, although the fact that the staircases were built of stone helped to reduce the risk. After one catastrophic fire in 1824 which gutted much of the south side of the High Street and wrecked the steeple of the Tron Church, the city fathers formed Britain's first-ever municipal fire brigade. In November 1861 the tenements between 99 and 107 High Street collapsed, killing 35 of the inhabitants. One man buried under the rubble told his rescuers to "Heave awa' chaps, I'm no' deid (*dead*) yet", words which are inscribed over the entry to Paisley Close.

In this late medieval version of Manhattan, the aristocracy, gentry, merchants and commons of Edinburgh lived cheek by jowl. Often they shared the same lands, the "quality" in the middle reaches, and hoi-polloi at the bottom and the top. Beggars and sedan-chair men lived in the closes where Earls and Dowagers had their apartments. They rubbed shoulders in the dark stairways, and knew one another in a way that was impossible in

Promotional balloons over the city centre.

England. Any Lord of Session (high court judge) whose verdict was unpopular could expect to be harangued, or even pelted with mud, as he made his way home.

Likewise, politicians, the aristocracy, church leaders and various power brokers came under close scrutiny. With the Scottish Parliament meeting in a building located in the middle of the High Street (just behind St Giles) it was impossible to avoid the eye of the public. When the Scottish parliament approved the Treaty of Union with England in 1707 the Edinburgh mob went on the rampage trying to track down the "traitors" who, they felt, had sold Scotland out to the "Auld Enemy" (the English). The English government's agent Daniel Defoe (the author of *Robinson Crusoe*) was pelted with stones when he ventured to look out of the window of his lodgings at Moubray House in the High Street. "A Scots rabble," Defoe wrote, "is the worst of its kind".

In fact the Edinburgh mob was a formidable political force. For part of the

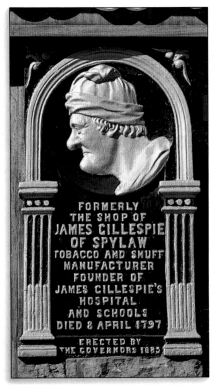

18th century it was led by one "General" Joe Smith, a bow-legged cobbler who believed passionately in the inferiority of women (his wife had to walk several paces behind him) and who could drum up a crowd of thousands within a few minutes. With the mob at his back Joe Smith could lay down the law to the Magistrates of Edinburgh, and ran a kind of rough justice against thieving landlords and dishonest merchants. His career came to an end in 1780 when he fell off the top of a stagecoach, dead drunk, and was killed outright.

Not that life in the Old Town was entirely dominated by the mob rule of General Joe Smith. Far from it. Until the end of the 18th century the Old Town was the epicentre of fashionable society, a tight little metropolis of elegant drawing rooms, fashionable concert halls, dancing academies and a bewildering variety of *howffs* (taverns), coffee-houses and social clubs. "Nothing was so common in the morning," wrote Robert Chambers, one of Edinburgh's liveliest chroniclers, "as to meet men of high rank and dignity reeling home from a close in the High Street where they had spent the night in drinking."

A peculiar Edinburgh institution were "the cadies", men and boys who acted as street messengers, guides and general factotums whose duties included the carrying of golf clubs. Although the poorest of the poor, and described as a "ragged, half-blackguard-looking set", the cadies were fiercely honest. One 18th-century English writer credited the cadies with the fact that "there are fewer robberies and less housebreaking in Edinburgh than anywhere else." The name lives on in a successful little company which runs guided tours of the Old Town from "The Witchery" restaurant on Castlehill.

Aa plaque in the wall of **Jenny Ha's**, a pub at the foot of the Royal Mile, informs that "on this site stood the tenement known as Golfer's Land". It was built in the 17th century by Bailie John Paterson the golfer with, it is said, his share of the stakes from a match when **Plaque in the Royal Mile.**

he partnered the Duke of York (later James VII) against two Englishmen.

The heady social life of the Old Town ended at the turn of the 19th century when it was progressively abandoned by the rich and the influential whose houses were inherited by the poor and the feckless. "The Great Flitting" it was called, and crowds would gather to watch all the fine furniture, crockery and paintings being loaded into carts for the journey down the newly-created "earthen mound" (now called The Mound) to the neo-classical New Town.

The fact that so many of the Old Town's finest houses were inhabited by the very poor may have been a blessing. Most of the people who took over were simply too hard up to make any "improvements", and many beautiful painted ceilings, elaborate plasterwork, and carved fireplaces in places like Chessel's Court and James's Court survived. This anomaly of the poor inheriting the houses of the rich is nicely drawn by James Bone in *The Perambulator in Edinburgh* (1911).

Soldiers and showbiz: Edinburgh Castle itself is well worth a visit and not only for the views out over the city. In many ways it is a very odd institution. Not only is it an ancient monument and one of Britain's major tourist attractions, but it is still heavily used by the British Army as a barracks and a school of piping, and stages one of the world's great showbiz events, the Edinburgh Military Tattoo. It has also been used, at one time or another, as a royal residence, a prisoner of war camp, an ordnance factory and a records office.

With its steep, easily defended sides, natural springs and excellent vantage points, the castle rock was squabbled over for thousands of years, by Picts, Scots, Britons and Angles, and by their successors. It has been taken by the English and retaken by the Scots more than once. It was the scene of the notorious "Black Supper" of 1440 when the young Earl of Douglas and his brother were hacked to death in front of the King. In 1618 the English poet John Taylor wrote

On display.

THE HERITAGE INDUSTRY

"For that is the mark of the Scot of all classes: that he stands in an attitude towards the past unthinkable to Englishmen, and remembers and cherishes the memory of his forebears, good or bad." — Sir Walter Scott's *Weir of Hermiston*

Robert Louis Stevenson was a good judge of his fellow Scots and their propensity for nostalgia, but could he have imagined his home town so obsessed with its own past? While Glasgow looks forward to a brighter future, Edinburgh is in the grip of an industry whose product is the celebration of auld lang syne. "Heritage Centres" have been opening on the Royal Mile at the rate of one a year: the city's past has become big business, with both public and private investors sinking money in expensive and prestigious attractions for tourists and locals alike.

The most expensive is "The Edinburgh Story", its doors opening in 1990 after building costs of £4 million. Housed in the magnificent old Tolbooth Church, whose gaunt, black pinnacles dominate the upper reaches of the Royal Mile, it aims to tell its tale through the sight, sound and smell of 16 "zone settings" illustrating the life of an ordinary Edinburgh family of 1594, and a multi-media presentation of 1,500 years of local history.

"What does Edinburgh offer the tourist?" asks Ann Miller, marketing manager of the Scotch Whisky Heritage Centre. "The castle and a palace which only opens at odd times". The Whisky Centre is a deliberate attempt to provide an all-weather, central tourist attraction which demystifies the national drink and provides an hour or so of entertainment for the family.

It is a bizarre experience. From the heady scent of heather on entering the former school building on Castlehill, to the cat which crouches beneath a barrel in the reproduction barrel-store, nothing is real. Fibre-glass pot stills and lifelike figures of crofters and blenders may facilitate a superficial understanding of the production method and history of the spirit, but give little flavour of the still thriving industry. And the only whisky you'll taste is what you buy from the well-stocked shop.

For authenticity, it's hard to beat the Scottish Mining Museum at Newtongrange, 10 miles (16 km) south of Edinburgh. Visitors to the museum don hard hats for the tour of the Lady Victoria Colliery, led by an ex-miner, whose explanation of working life down the pit may not trip off the tongue like a well-rehearsed speech, but has the authority of inside knowledge of the industry.

"Some of the new museums are advertising interactive computer technology," says Colin McLean, the museum's director. "But the only truly interactive technology is people. However good a computer is, it can't answer questions." Honesty rather than contrived authenticity is the key to the success of the Mining Museum. The Lady Victoria Colliery closed in 1981 and there is no attempt to hide the fact that mining is an industry in decline.

Back in Edinburgh, the staff of "The People's Story", in the Canongate Tollbooth, also feel cast in the role of bailiffs. "As soon as we hear a firm is closing down, we're on the phone right away," says Elaine Finnie who, as assistant keeper of social history, has been amassing memorabilia from the city's homes and workplaces.

"The People's Story" was conceived as a museum of Labour Party and trade union history, but has broadened its scope to reflect the housing, the workplace and the leisure activities of working people in Edinburgh over the past 200 years. It is told by the people of Edinburgh themselves. Hundreds of interviews with local pensioners were recorded and are the basis of the recreations of early 20th-century life.

The past is also seen through the living present at Edinburgh's last remaining Victorian brewery. Although plans to allow visitors to observe the Caledonian Brewery at work are at an early stage, it is in effect already a working museum. Stepping into the maltings or leaning over a tank of yeasty liquid is an experience with direct links with the past: beer is made here exactly as is has been since 1869. Tucked away at the city's west end, the Caledonian Brewery is a ray of hope for those who like their history real, not synthetic, flavoured and prettily packaged. ∎

that Edinburgh Castle "is so strongly grounded, bounded and founded, that by force of man it can never be confounded."

In later times, the Stuart faction tried (and failed) to defend the castle against the forces of William of Orange in 1690. The castle last saw action in 1745 when besieged by Bonnie Prince Charlie's Highland/Irish army, which failed to breach its defences. In fact the citizens of Edinburgh begged the Prince to lift the siege because the castle garrison were wrecking the city with cannon fire.

Many of the castle buildings are 18th and 19th-century, although the tiny Norman chapel dedicated to the saintly Queen Margaret dates back to the 12th century. It occupies the highest point on the castle rock, and stylish young army officers from Scottish regiments like to get married here. Also worth seeking out are the **Great Hall**, with its beautiful hammer-beam roof, and the **Scottish National War Museum** built in the 1920s by Robert Lorimer to commemorate the Scots killed in World War I.

The recently renovated **Crown Room** houses the Regalia (crown jewels) of Scotland which were locked away after the Treaty of Union with England in 1707 and forgotten about. In fact, no one was quite sure where they were until a commission set up by Sir Walter Scott in 1818 traced them to a locked chest in a locked room in the castle. In 1997 long lobbying paid off when the Regalia was joined by the Stone of Scone, Scotland's symbolic coronation stone which, in 1296, had been carried off to London's Westminster Abbey to sit beneath the throne of England for 700 years.

Also tucked away in the castle is "**Mons Meg**" a huge 15th-century cannon which was probably forged in Flanders, and may never have been fired in anger. In 1754 the great gun was hauled off to the Tower of London, but returned in 1829 with full military honours.

Immediately below the castle esplanade on Castlehill stands an iron fountain marking the spot where, from 1479 to 1722, Edinburgh used to burn its

The Edinburgh Military Tattoo in full swing.

witches. Beyond this is the extraordinarily romantic and picturesque cluster of tenements called **Ramsay Gardens**, designed by the late 19th-century planning genius Patrick Geddes on the site of land owned by the poet Allan Ramsay. Originally built to house students, the flats in Ramsay Gardens (especially the ones with the stunning views out over Princes Street and the Firth of Forth) are among the most sought-after properties in Scotland. The nearby **Outlook Tower** houses Geddes's "camera obscura".

Next, occupying a building that was formerly the Castlehill Reservoir, is a functional mill (**Edinburgh Old Town Weaving Company**) which reveals the magic of the making of tartan cloth. Visitors can try their hand at weaving, trace their clan and tartan, and admire a display of historical tartan dress. Across the road is **Canonball House**, a 16th-century house which gets its name from the cannonball half buried in the wall.

Next door is the **Scotch Whisky Heritage Centre**, built in what used to be a school. This venture sets out to explain how Scotch whisky is made, to which end there is a model of a distillery, and a slide show with an over-the-top commentary which makes some astonishing claims for the cosmic significance of Scotland's most notable export. The tour ends with a slow trundle around a series of waxwork tableaux in mobile whisky barrels. On the way out there is whisky for sale. The selection is decent enough – many good "single" malts – but the prices seem to be on the high side.

A few yards down the street is the imposing 19th-century Gothic bulk of the **Tolbooth St John's Church**. Until it was taken out of use in 1984, this was Edinburgh's "Highland Kirk" where the city's Gaelic-speaking population worshipped. They now sing their spine-chilling psalms at the Greyfriars Church. A Gaelic church service is one of Scotland's most beautiful and unique events.

Pots and paintings: Castlehill runs into the **Lawnmarket**, on the north side of which is **Gladstone's Land**, a 17th cen-

The one o'clock gun is fired at the Castle.

114

tury house and shop which has been completely restored by the National Trust for Scotland. The house is well worth a visit, and gives some insight into 17th-century Edinburgh life – dirty, difficult and malodorous.

Built in 1621 and called after the original owner, Thomas Gledstanes, the interior is stuffed with period oak furniture, carved mirrors, long-case clocks, Dutch paintings (no masterpieces) and an assortment of cooking pots, fire irons and other domestic bric-a-brac.

The ceiling of the "painted chamber" is embellished with well-painted roses, apples, pineapples and other flora and is dominated by an elaborately-carved four-poster bed (probably made in Aberdeen). The "green room" is an 18th-century interior, panelled in green-painted timber. One wall is taken up with a handsome display of porcelain and crockery.

Just off the Lawnmarket is **Lady Stair's House**, a handsome 17th-century pile which is now a museum dedicated to Scotland's three world-famous writers: Robert Burns, Walter Scott and Robert Louis Stevenson. Lady Stair was, in fact, one of the later inhabitants. The house was built by one William Gray of Pittendrum in 1622 who inscribed the lintel with the slogan "Fear The Lord & Depart From Evil". The house, restored by Lord Rosebery in 1897, now belongs to the City of Edinburgh.

The displays are interesting in a low-key way. Paintings, etchings, engravings and busts of the Big Three proliferate, along with such memorabilia as locks of hair, bibles, pipes, pocket books and walking sticks. The photographs of the gaunt, sickly Stevenson trying to recover his health in France, the USA and Polynesia are touching. And the enthusiasm of the Edinburgh *literati* for Burns is nicely caught in an engraving showing the ploughman-poet declaiming in front of Adam Ferguson, Dugald Stewart and the high court judge Lord Monboddo. The adulation was brief; within a few years Burns died in abject poverty.

On the corner of the Lawnmarket and

View towards the Camera Obscura.

George IV Bridge is **Deacon Brodie's Tavern**, one of Edinburgh's more famous pubs. It takes its name from an 18th-century villain called William Brodie who was a highly-respected master carpenter by day and an unscrupulous burglar by night. Brodie's life ended in 1788 on the gallows which he himself had designed for the City. From all accounts he made a brave end. This two-faced character fascinated Robert Louis Stevenson and was the model for the tale of "Dr Jekyll and Mr Hyde".

At this point, abandon temporarily the Royal Mile. Proceed along George IV Bridge for about half a mile, passing the National Library, towards a dramatic and controversial new building at the corner of Chambers Street. The new **Museum of Scotland** opened in late 1998 after nearly half a century of prevarication. (Prince Charles, it is said, resigned as president of the museum's patrons because he was unable to override the selection of the unashamedly modern design.)

To the east, linked to the new building, which is dedicated to the history of Scotland, is the original Royal Museum. Its main three-storey central hall with soaring, slender, steel pillars and glass roof – shades of Paxton's Crystal Palace in London – is a superb example of Victorian architecture. Exhibits in the original building include natural history, science, technology and decorative arts collections, not only Scottish but also ranging widely abroad.

Patron of beggars: Back on the Royal Mile, you are now on that section called **High Street**, whose dominant feature is **St Giles Cathedral**, the great Gothic church with its crown-shaped steeple where the reformer John Knox once preached and which remains the focal point of the established Church of Scotland. A church has stood on the site since the 9th century and parts of the existing building date back to 1120 or thereabouts. The church was dedicated to St Giles, the patron saint of beggars and cripples, in 1243, and has been knocked

Victoria Street through the looking-glass.

about a bit. It was burnt down by the English in 1385, rebuilt and extended in the following century; parts were restored in 1830 and it was then remodelled and "refaced" between 1872 and 1873. Work is going on to stop the fabric of St Giles falling apart.

St Giles has always been enmeshed in Scotland's religious turbulence. The Roman Catholic bishops and their trappings were ejected by Knox and the reformers in 1560, only to reappear in Anglican form in 1633 when Charles I tried to impose episcopacy on Scotland. There is a legend that a woman called Jenny Geddes hurled her stool at the Bishop of Edinburgh in 1637 for daring to "say the Mass in my lug (*ear*)". After the National Covenant was signed in 1638 bishops were again ejected, but they returned in 1660 at the Restoration of Charles II. Then, after the "Glorious Revolution" of 1688, bishops were banished for good and St Giles became the "Mother Church" of Scottish (and, to an extent, world) Presbyterianism.

Most of the stained glass in St Giles is mid- to late-19th century in origin. Before that the Church of Scotland took a sour view of such embellishments. One of the windows was installed in 1985 and is dedicated to the poet Robert Burns. The Thistle Chapel in the southeast corner was completed in 1911, and was designed by Robert Lorimer for The Most Ancient and Most Noble Order of the Thistle, an order of chivalry founded in the 17th century and Scotland's equivalent of the Order of the Garter. There is an agreeable café/restaurant in the basement much used by writers (*solicitors*) and advocates (*barristers*) from the courts on the other side of Parliament Square.

The courts themselves are worth a visit, particularly **Parliament House** with its great hammer-beam roof of Danish oak under which the Scots parliament used to meet. Nowadays it is where the writers and advocates foregather to discuss cases, usually while walking up and down. "The ritual is to march in pairs," noted James Bone in 1911, "facing to-

St Giles Cathedral; Robert Louis Stevenson's printing press at Lady Stair's House.

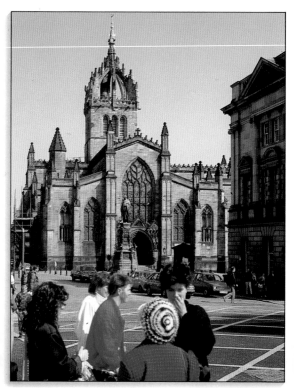

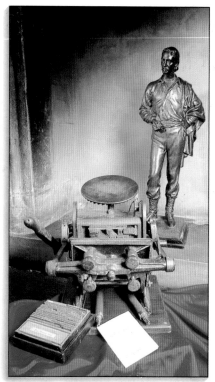

wards one another at the turn like officers on board ship." Parliament House is lined with some handsome paintings and sculpture by artists like Raeburn, Roubiliac, Steell and Turnerelli.

Outside St Giles is the **Mercat Cross** from which kings and queens are still proclaimed, and where a ghostly herald is said to have read the names of the men about to die at the battle of Flodden in 1513. It was here that the Marquis of Montrose was hanged in 1650, dressed in a new suit "of pure cloth all laid with rich lace". This fierce 17th-century warrior, whose military prowess rattled the Scottish establishment to its foundations, died with his "speech full of composure, and his carriage as sweet as ever."

Across the High Street is the **City Chambers** which is now the headquarters of the Edinburgh District Council but which was built as an "exchange" (i.e office block) in the late 18th century. It stands on the site of a house built by Sir Simon Preston of Craigmillar where Mary Queen of Scots spent her last night of freedom before being carted off to Leven Castle.

Running underneath the City Chambers is an old street called Mary King's Close which was devastated by fire in 1750, and where, it is said, strange chills are apt to descend on visitors and even stranger scratching noises can be heard.

At the corner of the High Street and North Bridge is the **Tron Church**, under which archaeologists have found some of the city's earliest streets. It is now an Old Town Information Centre and has an exhibition on Old Edinburgh.

Further down the High Street is Carruber's Close which leads to **Old St Paul's Church**. This was founded when the Episcopalian bishops were driven out of St Giles in 1690, and in the 19th century the church was a rallying point for Edinburgh's Jacobites. The **Museum of Childhood** contains a splendid collection of games, puzzles, models, teddybears, china dolls etc. which children usually find hard to get near because of crowds of wistful adults.

Interior of St Giles; John Knox's House.

Opposite is **Moubray House**, probably the oldest inhabited house in Edinburgh, and where Daniel Defoe lived in Edinburgh during his posting as an English spy. Adjacent is **John Knox's House**, now a museum run by the Church of Scotland and dedicated to the great 16th-century Protestant reformer. There is precious little evidence that Knox ever lived there, but the church tries to remind the world that the Reformation in Scotland was a lot less bloody than it was in England, and that John Knox, far from being a crazed fanatic, was in many ways an advanced, liberal thinker.

The foot of the High Street was the venue for a 16th-century street "rumble" that has gone down in Edinburgh lore as "The Cleansing of the Causeway." This bloody clash happened in April 1520 and was the result of dispute between two prickly border families, the Hamiltons and the Douglases. The latter prevailed, mainly because the Edinburgh mob supplied them with spears on which to spit the unpopular Hamiltons. The battle raged

in and out of the closes and wynds, and dozens of young men (especially Hamiltons) are reputed to have died. The shocked establishment rushed through a law banning the carrying of weapons in public places in Edinburgh.

Canongate and Holyrood: The **Canongate**, the street which forms the bottom part of the Royal Mile, is particularly rich in 16th- and 17th-century buildings. The **Tolbooth**, which served as an administrative centre and as a prison, is readily recognised by its clock, The building, with its towers and turrets, is from 1591, and the clock is from 1884. Today, it houses *The People's Story*, which traces, with smells, the lives, works and pastimes of the city's ordinary citizens from the late 18th century to the present.

Across the road is **Huntly House**, Edinburgh's museum of local history. This restored 16th-century mansion is packed with remarkable Edinburgh-made artefacts: silver, glass, pottery, long-case clocks, furniture and jewellery, plus intriguing collections of Edinburgh police

cudgels and batons, and three-dimensional shop signs made for hatters, tobacconists and instrument makers. Next door is **Acheson House**, once the residence of Charles I's Secretary of State for Scotland and now the **Scottish Craft Centre**.

Back on the north side of the street is the **Canongate Church**, built in 1691 for the congregation which was driven out of Holyrood Abbey to make way for King James VII's newly-created Knights of the Thistle. The Edinburgh mob took their revenge by wrecking the Thistle Chapel which the King had built at huge expense. The Canongate church is a handsome building, but no more intriguing than its churchyard: among the Great and Good buried here are the philosopher Dugald Stewart, the poet Robert Fergusson (whose headstone was paid for by Robert Burns), the visionary lord provost George Drummond and the artists Alexander and John Runciman. Monetarists can pay their respects to Adam Smith, who is buried under a suitably neo-classical monument.

Just below the Canongate Church is **Dunbar's Close Garden** (sometimes known as the "mushroom garden") a small walled plot laid out in the 17th-century style with gravel paths, stone seats and box hedges. It is almost completely unknown to the public. The Old Town used to contain many small gardens. In the 18th century a "physic plot" was the only source of medicinal plants, and flora such as lavender, hyssop, golden rod, celandine and wormwood were widely grown. Below the garden is **White Horse Close**, once one of Edinburgh's most important coaching inns and now a fetching courtyard of white-painted middle-class houses.

The **Palace of Holyrood House** began as an abbey in the 12th century, grew into a Royal Palace in the early 16th century, and was much added to in the late 17th century by Sir William Bruce for Charles II who never set foot in the place (although his father Charles I was crowned in the Abbey Church in 1633). In the 1650s Cromwell's troopers almost

The Tollbooth, an ancient entry into the city.

burnt the palace to the ground (by mistake) and then botched the restoration work. Like Hampton Court in London, Holyrood is now rather an odd mixture of late medieval and 17th-century buildings. Those parts of the interior open to the public are interesting in a gloomy way. The long Picture Gallery features 111 mostly mythical Scottish kings and queens all painted in short order by an energetic Dutchman called Jacob De Wit. They are a late 17th-century joke.

But Holyrood's history is long and often grisly. It was here that Mary Queen of Scots witnessed the butchery of her Italian favourite David Rizzio while she was pregnant with her son James (later the first king of Great Britain). It was here that the scattered remains of the Marquis of Montrose were reassembled prior to being given a decent burial in St Giles in 1661. Bonnie Prince Charlie held court at Holyrood in 1745 during his short-lived triumph.

Holyrood Palace, rich in grisly history.

And Holyrood Palace was used by George IV during his hilarious state visit to Edinburgh in 1822. The portly Hanoverian stalked the palace wearing flesh-coloured tights under an exceedingly brief Royal Stewart tartan kilt. "As he is to be here so short a time," remarked one waggish Edinburgh lady, "the more we see of him the better." An identical outfit was also worn by the Lord Mayor of London, a biscuit-maker from Wapping and one of the King's bosom drinking pals.

But George IV set a precedent which the British royals have been following ever since. Queen Victoria and Prince Albert favoured Holyrood as a stop-over on their way to and from Balmoral. And every June, when the Queen is in residence, the dress-hire business booms and polite Edinburgh goes into a flap over who has and who has not been invited to the Royal Garden Party in Holyrood's gardens. It usually rains.

Place of execution: Running roughly parallel to the Royal Mile, but at a lower level are the Grassmarket, the Cowgate and Holyrood Road. The Grassmarket –

TRIUMPH OF THE TRAVERSE THEATRE

The beginnings of things, particularly artistic things, become more difficult to pin down as time shrouds truth in rosy veils and wishes far too many thoughts. So you will hear, if you care to listen, at least a dozen different stories about the origins of the Traverse Theatre, that world-renowned cockpit of avant-garde drama, which opened its unlikely doors to the public on 2 January 1963.

Even the date, in retrospect, should have been significant. As a result of Hogmanay celebrations, most things in Scotland are unable to move, let alone open, on the sec-ond day of any new year. Yet there they were, a brave band of dedicated idealists, greeting their first audience in the tiny 60-seat theatre they had fashioned with their own hands out of a former brothel and doss-house in James's Court, just down the hill from the Castle.

For the record, the play was Jean-Paul Sartre's *Huis Clos*, the theme of which seeks to demon-strate that "hell is other people". Even before the doors opened and for many more years to come, the sourness of public squabbles was something the Traverse learned to live with.

Round about the same time a student wit in a Festival revue sang:

You can talk of Ionesco,
You can talk of Harold Pinter,
But if you think this town
Is culture's crown
You should come here in the winter.

That jolly jibe on the threshold of the liberated 1960s sums up the chief reason why the Traverse came into being. Edinburgh exasperated its intel-ligentsia with double standards and the ultimate contradiction of the Festival—for three weeks the city leapt to life and became the core of the artistic universe, then the lights went out for another year.

By creating a small club dedicated to present-ing the best of world drama that could be adapted to its tiny stage, the Traverse hoped to burnish the cultural lamp and keep it burning. Its director, Terry Lane, succeeded beyond all expectations by producing a programme which in the first year included a world premiere, eight British pre-mieres, and aired the work of Arrabal and Ionesco, Jarry, Grabbe and Betti. Membership rose to around 2,000.

Forbidding licensing laws and the heavy hand of the Lord Chamberlain had influenced the decision to make the Traverse a theatre club. Up that inhospitable close, in the hugger-mugger convivi-ality of theatre and restaurant, most things could happen and usually did. Membership implied a whiff of daring, a commitment to kicking over the traces.

By the mid-1960s, with Lane gone in high dudgeon and Jim Haynes – arguably the founder-father of the Traverse and certainly its spiritual guru – nearing the end of his tempestuous term as artistic director, the the-atre was attracting two kinds of headlines. The tabloid press rejoiced in nudity scandals, rows over foul language, and internecine punch-ups. Critics in the serious newspapers, such as Kenneth Tynan and Harold Hobson, held the Traverse up to the cultural world as a shining ex-ample of courageous ex-perimental theatre.

In 1969 the Traverse moved into a new 100-seat home in the Grass-market in the nick of time for that year's Festival. There, for the next 22 years, it produced inspir-ing work under a succes-sion of young directors such as Max Stafford-Clark, Michael Rudman and Mike Ockrent, all of whom went on to do notable work in London.

In 1991 the theatre moved to the new Saltire Court office block, which is invariably referred to as the Traverse rather than the Saltire. The main auditorium is a glorious affair with an extremely flexible stage and has been called "Britain's first purpose-built theatre for new writing since Shake-speare's Globe." (There is also a smaller studio theatre.)

Under the auspices of Ian Brown, who has been artistic director since 1988, the Traverse contin-ues to be innovative, willing to take a risk, and committed to new writing: 400 new plays have been mounted in the past three decades. Whether the works are world, British or Scottish premieres (for the Traverse is the home of new Scottish work), they attract a dedicated audience. ∎

now semi-pedestrianised – gets its name from its ancient function as a market-place for Lothian farmers selling hay, corn, and seed. But it has also seen some grimmer crops. The Grassmarket was one of Edinburgh's more important execution venues (along with Castlehill, the Mercat Cross, and the Gallowlees) and huge crowds used to flock into the street to watch convicted felons dancing at the end of the hangman's rope. And it was here in 1730 that the Edinburgh mob lynched William Porteous, the Captain of the City Guard, after he ordered his men to turn their muskets on the crowd.

At the south end of the Grassmarket is a memorial (erected in 1954) to the Protestant martyrs executed in the late 17th century when the Stuart kings Charles II and James VII tried to root out Presbyterianism from Scotland. These days are still remembered as "the killing times". The bodies of the hanged men and women were prepared for burial in the ancient Magdalen Chapel in the Cowgate, the only building in Scotland with pre-Ref-

The legendary Greyfriars Bobby.

ormation stained glass. The **Magdalen Chapel** is now the headquarters of the Scottish Reformation Society which has been involved in restoring the building.

Many of Scotland's Protestant martyrs are buried in the nearby **Greyfriars Churchyard**, which contains some of the most spectacular funerary sculpture in Britain. It also contains the grave of the West Highland terrier "Greyfriars Bobby" (immortalised by Walt Disney). So devoted was the little dog to its master, John Gray, a policeman, that it kept vigil over his grave for 14 years. The bronze statue of the dog outside the churchyard dates from 1873 and must be the most photographed piece of sculpture in Scotland.

Irish influence: Right into the 20th century the Cowgate – now a dismal street running under George IV Bridge – was known as the "Irish Quarter" after the thousands of immigrants who swarmed into the area, particularly after the 1846 Great Famine. James Connolly, a martyr of Dublin's 1916 Easter Rising, was born

and reared in the Cowgate. He worked as a printer on the *Edinburgh Evening News*, and did a spell of military service with the Royal Scots, the oldest regiment in the British Army.

Although most of the teeming population of the Cowgate was "decanted" out into the peripheral housing estates in the 1950s and 1960s, most names on the doors in the narrow streets and closes around the Cowgates are Irish (Mochan, O'Connor, Doyle, Flaherty, Boyle). And the Irish Catholic influence is exemplified by the huge but inelegant bulk of **St Patrick's Roman Catholic Church** (affectionately known as "Saint Paddy's").

St Patrick's has an intriguing history. It was originally built for a late 18th-century Episcopalian (Anglican) congregation who commissioned the painter Alexander Runciman to paint biblical scenes on the walls around the altar. In the 19th century the building fell into the hands of Presbyterians who immediately painted over most of Runciman's work. The church was then acquired by the Catholics who extended the building but couldn't afford to restore the paintings. A group of Runciman enthusiasts has been trying, with little conspicuous success, to persuade the Roman Catholic church to resurrect Runciman's art.

Almost next door to St Patrick's is **St Cecilia's Hall** which now belongs to Edinburgh University, but which was built by the Edinburgh Musical Society in 1762 as a fashionable concert hall modelled on the Opera House at Parma. Despite an unprepossessing exterior, St Cecilia's Hall has a stunning oval-shaped interior which is "remarkable for the clear and perfect conveyance of sounds, without responding echoes..."

According to Lord Cockburn, St Cecilia's "was the only public resort of the musical, and besides being our most selectly fashionable place of amusement, was the best and most beautiful concert room I have ever yet seen." The old hall is still well used for chamber concerts and recitals, and also contains Edinburgh University's magnificent collection of

Traditional shop survives in the Grassmarket.

harpsichords, spinets, clavichords and early pianos. St Cecilia is patron saint of music and musicians.

At the point where the Cowgate meets St Mary's Street, there is a restored fragment of the **Flodden Wall**. This is part of the defences built to keep out the English after the ruin of the Scottish army at Flodden in Northumberland in 1513. The English army did not arrive until 32 years later, by which time the Flodden Wall was complete, and proved to be useless.

The Cowgate runs into **Holyrood Road**, a dreary thoroughfare distinguished only by its view up to Salisbury Craig and Arthur's Seat. Neither the Dumbiedykes housing estate nor the new Moray House College of Education do the street any favours. Beer was brewed in this part of Edinburgh for more than 1,000 years. In 1900 there were 17 breweries in the area. But in 1987 Scottish & Newcastle Breweries closed down the last one, the Holyrood Brewery, which had been operating since 1743.

The abandoned 10 acres (4 hectares)

have been given by Scottish & Newcastle Breweries and British Gas to the Dynamic Earth Charitable Trust which plans to build, on part of the land, the William Younger Centre. This will house an exhibition presenting the story of the planet.

The rest of the site will be sold by the trust to commercial developers and the proceeds used to finance the exhibition project. A small hotel will be built, plus housing and workshops, and derelict closes will be opened up. This, the **Holyrood Project**, it is hoped, will inject new life into the bottom end of the Old Town.

There is no doubt that the history-bolstered Old Town is what distinguishes Edinburgh from Dublin or provincial English cities like Bristol, Bath or Nottingham. Outside London, no city in the British Isles is quite so pickled in affairs of state, church politics, factional plotting, intrigue and violence. Edinburgh is often bracketed with the city of Bath. But Bath is a demure 18th-century lady; Edinburgh is a beautiful old hag with blood on her teeth.

Organ collection at St Cecilia's.

THE NEW TOWN

Credit where credit is due. Just as London owes much of its power and grandeur to the white limestone carved out of the Isle of Portland in Dorset, so Edinburgh owes a huge debt to **Craigleith Quarry**, a mile or so west of the city centre. Craigleith Quarry produced some of the finest building stone on earth – blonde, fine-grained, non-porous and hard as iron – from which most of Edinburgh's "New Town" was built. And it is the neo-classical New Town that makes Edinburgh a world-class city, able to stand shoulder to shoulder with Prague, Amsterdam, Paris and Vienna.

The quarriers and labourers of Craigleith are the unsung heroes of Edinburgh. And the sandstone they carved was used to stunning effect by architects like Robert Adam, Thomas Hamilton, Robert Reid and William Playfair. Most of Edinburgh's finest buildings were built from Craigleith stone: Register House, the City Chambers, Charlotte Square, the Old College, Dean Bridge, St Stephen's Church, the Royal High School, the National Gallery and street after street of handsome houses. Every one of the clutch of buildings which bedecks the Calton Hill was built from sandstone hewn out of the Quarry.

If Craigleith had not been there, right on Edinburgh's doorstep, it is unlikely that the New Town would ever have been built, or at least built as well as it was. The quarry was one of the reasons why, in the words of the historian Arthur Youngson, "a small, crowded, almost medieval town, the capital of a comparatively poor country, expanded in a short space of time, without foreign advice or foreign assistance, so as to become one of the enduringly beautiful cities of Western Europe."

Built in an extraordinary explosion of creativity between 1766 and 1840, the New Town is one of the biggest unspoiled Georgian developments on earth.

It now consists of the northern half of central Edinburgh, 785 acres (318 hectares) in area containing more than 11,500 individual flats, houses, shops, studios and offices. An estimated 24,000 people live within its boundaries. It is the biggest single "Conservation Area" in Britain, and one of the biggest in Europe. In 1987 the New Town won the "Europa Nostra" award.

The whole intricate pattern of terraces, squares, streets and circuses stretches from Haymarket in the west to Abbeyhill in the east, and from Canonmills in the north down to Princes Street in the south. While most of the original New Town (especially Princes Street and George Street) is commercial, 75 percent of the area remains residential, which is remarkable for an inner-city district in a modern city.

Neo-classical Edinburgh is often compared to the English city of Bath, but this is a misleading comparison. Georgian Bath is much smaller than Georgian Edinburgh, and is built from a

Preceding pages: Holyrood Abbey. **Left,** National Trust restorers. **Right,** feeding time in Bellevue Crescent.

sandstone so soft that the city seems about to melt into the River Avon. Dublin is also held up for comparison, but Georgian Dublin (like much of Georgian London) is built of brick and lacks Edinburgh's gravitas. According to Desmond Hodges, the director of the New Town Conservation Committee (NTCC) only St Petersburg in Russia has a similar concentration of well-built Georgian architecture.

The English poet and critic Sir John Betjeman regarded neo-classical Edinburgh as unique. Georgian Edinburgh, he wrote, "is nearly always more three-dimensional than architecture in Ireland, for instance, where you get a splendid facade, but it's rather thin behind. In Italy you often find this stage scenery effect, and in France too..." But not in Edinburgh where "even if you're being Greek, you usually carry the design round all sides of a building."

The New Town is one of Europe's urban success stories. It is why Edinburgh was dubbed the "Modern Athens", and modern Athenians have included, at one time or another, Sir Walter Scott (39 Castle Street), Robert Louis Stevenson (17 Heriot Row), Sir Arthur Conan Doyle (11 Picardy Place), David Hume (St David Street), Sir James Clerk Maxwell (14 India Street), Alexander Graham Bell (South Charlotte Street), Earl Haig (24 Charlotte Square), Sir J.M.Barrie (3 Great King Street), Sir James Simpson (52 Queen Street), Thomas De Quincey (9 Great King Street) and Sir Compton Mackenzie (31 Drummond Place).

Birth pangs: It all began in 1752 with a pamphlet entitled "Proposals for carrying on certain Public Works in the City of Edinburgh". It was published anonymously, but was engineered by Edinburgh's all-powerful Lord Provost (Mayor), George Drummond. A dedicated unionist, Drummond was determined that Edinburgh should be a credit to the Hanoverian-ruled United Kingdom which he had helped create, and should rid itself of its well-justified repu-

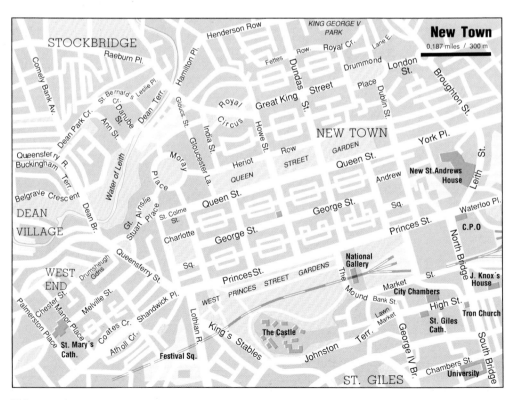

tation for overcrowding, squalor, turbulence and unruly Jacobitism.

What Edinburgh needed, the pamphlet proclaimed, was room to expand. "Confined by the small compass of the walls and the narrow limits of the royalty (*city boundaries*)... the houses stand more crowded than in any other town in Europe, and are built to a height that is almost incredible. Hence necessarily follows a great want of free air, light, cleanliness and every other comfortable accommodation... No less observable is the great deficiency of public buildings... There is no exchange for our merchants; no safe repository for our public and private records; no place of meeting for our magistrates and town council..."

Within a few years of the publication of the "proposals" George Drummond and his resourceful colleagues had raised the money to build an "exchange" (now the City Chambers) in the High Street, had started draining the noisome Nor' Loch (now Princes Street Gardens) and,

most importantly, had invited tenders for a bridge linking the crowded Old Town with the empty lands to the north. By 1772 the bridge – still known as the North Bridge – was complete at a cost of around £16,000.

George Drummond died in 1766 and never lived to see the "New Town" he longed for and did so much to conjure into existence. But that very year the City Fathers organised an architectural/planning competition to develop the land they owned north of the new Bridge. The competition was won by a 22-year-old unknown called James Craig who devised a conventional but highly effective "gridiron" of wide streets running east to west (Princes Street, George Street and Queen Street) and north to south (Castle Street, Frederick Street, Hanover Street and St David Street). There were grand squares at either end (now known as Charlotte Square and St Andrew Square).

Craig's plan was dedicated to that "Patron of Every Polite and Liberal Art"

Two's company in St Andrew Square.

George III, and was headed by a few lines of poetry (doggerel really) written by his uncle James Thomson: "Lo! stately streets, lo! squares that court the breeze!" To some extent, Craig's new town is Scotland's tribute to the Hanoverian ascendancy. The street names are resoundingly Germanic and royal: Hanover Street, George Street, Queen Street, Princes Street, Charlotte Square.

This tradition was carried on by later developers in Cumberland Street, William Street, Frederick Street, Saxe-Coburg Place, and so on. George Drummond would have approved mightily: the New Town is his monument. As was said of the aesthetic debt owed by London to Christopher Wren and as will be said about Singapore's Lee Kuan Yew: "If you would see his memorial, look about you."

Rise, fall and rise: Craig's street plan (which has been dubbed the "First New Town") was a great success, particularly when the gifted Robert Adam was brought in to design the elevations of the buildings. Anyone wanting to build a house in, for example, Charlotte Square had to build it to Adam's design. It was a form of planning control which was highly effective, if occasionally resented. And it produced an architecture which is austere in outline but intricate in detail. The facades in Charlotte Square may look repetitive, but the stonework is usually rock-faced at basement level, rusticated at ground floor, and consists of polished ashlar above. Within the severe Adam framework are pediments, pillars, swags of laurel, Grecian urns and even Egyptian sphinxes.

And the gentry and professional classes loved it. They could hardly wait to abandon their crowded roosts in the Old Town for the grandeur of the New Town. Everyone who could scrape together the cash bought a house on the other side of the "North Bridge". By the 1790s the exodus of the well-heeled from the Old Town was under way, and went down in Edinburgh history as "the

Elegance in Charlotte Square.

THE MONEY MEN OF CHARLOTTE SQUARE

One of the most remarkable facts about Edinburgh is that it is the biggest financial centre in Europe apart from the City of London. Occasionally the bankers of Frankfurt, the Gnomes of Zurich or even the upstarts of Manchester dispute Edinburgh's claim, but their protests are half-hearted and never conceded. How much money is handled is hard to determine, but figures of £50 billion and upwards are bandied about.

Naturally, Edinburgh's huge community of bankers, investment-fund managers, stockbrokers, corporate lawyers, accountants, insurance executives and unit-trust operators has to be "serviced". Which means nice business for the city's glossier public relations firms, advertising agencies, design studios and photographers – not to mention restaurants, wine bars and auction houses like Sotheby's, Phillips and Christie's.

Just as "the City" is shorthand for London's vast financial community, so Edinburgh's is known as "Charlotte Square". But the financial district it inhabits extends far beyond the elegant boundaries of the square itself. It now takes in much of George Street, St Andrew's Square, Queen Street, Melville Street and various other large chunks of the New Town.

Edinburgh's star role in the financial world can be traced back to the enthusiasm of the Scots for making and then keeping money. They have always been among the modern world's best and canniest bankers. Which is why the Scottish clearing banks have a statutory right (dating from 1845) to print their own distinctive banknotes. This is a right the Scottish banks relish, particularly as the English banks were stripped of it following a series of 19th-century bank failures.

And the Scots are remarkably attached to their Edinburgh-based banks, as the powerful Hongkong & Shanghai Bank found to its cost when it tried to take over the Royal Bank of Scotland in 1981. The men from Hongkong were stunned by the ferocity of the opposition drummed up in Scotland, and were forced to back off. But in 1987

the Clydesdale Bank (a Scottish subsidiary of England's Midland Bank) slipped into Australian hands with hardly a murmur of objection. "Everybody felt the Clydesdale was probably better off belonging to some hard-changing Australians than the dozy English," was the opinion of one Edinburgh financier.

Probably the biggest fish in Edinburgh's financial pond are the giant Scottish insurance companies which handle funds of more than £30 billion. The most important by far is the Standard Life Assurance Company which has offices all over Britain, Ireland and Canada and is now Europe's biggest "mutual fund". Like most of Edinburgh's insurance companies, the Standard Life is a vintage operation (1825). Some rivals are even more venerable, with names that have a satisfyingly old-fashioned ring, like the Scottish Widows Fund & Life Assurance Society or the Scottish Provident Institution for Mutual Life Assurance.

Although Charlotte Square has taken a lot of stick over the past 25 years for being slow to get in on the booming unit trust business, there's no shortage of traditional investment trusts. It was with money from these trusts that much of the American west was built up. In the 19th century Charlotte Square was heavily into cattle ranching, fruit farming and railways in the USA. Nowadays it prefers to sink its "bawbees" into the hightech wizardry of Silicon Valley. And while Edinburgh as a whole has benefitted little from North Sea oil, parts of Charlotte Square did very nicely.

For all its clout, though, Edinburgh doesn't have a financial monopoly in Scotland. There's a thriving little financial community in Dundee (mainly investment trusts built from old jute money), and the businessmen of Glasgow have been throwing up glitzy new office buildings in a way that makes Charlotte Square nervous.

"A bit worrying," says one Edinburgh stockbroker. "If the Japanese or the Americans start to move out of London in a big way, there'll be a lot more room for them in Glasgow than there will be in Charlotte Square. The New Town is beautiful, but it ain't very big. And our chances of getting permission to put up offices in the centre of Edinburgh are zero." ∎

great flitting". And when they moved out the poor swarmed in, many of them Gaelic-speaking immigrants from the Highlands and Ireland.

In one respect "the great flitting" was a step in the wrong direction. The New Town resulted in Edinburgh becoming more of a class-divided city than it had ever been. It spelled the end of the social system whereby aristocrats and high-court judges rubbed shoulders in the same narrow tenements with fleshers, baxters, booksellers, caddies and se-dan-chair men. In the New Town such people and their businesses were tucked out of sight in narrow streets and lanes such as Rose Street, Thistle Street, Hill Street and Young Street. Some tene-ment streets – Cumberland Street and Jamaica Street – were specifically de-signed to accommodate "the better class of artisans."

The Craig/Adam "first" New Town was quickly followed by a "second" New Town to the north based on **Drummond Place**, **Great King Street** and **Royal Circus**. It was then extended to the west into land owned by the Earl of Moray who hired the architect James Gillespie Graham to create a street pat-tern very different from Craig's "gridi-ron". Graham devised a series of interlinked circuses and crescents at Moray Place (which has 12 sides), Ainslie Place and Randolph Crescent. The Moray Estate development was strictly controlled so as "to render the plan ornamental to the City and conven-ient for the inhabitants."

The New Town crept down to the Water of Leith into **Stockbridge**. Here the painter Sir Henry Raeburn created the beautiful Ann Street where the houses have front gardens (very rare in the New Town) and which was called after Raeburn's wife. **Ann Street**, **Danube Street** (where property values were held down for years by Edinburgh's most flourishing brothel) and **Carlton Street** run into the handsome terraces of **Dean Terrace**.

The New Town also climbed east,

Graceful curve in Moray Place.

past **York Place**, **Broughton** and **Gayfield** up the Calton Hill where a brilliant, but short-lived, architect/planner called William Stark argued that any development should use the lie of the land and cherish those trees "which enrich and give interest to the whole surrounding scene." Stark's remarkably advanced philosophy was put into practice by his pupil William Playfair in the layout of Royal Terrace, Calton Terrace and Regent Terrace.

And to the west, neo-classical Edinburgh extended out past Princes Street to form wide boulevards like **Shandwick Place**, **Manor Place** and **Melville Street**, which is brought to a startling (and atypical) full stop by the Gothic bulk of **St Mary's Episcopal Cathedral**. The cathedral was designed by Sir George Gilbert Scott and was paid for by the Walker family of Easter Coates, who made their huge fortune by selling and letting land to the New Town builders. St Mary's is the largest post-Reformation church in Scotland.

Although Edinburgh's New Town is now regarded as one of the great achievements of the Scottish Enlightenment, it has had its critics. Nineteenth-century Romantics found many a fault with its urbane classicism. John Ruskin, for example, took a dim view of what he saw as the over-regimentation of the streets. The popular Victorian novelist Mrs Oliphant (who used to live in Fettes Row) complained about "those doleful lines of handsome houses which weigh down the cheerful hillside under tons of monotonous stone." Even that great lover of Edinburgh Lord Henry Cockburn saw much of the New Town as a "blunder of long straight lines of street… every house being an exact duplicate of its neighbour."

In fact, by the latter half of the 19th century the New Town had fallen from aesthetic grace. In his *Edinburgh: Picturesque Notes,* Robert Louis Stevenson observed: "It is as much a matter of course to decry the New Town as to exalt the Old; and the most celebrated

Ann Street.

authorities have picked out this quarter as the very emblem of what is condemnable in architecture." And, writing in 1911, that astute observer of the urban scene James Bone found it "not a little curious that in the last half-century there has been a certain fall in the world's appreciation of the New Town." Indeed, in the first half of the 20th century, the New Town was allowed to decay alarmingly. James Craig's original New Town (based on Princes Street, George Street and Queen Street) rapidly became commercialised and many handsome Georgian buildings were felled to make way for 19th- and 20th-century shops and offices. Elsewhere, private houses were converted into hotels, boarding houses and offices. Splendid neo-classical interiors were chopped about to make dingy bed-sits.

Structural problems, particularly differential settlement, began to plague steeply-inclined streets like **Dublin Street** and **Scotland Street**. Buildings began to shift as underground drains cracked open and underground streams cut the ground from beneath them. In many buildings the sandstone sills and lintels were neglected. Gutters overflowed and rot set in. Many of the lawyers, doctors, accountants, bankers and merchants who made up the bulk of the New Town's population fled to villas in Ravelston, Morningside or Newington. By the 1950s building societies and banks were proving reluctant to lend money on houses in some parts of Georgian Edinburgh.

The New Town reached its nadir in the 1960s when St James's Square behind the east end of Princes Street and the surrounding Georgian streets (King Street, East Register Street, Leith Street, Union Street) were cleared to make way for the grey concrete excrescence known as the **St James's Centre**. There's irony – but little comfort – in the fact that most of the rubble and building stone from St James's Square was used to infill Craigleith Quarry, where it came from in the first place.

The light touch in a National Trust repair shop.

But in the 1970s things began to change. The watershed was a conference on "The Conservation of Georgian Edinburgh" organised by the Scottish Civic Trust, the Civic Trust of London and the Edinburgh Architectural Association. Speakers included Sir John Betjeman, Sir Robert Matthew, Lord Holford and Count Sforza from the Council of Europe. They were at one in declaring the New Town a wonder of the world and an urban landscape which had to be rescued at all costs.

The 1970 conference led to the setting up of the 16-strong New Town Conservation Committee (NTCC) which now has a full-time director and staff, and which by 1997 had doled out around £13 million of public money, mainly on grants to repair dodgy masonry. From the NTCC offices at 13A Dundas Street Richard Griffith operates an aid and advice centre for distressed architecture. Most of the £1 million-plus which the NTCC has to spend every year goes on peripheral areas where the owners and/or landlords have no money to spend on renovation themselves. The lower the rateable value, the higher the grants given.

Griffith and his staff also locate fireplaces, street lamps, plaster mouldings, bits and pieces of joinery, brass chandeliers. They do what they can to ginger up tenants and owner-occupiers to get together to stop some cherished building falling down. They liaise with the 50 or so street associations, some of which are adept at raising large sums of cash for such things as railing-mounted street lamps. Hodges, an Irishman, is also adept at banging the drum for the New Town.

All the money and effort seem to have paid off. The New Town is once again one of the most sought-after areas in Edinburgh. Advocates, doctors, accountants and stockbrokers have returned in large numbers. Even the narrow back streets and mews lanes, once the province of the "artisan classes", are now roosts for young corporate lawyers

Fanlight in Queen Street.

and investment-fund managers. Restaurants and wine bars abound. And the grander houses in streets like Moray Place, Drummond Place and Ann Street are changing hands at London-style prices.

Social life: Some insight into the lifestyle and domestic arrangements of a well-off New Town family can be gleaned from the "**Georgian House**" at 7 Charlotte Square, which has been decked out by the National Trust for Scotland (NTS) in the style of the late 18th century. Although some historians argue that it is more of a Georgian "ideal home" than a real household, the NTS has done a comprehensive job. The furniture, carpets, soft furnishings and fittings are all of the period, the walls are decorated with paintings by Raeburn, Reynolds, Hoppner and Allan Ramsay, and the tables and sideboards are laden with Georgian plated silver and Wedgwood china.

The basement kitchen is a masterpiece of late 18th-century domestic technology. The range features a roasting spit which is linked by a system of gears and pulleys to a fan in the chimney which rotated from the heat of the fire. The hotter the fire, the faster the fan turned, the quicker the spit revolved. To save energy, the heat could be boosted by a mobile polished-metal reflector.

The NTS has also produced a short video which reconstructs a day in the life of the house's original owner, an Argyllshire gentleman called John Lamont of Lamont. According to the NTS and its amateur actors, the Lamont family's day consisted of a brief spell of business, much preparation for the evening and ended with a decorous dinner party for six and a spot of light dancing (Strathspeys etc) under the chandeliers in the drawing room. Coaches at the door by eleven.

This is almost certainly a too genteel version of events. Edinburgh society of the time was notorious (among the English at least) for its rough-hewn manners. Most 18th-century dining room

The Georgian House in Charlotte Square.

sideboards contained a chamber pot which the gentlemen used without interrupting their conversation. (This may be why the ladies fled to the drawing-room as soon as the meal was over). Huge quantities of claret were sunk to the accompaniment of a string of toasts: "Thumpin' luck and fat weans"; "When we're gaun up the hill o' fortune may we ne'er meet a frien' comin doun"; "Here's health to the sick, stilts to the lame, claes to the back, and brose to the wame"; "Mair sense an' mair siller".

Serious drinking and serious thinking were not mutually exclusive. The great philosopher David Hume, who lived on the corner of St David Street and St Andrew Square, was a renowned tippler. It's said that, while Hume was making his way home, he toppled into a bog in what is now Princes Street Gardens. When the overweight genius found he was hopelessly mired, he begged a passing woman for help. She recognised him immediately as "Hume the Atheist" and refused to proffer her umbrella until he recited both the Lord's Prayer and the Creed. This he gladly did.

But the days when David Hume and Adam Smith locked horns over endless bottles of claret have gone. Nowadays New Town social life is much more decorous. Dinner table conversation is dominated by the price of property, the cost of school fees and the moral dilemmas of private medicine – or, more likely – by marble fireplaces, anthemion and palmette friezes, wrought iron street lamps, brass fire dogs, the soaring price of pine shutters and the delights of moulded pine astragals.

The reason is that the denizens of the New Town are passionate restorers and renovators. They are people beguiled by the elegance and history of the place. The New Town generates a rare zeal. When thieves ripped out the fireplaces from a house being renovated in Malta Terrace in Stockbridge, the lady of the house spent the next six weeks haunting every dealer and junk shop in Edin-

Traditional knees-up at the Assembly Rooms.

How Schools Score in Snobbery

Glaswegians, when asked "which school did you go to?" know perfectly well that, if their answer is something like Our Lady of Lourdes or St Aloysius Primary, there's very little chance – no matter how skilled they may be as footballers – that they'll ever play for Glasgow Rangers, a defiantly Protestant team. In other words, in that sectarian city the question has little or nothing to do with education and a great deal to do with identifying a person's religious heritage.

The same question in Edinburgh has a different motive. An answer like St Augustine's or St Thomas of Aquin's would raise few eyebrows and one would be extremely unlucky if it provoked any sectarian bias. Indeed, such is Edinburgh's indifference to these matters that sheer ignorance might even encourage some positive discrimination. These saintly State comprehensive schools sound like private educational establishments – St Denis and Cranley, St George's, St Hilary's – and to have one of these in your *curriculum vitae* would, by Edinburgh's lights, set you apart.

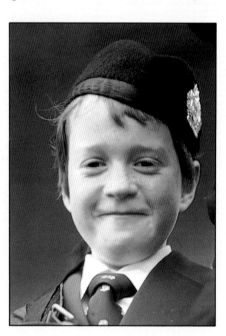

Which school you went to can still plot your position in Edinburgh's pecking order. The discrimination might not be as fierce as the racial and sexual bias that prevails, despite legislation to counter it, but there is no court of appeal when an employer decides against a former pupil of Craigroyston Community High School in favour of an applicant with a Heriot's background and no other superior distinction.

Parents who have bought such an expensive education, often at considerable personal cost, will argue that it was their only way to buck the Edinburgh system and give their offspring a lift up the hierarchical ladder as well as the chance of superior schooling. Some Edinburgh parents who could afford to, choose not to, and take the democratic gamble on getting the best out of the State system. Most Edinburgh parents have no choice.

At the top of the heap are Fettes College (where the British prime minster Tony Blair was a pupil), Loretto School (in far-flung Musselburgh), and Merchiston Castle School, all of which have proud traditions and enviable facilities as Scottish public schools, predominantly for boarders.

Edinburgh Academy, George Heriot's School, and the Merchant Company schools – George Watson's College, Daniel Stewart's and Melville College, and the Mary Erskine School – are the principal fee-paying establishments. Each has several claims to stake: antiquity and tradition versus hi-tech modernity, superb playing fields and sports facilities versus track records in music and the arts, emphasis on science and mathematics versus the humanities. In their advertisements for themselves they would doubtless claim all of these distinctions, but high academic attainment and the nurturing of character is their most heavily articulated common goal.

Fortunately for Edinburgh, it has a score of State-run comprehensive schools whose headmasters and staff share exactly these ambitions for their pupils. Boroughmuir and Broughton, Trinity and Leith Academy have in the past produced members of the Scottish judiciary, newspaper editors, bankers and shipping magnates, captains of commerce, actors, composers, and Scotland's greatest poet since Burns. They will do so again.

Meanwhile, snobbery creates all sorts of traps for the unwary. You might buy a tie at a jumble sale, for example, because you rather like its subtle veins of purple and orange against a black background. Suddenly strangers start greeting you in the street and making incomprehensible remarks which, when you finally decode them, reveal that you have been masquerading as a former pupil of Daniel Stewart's College.

Far and away the most famous Edinburgh school is its oldest, the Royal High School – the "town school" since the 12th century. Its former pupils include Robert Adam, Alexander Graham Bell, James Boswell, Lord Cockburn, Drummond of Hawthornden, and Sir Walter Scott.

A highlight in its history – pupils hug themselves with glee when they hear about it – is the incident when a town bailie (*municipal magistrate*) came to the school to intercede in a dispute over a holiday. A boy settled the matter by shooting him dead at the school gates. ∎

burgh waiting for the fireplaces to turn up. And turn up they did, with the result that the dealer got done for "reset" (selling stolen goods) and some fireplace bandits got a nasty shock when the Lothian & Borders police turned up.

At the other end of the economic scale, the millionaire businessman Sir James Gulliver has spent large sums restoring a house in **Heriot Row**. Money has been no object. There is watered silk fabric on the walls, genuine Georgian furniture in most rooms, handsome gilt-framed paintings throughout, and the light bounces off gilded French mirrors. According to the New Town cognoscenti, Gulliver's ambition is to make his New Town residence Edinburgh's first "million pound" family home.

But the historians say the conservationists usually get it wrong. "For one thing the original interiors were painted in colours we'd consider hideous," says writer and collector David Black (himself a New Town resident). "It was all much richer and more colourful then.

Target for conservation: Heriot Row.

Heavy curtains, heavy carpets, heavy upholstery. They certainly didn't go in for light-coloured paints to set off natural timber. That's a very recent taste. The bright, airy flats and houses we see in the New Town now are absolutely nothing like the originals."

But, for all that, the New Town offers some of the most elegant living in Britain. Glimpses of New Town domestic life can be obtained by pounding the pavements and peering into windows. Alternatively, the New Town walks run by the New Town Conservation Committee every summer usually end with a glass of wine in some proud conservationist's lovingly restored home. The NTCC say that some New Town owners join the walks just to see how others are decorating their houses.

Private pleasures: One of the more dismal sights of an Edinburgh summer is to see puzzled tourists shaking the locked iron gates to the "**pleasure gardens**" of the New Town. They are Edinburgh's great unused resource and most

miserable anomaly. There are many acres of well-tended greenery and trees, right in the middle of the city and all of them are barred to the public. They are for the exclusive use of the "keyholders", usually people who own property in the surrounding streets. They are almost always empty, even in summer. (The Charlotte Square Gardens are an exception, being open to the public.)

Such privately-owned pleasure gardens can be found in Queen Street (17 acres/7 hectares in all), Moray Place, Drummond Place, Ainslie Place, Charlotte Square, St Andrew Square, Royal Circus, Saxe-Coburg Place, Belgrave Crescent and many other corners of the New Town. The Earl of Moray's pleasure garden behind Moray Place and Ainslie Place, on a steep slope running down to the Water of Leith, is one of the most beautiful hanging gardens in Scotland. It is hardly ever used. At the other end of the New Town, the 9-acre (3.6-hectare) Regent Gardens offer superb views over the Firth of Forth to the north

and Arthur's Seat to the south. They are used by the occasional dog-walker.

It is a system which made some sense when the New Town houses were occupied by large families (eight to 10 children was quite common) and their many servants. Then the pleasure gardens of Queen Street, Moray Place and Drummond Place were well used for picnics, games, concerts or just strolling. It's said that Robert Louis Stevenson, who lived in Heriot Row, dreamed up *Treasure Island* while playing by the little pond in west Queen Street Gardens.

But nowadays, when many (probably most) of the large houses around the gardens have become institutions, offices, studios, hotels and foreign consulates, these beautiful corners of Edinburgh are scandalously unused. A few half-hearted attempts to change the system have been made by the Edinburgh District Council over the years, but they came to nothing.

Desmond Hodges, formerly of the New Town Conservation Committee,

Burning leaves in Randolph Crescent.

says that any attempt to open up the pleasure gardens to the public would be bitterly resisted by New Town residents on the grounds that it would lead to the deterioration of the landscape. "It's much better that the gardens are well maintained so that everyone can enjoy them as they walk around Edinburgh," Hodges says. Others feel this is a ludicrously élitist view of a valuable asset, although they appreciate that any public "takeover" of the gardens would be expensive.

Public pleasures: As more than 75 percent of the New Town is still in domestic use, it follows that public buildings are relatively thin on the ground. An eccentric, romantic red sandstone building at the corner of Queen Street and North St David Street, which looks as if it had strayed in from Venice, is the home of the **Scottish National Portrait Gallery**. Flamboyance is not confined to the exterior. Within the gallery, the square, arcaded central hall is decorated with a painted and gilded frieze showing almost 150 full-length figures from Scottish history. The rather gloomy portrait gallery is well stocked with pictures of generations of Scots worthies, while the museum contains many an intriguing artefact.

The Pictish and Gaelic cross stones and carvings are extraordinary. The children's favourite appears to be "the maiden" – the guillotine that stood in the Old Town and was used to shorten malefactors.

One of the most outstanding buildings is **West Register House** on the west side of Charlotte Square. This was originally St George's Church, built by Robert Reid in 1824, until it was taken over by the Government in the 1960s as part of the Scottish Record Office. Much of Scotland's history is kept under its domed roof, including many government files closed for 100 years. There is often an exhibition in the foyer.

Round the corner in George Street is **Henry Duncan House**, the Scottish headquarters of the TSB Bank and called after the Rev. Henry Duncan, the Church

of Scotland minister who founded the savings bank movement in Dumfrieshire in 1810. The TSB has contrived to retain the Georgian facade of the building while constructing a glitzy Dallas-type atrium to the rear, complete with glass lifts soaring to the ceiling.

Also worth a visit are the **Assembly Rooms and Music Hall** at 54 George Street, built between 1784 and 1787 but with the 1818 addition of a Doric portico and arcade projecting into the street. It was once the social focus of the New Town; it was heavily used by 19th-century musicians and entertainers, including Chopin and Dickens. Thackeray was hissed here in 1856 for making disparaging remarks about Mary Queen of Scots, and here Walter Scott finally announced what had been an open secret: that he was the author of the Waverley novels. Still owned by the city, this is the biggest and most successful venue of the Festival Fringe.

The best building in **St Andrew Square** is the one belonging to the Royal Bank of Scotland. In Craig's New Town plan, a church was projected for this site to balance St George's church in Charlotte Square. However, Sir Lawrence Dundas, who onwed the land, quickly proceeded to build a splendid townhouse designed by Sir William Chambers. It became an excise office in 1794 and a bank in 1825. The beautiful domed banking hall was added in 1858, and is one of the treasures of Edinburgh. The equestrian statue in front of the bank is of the Earl of Hopetoun who took command of the British forces in Spain when Sir John Moore was killed on the retreat from Corunna.

Register House at the east end of Princes Street is Robert Adam at his best. Designed in 1772 and built between 1774 and 1788, it was the first custom-built depository in Europe and is dominated by a magnificent domed interior. It is a public record but it stores details of all Scotland's property and land transactions and is heavily used by lawyers and researchers who tend to

Behind the news: Register House.

look askance at tourists. The bronze statue in front of Register House is the Duke of Wellington on horseback.

The old **Royal High School** in Regent Road was designed by Thomas Hamilton and built between 1825 and 1829. It has been described as "the noblest monument of the Scottish Greek Revival" and was until recently the headquarters of the Crown Office (Scotland's prosecution service). In the 1970s it was talked about as a possible home for a devolved Scottish Assembly, but recently has been declared unsuitable for that purpose. It is occasionally used for debate by the Scottish Grand Committee. Also on Regent Road is a handsome memorial to **Robert Burns** designed by Thomas Hamilton in 1830.

On the crest of the **Calton Hill** (333 ft/100 metres) is **Observatory House** (the only building by James Craig left standing), the **City Observatory** (1818) the **Dugald Stewart memorial** (1831), the **John Playfair memorial** (1825) – all three designed by William Playfair –

and the **Nelson Monument** (Robert Burn, 1807). The huge **National Monument** (William Playfair, 1823) was to have been a version of the Parthenon until the cash ran out with only 12 columns completed. It is often called "Scotland's Disgrace".

God's houses: What it lacks in public buildings, the New Town makes up for in churches, some of which are the height of neo-classical elegance.

One of the best is **St Andrew's and St George's** at the east end of George Street which was designed by Major Andrew Frazer of the Royal Engineers between 1782 and 1784. The beautiful oval-shaped interior was the first of its kind in Britain and has been maintained more or less intact. This building was the site of the Great Disruption of the Church of Scotland in 1843 when almost 500 ministers walked away from homes and salaries to form the Free Church of Scotland. One of those who joined the rebels was the Rev. Henry Duncan, after whom the TSB named

their Scottish HQ. "The Undercroft" is a café/meeting place below the church.

Also in the "first" New Town is what is left of **St George's (Episcopal)** chapel in York Place. This architectural oddity – a kind of castellated gothic – was designed by James Adam in the 1790s along the lines of St Bartholomew-the-Less in London. The building was, until recently, a casino and is now offices.

Another Georgian church in York Place is **St Paul and St George**, designed in 1816 by Archibald Elliot and a very effective essay in the neo-perpendicular style. More conventionally neo-classical is **St Mary's Church** in Bellevue Crescent. Designed in 1824 by Thomas Brown, the City Superintendent of Works, the church forms the centre piece of one of the eastern New Town's more amiable crescents. The portico of St Mary's features six columns with Corinthian (rather than the usual Ionic or Doric) capitals. The slender clock tower is topped by a lantern.

Probably the best of the New Town churches is the huge **St Stephen's Church** at the bottom of St Vincent Street. It was built by the City of Edinburgh "to make provision for the supply of religious ordinances to the people." Designed by William Playfair and finished in 1828, the church is described as being "a design of vast scale, Baroque power and Grecian severity." The square clock tower is more than 160 ft (49 metres) high, and contains the longest clock pendulum in Europe.

Like much of Edinburgh, St Stephen's faces two ways: into the comfortable elegance of the New Town, and down to the brash, upwardly mobile area of Stockbridge. The Rev. William Muir, the first minister of St Stephen's, appointed a Gaelic-speaking "missionary" to look after the moral welfare of the Highland and Irish sedan-chair men of Stockbridge. Many of these immigrants had no English, and Muir feared (with some justification) that they were becoming increasingly dissolute and alienated from the establishment.

Of course, Edinburgh's climate can be damp...

EDINBURGH FOOD: A SURVIVAL GUIDE

Edinburgh's fashionable restaurants may differ little from their English counterparts – though steak and game, if not vegetables, do tend to be better north of the River Tweed – but historically the Scots kitchen is no more like the English than the Portuguese is like the Spanish.

That expert in Scots gastronomy, F. Marian McNeill, has rightly scolded that expert in the art of French gastronomy, André Simon, for referring to Scottish dishes as "English fare". Many good things come out of England, she admitted, but porridge isn't one of them.

If flour, even in these days of *nouvelle cuisine*, and meat still form the basis of English cookery, meal and fish form the basis of Scottish, along with bakery, which can sometimes be stodgy, heavy and mass-produced but is often really delectable. Not too long ago in Scotland there were fewer restaurants than tea rooms, where people ate not only lunch and afternoon tea but also "high tea". The latter consisted perhaps of fish and chips and an array of scones and cakes. Such establishments, sometimes with a piano trio providing gentle music, flourished in Edinburgh until after World War II.

Biscuit-making remains an extensive industry, and orange marmalade is a renowned export – though the theory that the name "marmalade" derives from the words *Marie est malade* (referring to the food given to Mary Queen of Scots when she was ill) is still hotly debated.

Kippers, too, are a treat. The best are from Loch Fyne or the Achiltibuie smokery in Ross and Cromarty, where their colour remains properly golden, not dyed repellent red as they are in so many places. Finnan-haddies (*alias* haddock) are a tasty alternative, boiled in milk and butter. Salmon and trout, sadly, are just as likely to come from some west-coast or northern fish farm as fresh from the river, but the standard remains high. If buying from a fishmonger, ask for "wild" salmon, more flavourful than the farmed variety.

Venison, pheasant, hare and grouse are equally

established features of the Scottish kitchen. Admittedly, the romance of eating grouse after it has been ritually shot on or around 12 August should be tempered by this bird's depressingly fibrous toughness, which makes grouse shooting seem, to a gourmet, an unutterable waste of time.

As for haggis – though it, too, is hardly a gourmet delight – it does offer a fascinating experience for brave visitors. Scotland's great mystery dish is really only a sheep's stomach stuffed with its minced heart, liver and lights, along with suet, onions and oatmeal. After being boiled, the stomach is sliced open, as spectacularly as possible, and the contents served piping hot. Butchers today often use a plastic bag instead of a stomach; this has the advantage that it is less likely to burst during the boiling process, ruining the meat. But no haggis devotee would contemplate such a substitute.

The tastiest haggis, by acclaim, comes from Macsween's of Edinburgh, who also make a vegetarian haggis. Small portions of haggis are sometimes served as starter courses in fashionable restaurants, though an authentic way to eat it is as a main course with chappit tatties (potatoes), bashed neeps (mashed turnips) and a number of nips (Scotch whisky, preferably malt).

This is especially so on Burns Night (25 January), when supper is ceremonially accompanied by poetry reading, music and Burns's own *Address to the Haggis*; or else on St Andrew's Night (30 November), when haggis is again attacked with considerable gusto.

No adventurous eater should pass up such exotic-sounding fare as feather fowlie (a chicken soup), cock-a-leekie (a soup made from chicken and leeks, but authentic only if it also contains prunes), hugga-muggie (Shetland fried haggis, using the fish's stomach), Arbroath smokies (smoked haddock stuffed with butter), crapit heids (haddock heads stuffed with lobster), stovies (potatoes cooked with onion), and cream crowdie (a mixture of oatmeal, sugar and rum).

Though the Scots are said to like far more salt in their soup – and with their fish and vegetables – than the English, they also possess an exceptionally sweet tooth. This is also evidenced in their penchant for fizzy lemonade. ∎

GRAVEYARDS WITH TALES TO TELL

In the early 19th century Edinburgh's graveyards were famous for being infamous. As many a surviving cemetery watchtower testifies, they became the hunting ground of "resurrectionists" – those body-snatchers who plundered fresh graves for corpses to sell to research and demonstration classes in the city's medical school.

This trade – often encouraged by the no-questions-asked attitude of the distinguished men of medicine in receipt of its supplies – was taken to its logical, if nefarious, conclusion by the notorious duo William Burke and William Hare. They cut corners by assisting the anatomical specimens of Robert Knox, Fellow of the Royal College of Surgeons, into the condition required for his highly popular lectures.

When it was discovered that Burke and Hare had murdered at least 16 people and sold their bodies to Knox for seven pounds 10 shillings (£7.50) each, the anatomist's reputation was permanently tarnished. A mob attacked his house and burned his effigy and his colleagues indicted him for the zeal which made him indifferent to the source of his clandestine corpses.

It's impossible to visit any of Edinburgh's graveyards without reflecting on these events; but the most celebrated have associations which eclipse this grisly episode in the city's history.

Disney world: Popular fame – disseminated worldwide by Walt Disney and the cinema—is the lot of the historic **Kirkyard of Greyfriars**, which lies close to the west side of George IV Bridge. At the junction of the bridge and Candlemaker Row is a fountain topped by a statue of a Skye terrier – Greyfriars Bobby, the little dog which has become a saint in the iconology of canine loy-

Left, the Lincoln Monument in Old Calton Burial Ground.

alty. Bobby belonged to John Gray, a Pentlands shepherd who brought him to Edinburgh every market day. The two would have their midday meal in the tavern opposite the kirkyard gate (now called Greyfriars Bobby).

When Gray was buried in the old cemetery in 1858, the dog refused to leave his grave. He "kept watch" there for 14 years, leaving his post only at midday to continue his custom of lunching at the local inn. When Bobby died in 1872, his statue was designed in bronze by William Brodie and paid for by Baroness Burdett-Coutts.

But sentimental pilgrims to Greyfriars should know that the kirkyard was the scene of a key event in Scottish history, and that it contains the country's best and most bizarre collection of 17th-century monuments. It was here that the National Covenant was signed in 1638 – an act of religious defiance which precipitated a bitter internecine war.

In 1679, 1,200 Covenanters were taken prisoner at the Battle of Bothwell Bridge and held for five months in an enclosure (which you can still see) in the south of the graveyard, with no shelter and very little food. The courage of the Covenanters was, in today's terms, the blind heroism of the zealot. These rigorous Presbyterians refused to accept the episcopalian form of church government which was being forced on the Church of Scotland by Charles I.

Notable occupants of Greyfriars Churchyard, which was a burial ground on the site of a 15th-century Franciscan friary even before the Old Greyfriars Kirk was built in 1612, include the poet Allan Ramsay and his eponymous son, the painter; George Buchanan, adviser to Mary Queen of Scots and tutor to her son James VI; Captain Porteous, whose actions provoked the Porteous Riots of 1736; and the Earl of Morton, who was Regent during the minority of James VI but who was executed for his part in the earlier murder of Lord Darnley.

If less ancient in history, Edinburgh's other two cemeteries of distinction are **Greyfriars.**

worth visiting for their situations and memorials. Just below Waterloo Place, on a lower slope of the Calton Hill, is the **Old Calton Burial Ground**, which dates from the 18th century and contains some impressive monuments to Edinburgh citizens who made their mark both locally and internationally. The finest of them is Robert Adam's tomb for the philosopher David Hume. (Adam's first sketches suggest his inspiration was the tomb of Theodoric at Ravenna, in Italy.)

This burial ground is also home to the **Lincoln Monument**, built in 1893 and dedicated to Scottish-American soldiers who died in America's Civil War. In the centre is an obelisk which pays tribute to five political martyrs, bent only on reform, who were found guilty of sedition in 1793 and sentenced to transportation. The government was edgy about revolution (in the aftermath of the French Revolution of 1789) but it had recovered its nerve when the obelisk was raised in 1844.

In the West End of Edinburgh, across the Dean Bridge in the old parish of Dean, is Edinburgh's answer to Glasgow's grandiose Victorian Necropolis. The **Dean Cemetery**, surrounded by high walls, is not a conspicuous landmark like the Necropolis but it does contain tombs and memorials which are similar expressions of Victorian self-regard, and which try to defy mortality.

It was laid out in 1845 on the policies of Dean House, a significant 17th-century mansion which fell victim to the redevelopment of the Dean estate. Some of its more interesting stones are preserved in the cemetery's boundary wall. Enthusiasts for spectacular tombstone sculpture should look out for the Grecian temple of James Buchanan, founder of the Educational Institute of Glasgow; the 30-ft (9-metre) granite obelisk which marks the grave of Alexander Russell, editor of *The Scotsman*; and the confident pyramid of red polished granite which is raised above the remains of Lord Rutherfurd of Lauriston Castle.

Canongate Churchyard, with Arthur's Seat in the background.

THE TENEMENT LANDSCAPE

Not many people know this, but the cartoonist Ronald Searle's fictitious centre of mayhem and chaos, St Trinian's School for Young Ladies, sprang from the south Edinburgh suburb of Marchmont. Between 1922 and 1946 an Edinburgh schoolteacher called Miss C. Fraser Lee ran an establishment there called St Trinnean's School for Girls (motto: "Light and Joy") along the lines of the liberal "Dalton" system of education. In some straight-laced Edinburgh circles this was seen as anarchy, and Miss C. Fraser Lee's college for middle-class young ladies acquired a totally unjustified reputation as an educational free-for-all.

Searle learned all about St Trinnean's school from two of Miss C. Fraser Lee's pupils when he was posted to Scotland as an army engineer in 1941. The combination of female gentility and utter chaos was a notion that appealed to him hugely, and he immediately dashed off a cartoon to the magazine *Punch.* When the war was over, Searle returned to the subject of St Trinian's with a vengeance. The rest, as they say, is history.

Which is, somehow, typical of the respectable suburbs of inner Edinburgh. Nothing is quite what it seems. The well-crafted tenements of **Marchmont**, **Bruntsfield**, **Morningside** and **Merchiston** throw up many contradictions and surprises. Another fictional monster from the inner suburbs of Edinburgh is Miss Jean Brodie, Muriel Spark's demure schoolteacher with advanced ideas who taught her *crème de la crème* to thrill to the iron hand of the Italian dictator Mussolini.

The tenemented inner suburbs of Edinburgh are a fascinating landscape. They were built for, and are still largely inhabited by, hard-working, reasonably well-off schoolteachers, bank clerks, insurance under-managers and shopkeepers. The bigger flats contained enough rooms to house a servant or two. It is probably from these suburban tenements that Edinburgh acquired its reputation for gentility and sniffishness. "All fur coats and nae drawers (*no underwear*)" is a traditional Edinburgh opinion of the denizens of the city's posher inner-city tenements.

In some parts of Britain the word "tenement" is synonymous with poverty and hard times. Not in Edinburgh. The citizens of Edinburgh have long been used to living high. In the Old Town the "quality" and hoi-polloi lived cheek-by-jowl in narrow tenements, rubbing shoulders on the common stairs. And even when the Scottish gentry moved north into the purpose-built elegance of the New Town, most of them continued to live in flats.

The enthusiasm of Edinburgh's middling-classes for suburban villas with gardens front and rear is a recently-acquired taste. Which is why Edinburgh's inner suburbs – unlike the inner suburbs of, say, London, Liverpool or

Manchester – are overwhelmingly a landscape of stone-built tenements. The long rows of three-up two-down houses which characterise so many English cities, hardly appear in Edinburgh. Much of the inner city consists of great cliffs of blonde (and sometimes red) sandstone, usually four or five storeys high, and often elaborately modelled.

The effect varies. In a setting sun against a blue sky, the tenement cliffs of Edinburgh can be stunning; in a lowering drizzle, the streets can seem like the dankest of canyons. But it is a cityscape full of surprises.

The quality and style of the tenements vary, depending on who they were built for. Those built to house Edinburgh's working-classes (at Tollcross, Leith, Tynecastle and Fountainbridge) tend to be flat-fronted, unadorned, and about as interesting as cold porridge. They contain pokey flats which have precious little in the way of embellishment. On the other hand, the Edwardian buildings run up for the middle-classes (at Spottiswoode, Comely Bank, Goldenacre) tend to be restrained but handsome, with bay windows, ceramic-clad common stairways and excellent plasterwork and joinery.

But by far the best are the tenements built in the exuberant "Scottish Baronial" style of the late 19th century. These are some of the city's unsung splendours. Inner suburbs like Marchmont, Bruntsfield, Morningside, Polwarth and Merchiston (and, to a lesser extent, Abbeyhill, Leith and London Road) are crammed with elaborately-modelled tenement blocks, most of them bristling with spires, corner turrets, crow-stepped gables, mock cannons, skewputts and mock gargoyles, all topped with wrought-iron roof ridges, fancy lightning conductors and weather vanes.

It all forms, in the view of architectural historian-critic Colin McWilliam, "large-scale splendour that can speak from a distance, with carefully composed elevations and majestic corner towers." For aficionados of architec-

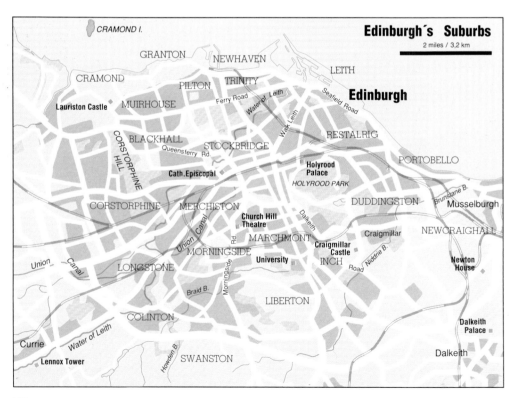

tural detail, inner-city Edinburgh is a veritable paradise. The city owes this fantasy-land to a handful of energetic practitioners like John Pyper, George Wilson, Edward Calvert, John C. Hay and the resoundingly named Hippolyte Jean Blanc (who was born and bred in Edinburgh of a French father and an Irish mother).

Marchmont's majesty: Baronial Edinburgh is probably at its finest in the district of **Marchmont**, which is situated about a mile south of the High Street, on the edge of the handsome public park known as The Meadows. Marchmont owes its existence to the commercial shrewdness of Sir George Warrender of Lochend, whose family had owned the land around the area since 1695. When Warrender realised, in the middle of the 19th century, that he could get a lot more money by "feuing" (leasing) his land out for housing instead of renting it out for grazing, he hired a clutch of experts (among them the architect David Bryce) to put together a development plan for the area.

By 1869 the first of the Marchmont feu plans was drawn up. But Warrender laid down conditions. All the street names (Marchmont, Warrender, Arden, Lauderdale, Thirlestane and Alvanley) were to be called after the various branches of his family and all the tenements were to be designed on flamboyant Scottish baronial principals. Elevations were to be approved by Warrender himself. And to maintain the respectability of the area – not to mention the property values – none of the shops in Marchmont were to be rented to purveyors of hard liquor. Although that last condition has long since lapsed, there are still remarkably few pubs.

The construction of Marchmont between 1869 and 1914 was a huge building programme. But it produced the greatest concentration of baronial tenements anywhere in Scotland. Streets like Warrender Park Road, Warrender Park Terrace and Marchmont Road positively bristle with turrets, spires, can-

Tollcross: civic design is apparent from the air.

dle-snuffer roofs, ogee-shaped domes and other architectural features.

Many of the architects (and some of the builders) tricked the buildings out with fancy plaques bearing their own initials (EC is Edward Calvert, ABC is the Argyle Building Company, JP is John Pyper and so on). Probably the best – or at least the most vigorous of the designs – were Edward Calvert's who was responsible for most of the astonishing Warrender Park Terrace facing The Meadows.

The whole development was a great success. Edinburgh's expanding middle-classes fell over themselves to buy the roomy flats of Marchmont. Sir George Warrender and his family became even richer, and continued to live in the 16th- and 17th-century splendour of Bruntsfield House, which is now a part of James Gillespie's High School. And to educate Marchmont's booming child population, the Edinburgh School Board ran up James Gillespie's primary school, among whose alumni are TV comedian Ronnie Corbett, the late film actor Alistair Sim and former Liberal Party leader David Steel. (Gillespie himself was an 18th-century snuff merchant turned philanthropist, whose homely bust can be seen in the Merchants' Halls in Hanover Street.)

Bruntsfield and Merchiston: The district of **Bruntsfield** lies to the west on the other side of the Bruntsfield Links, which is about all that is left of the "burgh muir" (town's land) where James IV assembled the huge Scots army which he marched to ruin and to dreadful defeat at Flodden in the north of England in 1513. Many of Edinburgh's plague victims were also buried on the "burghmuir", and human remains used to turn up regularly in suburban gardens all over south Edinburgh.

Although the sandstone tenements of Bruntsfield are generally less flamboyant than those in Marchmont, there are handsome examples by architects such as MacGibbon & Ross (Bruntsfield Crescent) and Hippolyte J. Blanc (Brunts-

No smoke without fire: the Victorians didn't stint on chimneys.

158

field Terrace). The great sandstone cliffs march down the hill to Polwarth to the north and Merchiston in the west.

Good-looking tenements abound, especially in Viewforth Square, but public buildings are few, although some are worth searching out. One such is Edward Carfrae's **Boroughmuir School** (1911) in Viewforth.

Another building well worth a look is **Merchiston Tower**, a recently-restored 16th-century tower house now surrounded by the uninspired 1960s modern of Napier University. (Until 1992 Napier was a college rather than a university; with 9,000 students, it is one of Scotland's large higher educational institutions.) This is the family home of John Napier of Merchiston (1550–1617) the Presbyterian theologian and mathematical genius who not only devised logarithms and cooked up the idea of the decimal point, but published a paper entitled "Secrette Inventionis" which gave the world the notion of the armoured tank and the military subma-

rine. John Napier may have been a favourite of King James VI, but to the locals he was some kind of necromancer and adept in the black arts. So one of the world's great original mathematicians (who ranks with Newton, Copernicus and Kepler) went down in Scots history as "The Wizard of Merchiston".

Churchill and Morningside: Churchill (or "holy corner") is so called because of the assortment of churches which stand at the four corners of the crossroads at Bruntsfield Road, Colinton Road and Chamberlain Road. None of the churches is of any particular architectural or historical interest, except perhaps Hippolyte J. Blanc's exercise in elaborate French-style Gothic at **Christ Church** (Episcopal) on Bruntsfield Place where Blanc was a member of the congregation. The church was built between 1875 and 1878.

A much more interesting history is attached to the Italianate **St Peter's Church (Roman Catholic)** in Falcon Avenue. St Peter's is a product of that

A fine day in Logregreen Road.

bizarre conjunction of circumstances which seems to underpin so much Edinburgh history. The church was set up in 1907 in one of the most staunchly Protestant parts of Edinburgh by Canon John Gray, an English-born priest. It was funded by his friend Andre Raffalovitch, a wealthy Russian-born Jew who had fallen in love with the city. The building was designed by Sir Robert Lorimer, probably the most important Scots architect of his time.

Another building with some ecclesiastical resonance is the **Churchill Theatre** on Morningside Road. Built in 1892 to a design by Hippolyte Blanc, this was the last building occupied by the Morningside Free Church congregation, one of whose ministers (until his death in 1847) was the great Thomas Chalmers. A brilliant theologian, orator and mathematician, Chalmers was the leading light of the 1843 "Disruption" which split the Church of Scotland.

One of the many buildings the itinerant Free Church congregation used before they found a home was the tiny schoolhouse on the opposite side of Morningside Road. For most of its working life this handsome little building (1823) was known as the "cuddy" school after the number of country children who travelled to the school on their "cuddies" (the Scots word for horses and ponies). The animals were tethered in the lane beside the school which is still known as Cuddy Lane.

On the other side of the road is a lump of grey stone which is claimed (without a shred of evidence) to be the "bore stone" on which James IV raised his banner in the pre-Flodden gathering.

Morningside has had its share of unlikely residents (permanent and temporary). Jane Welsh Carlyle was one, as was David Deuchar, the jeweller who discovered the genius of Henry Raeburn. George Meikle Kemp, the architect/builder who designed the Scott Monument in Princes Street, lived in Morningside, as did Susan Ferrier, the 19th-century novelist who was regarded

Left, night falls on Morningside. Below, languid afternoon in London Road.

THE OUTER DARKNESS

Edinburgh may be one of Europe's most handsome cities, but it is not without blemish. It may not have an "inner city" problem, but it certainly has its "outer city" difficulties, being ringed to the east, south and west with some of Britain's most depressing and crime-ridden municipal housing estates. Indeed, the odd, rather spiky names of Craigmillar, The Inch, Niddrie, Oxgangs, Dumbiedykes, Pilton, Muirhouse and Hailes have become bywords for problems of crime, vandalism and misery which the decent communities they house are now struggling to overcome.

Some of Edinburgh's housing estates are a formidable size. North and South Hailes, for example, contain more than 5,000 houses. There are 2,600 dwellings at Craigmillar, 2,500 at Stenhouse, 2,500 at Muirhouse, 2,200 at The Inch, 2,100 at Kaimes, and so on. In all, there are more than 50,600 houses, but most are concentrated in a huge arc running from Craigmillar and Niddrie in the east, round the city to Muirhouse and Pilton in the west.

Because 70 percent of them were thrown up in the great building boom of the 1950s and 1960s, they tend to suffer from bad design and poor workmanship and are now plagued with damp, condensation, mildew, sprawled concrete, faulty wiring, dire sound insulation, rotten security and eternally broken lifts. The Edinburgh District Council (EDC) says it needs at least £200 million to lick its housing stock into some kind of shape.

Yet, despite all the problems that beset the estates, the EDC has a list of 13,000 people waiting for council houses, and another 10,000 or so who have them but want to "exchange" to another part of the city. What's more, 3,600 council houses are lying empty, mostly because they are about to be repaired, but many because "there is no apparent demand from anyone on the waiting list". In other words, they are unacceptable even to people who are desperate to have a roof over their heads.

These boarded-up properties are now known in chilling bureaucratese as "long-term voids", and often fall prey to squatters, glue sniffers and drug abusers, or become "headquarters" for teenage street gangs like the Granton Young Parkie, the Drylaw Mental or the Bar-Ox. (Street gangs are an old problem in many parts of Edinburgh; in 1981 there was a nasty outbreak of "copy-cat" rioting on some of the Edinburgh housing estates when Brixton in London and Toxteth in Liverpool went up in flames.)

But the fact is that about 25 percent of the population of Edinburgh – or around 108,000 people – live in council housing estates, some of which have devastatingly high levels of poverty and unemployment. At the last count, more than 25 percent of the people in Craigmillar, for example, were out of a job, 24 percent in nearby Niddrie, 23 percent in Pilton and 22 percent in Muirhouse.

These figures hide a male unemployment rate of around 40 percent, and a level of youth unemployment which is appalling. A recent survey of 16 to 21 year-olds on the Muirhouse estate revealed that more than 80 percent of them were workless and living entirely on state benefit.

The EDC also says that more than 33,000 of its tenants (roughly one in three) are living below the poverty line. And the Council is frank about the effect of such miserable housing on the health of Edinburgh's citizens. A recent report cited research that linked dampness "with the physical ill-health of children and the mental ill health of mothers" and poor housing with serious health problems ranging from "mental and emotional stress to drug abuse (with possible links to Hepatitis B and Aids)."

In fact, Edinburgh has the worst incidence of Aids in Britain outside of London, almost all of it confined to the drug-abusers on the big housing estates. One Member of Parliament complained that "in some streets in Muirhouse drugs are being pushed quite openly at times."

In Muirhouse and Pilton an estimated 33 percent of the area's "junkies" are HIV-positive, and could develop full-blown Aids at any time. "That's a serious problem for the future" is the view of one doctor who works in the area. "I just don't know if we would be able to cope with an Aids problem like that." ∎

as "Scotland's Jane Austen". Morningside House (now replaced by a supermarket) was home to the eccentric high-court judge Lord Gardenstone, a man who "increased the mirth of the company" and who liked to warm his bed with piglets and to ride into town with a servant dressed in full Highland dress trotting behind him.

Further down Morningside Road, on the opposite side, is Morningside's liveliest and most famous hostelry, officially called the "**Volunteer Arms**", but always known as "The Canny Man's". The pub owes its official title to the fact it was used by the Edinburgh Volunteers (the local militia) on their way to and from the musket range at Blackford Hill. The title "Canny Man's" is ascribed to James Kerr who bought the pub in 1871 and used to instruct his hard-drinking customers to "*Ca' canny*" (i.e. take it easy). The Canny Man's is worth a visit for a large selection of clocks, pictures, posters, bridles and hunting horns – indeed, anything that can be hung – which bedeck the walls.

James Kerr is still remembered by the old folk of Morningside as a generous man and a great attender of funerals at the Morningside Cemetery. "My mither used tae say ye could aye be sure o' a send off fae the Canny Man," says one old lady. And Morningside has a long connection with poverty and madness. It was the site of Edinburgh's "poorhouse" and still contains the Royal Edinburgh Hospital (one of the biggest mental hospitals in Scotland) and the Thomas Clouston Clinic (better known as Craig House).

At the beginning of the 19th century the notorious Edinburgh "bedlam" at Darien House (where the poet Robert Fergusson died) was closed down and replaced, in 1813, by "an asylum for the cure and relief of mental derangement". The guiding light behind this project was an energetic doctor called Andrew Duncan, who gave his name to one of the Royal Edinburgh Hospital's clinics. In 1782 Duncan had proposed that a properly-run public asylum should be built in Edinburgh, a plan which raised some bitter hostility. But Duncan persisted and obtained a Royal Charter in 1807 plus a useful £2,000 from the fund built up from the Highland Estates forfeited after the 1745 Jacobite rebellion.

The original building (by Robert Reid and known as "The East House") was opened in July 1813 on what is now Millar Crescent and Morningside Terrace. The enlightened tradition established by Andrew Duncan was continued by Thomas Clouston who set up the spacious Craig House hospital in Morningside Grove in 1894. This building, which is now part of Napier University, was designed by Sydney Mitchell to ideas of Clouston and sits in its beautiful grounds like a French château. It contains some palatial public rooms. In Thomas Clouston's view the mentally ill deserved the best that money could buy, because "nothing we can do for the comfort of our patients is too much to atone for the cruelty of past ages."

Below, game of shinty. Right, mobile art.

LEITH AND NEWHAVEN

Although Edinburgh has a powerfully-etched world image, for some reason it never seems to include the city's formerly important harbour on the Firth of Forth. Edinburgh's maritime dimension has almost always been overlooked or underrated by guidebooks. Yet the Port of Leith, which lies only a few miles north of Princes Street, has always been crucial to Edinburgh's economic and strategic well-being.

Leith was (and to some extent still is) Edinburgh's window on the outside world, the point through which the Scots ploughed their way into the North Sea to swap goods, do deals or make war with France, Holland, Germany, Russia or England. Right up into the 1960s Leith was a tough, vigorous dockland, brimming with mildly dangerous pubs, seamen's flophouses, bookies and brothels.

All that has changed. Like most British ports (such as London, Liverpool, Glasgow and Bristol) the Port of Leith is a shadow of its former self. Most of the ships have gone, the few cargoes that do come through the harbour mouth are in giant containers and are disposed of by a handful of men, and Leith's ancient tradition of shipbuilding ground to a halt when British Shipbuilders closed the Robb Caledon yard in 1984. On the brighter side, more and more cruise ships are now dropping anchor at Leith.

By way of compensation – although not many Leithers see it as such – parts of the port have been discovered by the more raffish parts of the Scottish middle class. Old warehouses, maritime offices and at least one cooperage have been converted into expensive flats. New housing (coyly labelled "**King's Landing**") has sprung up on an infilled dock. And the area around **The Shore** (probably Leith's oldest street) is now peppered with fashionable watering-holes with vaguely maritime names like "Skippers", "The Waterfront Wine Bar" and

the "King's Wark" (a pub which used to be known as "The Jungle" and to which the police only travelled mob-handed).

The government (via the Scottish Development Agency) has spent millions cleaning up Leith's handsome 18th- and 19th-century public buildings. Graphic designers, advertising agencies, public relations consultancies and assorted craftworkers have been moving into Leith in a big way. All of which is no doubt a Good Thing, and it is a process which has certainly saved many a handsome industrial building from collapsing into ruins.

But the "gentrification" of Leith is a transformation that many Leithers lament. "I suppose it's nice enough," says 78-year-old retired docker James Dick. "But it's hell of a quiet. I miss the noise. Where's the noise o' the ships? Where's the noise o' the cranes? Where's the noise o' the shipyard whistles? Where's the noise o' the lassies going to their work at the bonds (bonded warehouses), Duncan's sweetie works or the roperie

(*rope works*)? And what are oor bairns going to work at when they come out of school? They canna' a' be advertisers, can they?"

According to veteran Leithers like James Dick, the centre of Leith was "The Kirkgate", the heart of which was ripped out by the planners in 1960. Leithers still mourn the passing of the Kirkgate. The narrow street used to house the Gaiety Theatre (venue for music hall greats like Will Fyfe, Harry Gordon and Lex Mclean), Sam Ret's huge fish and chip shop and businesses such as Hendrys the offal butcher, Millar's arcade (and billiard saloon), Kinnaird's pie shop, the Maypole Dairy.

They still talk affectionately of Wee Jaikie the Barber; "Tatty Jock" the policeman who kept order with fists and feet; "Doctor" Fahmy, the Egyptian street dentist; and Baillie Keddle, the prosperous egg merchant-cum-magistrate who believed the answer to most problems was good birching. They recall the days when Leith had more pubs than was good for it, and men and women were often carted home, drunk and unconscious, on handcarts. "Leith'll never be what it used to be" is the opinion of old James Dick. "It's just another part of bloody Edinburgh now."

This resentment that Leith is now "just another part of bloody Edinburgh" is an expression of an ancient (and not always good-natured) feud between Edinburgh and Leith which has been going on since medieval times. Like the many Scots who refuse to regard Scotland as just another region of Britain, many (and probably most) native-born Leithers refuse to accept that the port is just another suburb of Edinburgh.

Leith's turbulent relations with Edinburgh date back to medieval times when only Scotland's "Royal Burghs" (like Edinburgh) had the right to trade abroad. As Leith was not a Royal Burgh, the "traffickers" (i.e. merchants) of Leith were supposed to stand back and let the "traffickers" of Edinburgh do all the lucrative foreign trading with the Bal-

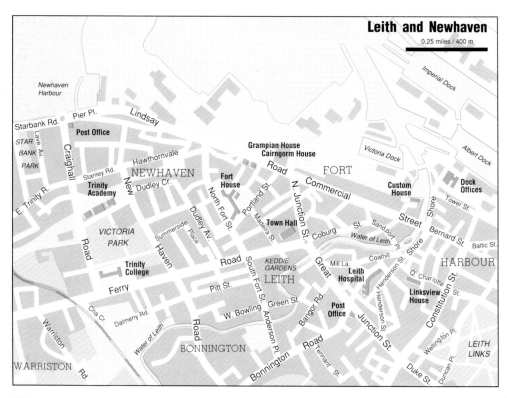

Leith and Newhaven

0,25 miles / 400 m

tic, France, the Low Countries, Scandinavia and England. It was a monopoly that Edinburgh relished and Leith bitterly resented. And it was a law that was much ignored; the Leith men preferred to risk the wrath of the kings rather than let Edinburgh take all the business.

Leith's resistance to Edinburgh's overweening ways irritated the Edinburgh mercantile establishment so much that in 1510 they tried, with some success, to turn Leith's flank by buying the nearby fishing/shipbuilding village of Newhaven from King James IV. It was an ominous start to what was a very nasty century for Leith.

In 1544 an English fleet led by the Earl of Hertford came ploughing up the Forth with specific instructions from Henry VIII to "Sack Leith, and burn and subvert it..." This the English troopers proceeded to do with great enthusiasm, and returned three years later (in 1547) for a repeat performance.

Leith was Scotland's major port.

In 1554 the English army was back this time to help the Protestant Scots, "Lords of the Congregation", winkle out a French army which had dug itself into Leith at the behest of the Catholic queen Mary of Guise (mother of Mary Queen of Scots). After a protracted siege and artillery duel, which did the fabric of Leith no good at all, the French surrendered and were shipped home.

If the 16th century was something of a disaster for Leith, the 17th century was not much better. In 1603 King James VI of Scotland (James I of England) confirmed Edinburgh's grip on the trade coming through Leith, in 1645 the port was hit by an outbreak of bubonic plague which wiped out two-thirds of the population, and in the 1650s Leith was occupied by Cromwell's army (who built a "citadel" in Leith to house their troops).

But in the 18th century the affairs of Leith – like the affairs of the rest of Scotland – began to improve (despite the Jacobite insurrections of 1715 and 1745). By the tail-end of the 18th century, Leith had become not only Scotland's major port, but also an important centre for

shipbuilding, shiprepairing, glass making, sugar refining, rope making, brick making, tanning and whisky distilling.

Edinburgh's grip – some say stranglehold – on Leith was loosened in 1833 when Parliament passed an act setting up Leith as an independent burgh with "the number sixteen Councillors, whereof one shall be Provost (i.e. Mayor), four shall be Baillies (i.e. magistrates) and one a Treasurer. Proudly, Leith set up all the trappings of a municipality: a Town Hall, Burgh Court, Police Office and Police Force.

Edinburgh, however, tried to subvert the fledgling municipality by refusing to transfer the income from Leith's customs dues. The Edinburgh City fathers justified this shabbiness by claiming that the Act which set up Leith made no mention of customs duties. (Halfway up Leith Walk there is a pub called the "Boundary Bar" through which the Edinburgh/Leith border used to run. As the two municipalities had different drinking hours, customers could extend their happiness by moving from one end of the bar to the other when the time came. This was only one of many anomalies which used to irritate the burghers of Edinburgh and delight the imbibers.)

By the end of the 19th century Edinburgh was plotting to resume its grip on the increasingly prosperous Port of Leith. In the 1890s "amalgamation" was being mooted on the grounds of municipal efficiency, despite the fact that Leith was in no mood to return to the Edinburgh fold. In 1919 Edinburgh finally persuaded Parliament that its boundaries should be extended to include Leith.

Yes or No?: The Leith town council did their best to fight back with a noisy propaganda campaign and a (probably rigged) plebiscite among the 50,000 or so Leithers. Pamphlets were circulated declaring that a merger would be "distinctly harmful to the best interests of the Burgh of Leith" and pleading with the Leithers to return "an unmistakable No" in the plebiscite.

When the votes were counted (in Janu-

Echoes of Leith's maritiime tradition.

ary 1920) only 5,357 voted in favour of a merger compared to 29,981 against. But it made no difference; the merger prevailed. The plebiscite carried no legal or constitutional weight.

In the end, Edinburgh had its way. Leith was stripped of its municipal powers and privileges. The famous Leith Police – saying the name aloud was a test of sobriety – became a division of the Edinburgh City (now Lothian & Borders) police force, and the Leith Town Hall became a concert venue. The Port of Leith lapsed into its role as one of Edinburgh's most intriguing northern suburbs. (Not that Leith's independence has been forgotten; not long ago, *The Scotsman* carried an article urging the people of Leith to reassert their old autonomy because the merger with Edinburgh "was a union foisted on them by Westminster in the first place.")

Leith: still an intriguing northern suburb.

Edinburgh's enthusiasm for clutching Leith to her bosom is understandable. The port has always been economically important. All through the 19th century Leith expanded as dock after dock was built: the Victoria Dock in 1851; the Albert Dock in 1881; the Imperial Dock in 1903. Ships from Leith exported coal, salt, fish, paper, leather and Scots ale, and returned with (among much else) grain, timber, wine, foreign foods and Italian marble. They traded with Hamburg, Bremen, Amsterdam, Antwerp, Copenhagen, Gothenburg, occasionally North America and Australia, and did a brisk coastal business with ports in eastern England.

Shipbuilding and ship-repair firms flourished too; Ramage & Ferguson, James G. Man & Son, Menzies & Co, Crann & Somerville, Hawthorns (who also made railway engines) and latterly Henry Robb Ltd. In fact, Henry Robb, which ate up most of the competition, was one of Britain's most energetic shipbuilders. In the 65 years of the firm's existence the yard built over 500 ships, mostly specialised vessels like crane-barges, rescue tugs, passenger ferries, and naval frigates.

"Always a great occasion" is how Margaret McIntyre (whose husband was a crane driver) describes a launching at Robb's yard. "Everybody used to go down to the yard and cheer the ship into the water." And around the docks and shipyard grew up a complex "infrastructure" of shipping agents, marine engineering shops, cooperages, marine insurance firms, grain merchants, coal merchants, and ships chandleries (not to mention pubs, clubs, flophouses, bookies and whores).

Recently restored buildings such as the old **Corn Exchange** in Baltic Street, the **Leith Assembly Rooms** and **Exchange** in Constitution Street, the **Old Leith Bank** in Bernard Street, **Trinity House** in the Kirkgate and Robert Reid's beautiful neo-classical **Customs House** on The Shore are a testament to Leith's mercantile vigour.

Fishing loomed large, too. Until the mid-1960s four fleets of deep-sea trawlers plied out of Leith and the nearby harbour of Granton, owned by local dynasties like the Croans, the Patons, the Devlins and the Carnies. The two mile stretch of shore between Leith and Granton used to be littered with shipyards, ship-repair yards, a ship-breaking yard, a dry dock, a ropeworks, a wireworks and a networks.

The women of Leith and Granton could earn extra money by making fishing nets at home (on hooks attached to the backs of cupboard doors). A nimble-fingered woman who knew what she was doing could rack up an extra £3 or £4 a week, which was good money in the depressed 1930s.

One of the reasons that Edinburgh Zoo has one of the world's finest collections of penguins is that Leith was one of the world's more important whaling ports. And for much longer than is generally realised. In 1615 James VI granted Sir George Hay and Sir Thomas Murray a monopoly on the Greenland (Arctic) whale fishing, to be operated out of Leith. In the 1750s the Edinburgh Whale Fishing Company picked up where Hay

Edinburgh is affectionately known as "Auld Reekie".

172

and Murray left off, and began to kill the Greenland whales in a much more systematic and efficient way, from much bigger boats.

At the end of the 19th century the Scots-Norwegian firm of Christian Salvesen & Co of Leith began large-scale whaling in the waters of the Antarctic. In 1908 a Leith Harbour was established on the bleak coastline of South Georgia, and generations of Leith and Edinburgh seamen spent their working lives risking life and limb on whale-catchers in the Antarctic, or as "flensers" hacking evil-smelling fat and blubber from the corpses of the giant beasts. "When one of Salvesen's factory ships put into Leith," says one old seaman, "you could smell the bloody thing from Princes Street."

Leith's ecclesiastical history is very old, and the area has its share of handsome church buildings. The best is probably **North Leith Parish Church** in Madeira Street, an elegant piece of neo-classical architecture built in 1816 to a design by William Burn. Another classical essay is **St Thomas's** in Great Junction Street.

Much more common are Victorian Gothic buildings such as the **South Leith Parish Church** in the Kirkgate and **St Mary Star of the Sea** in Constitution Street (designed by Edward Pugin and Joseph Hansom) in 1854. **St Thomas's Church** in Sheriff Brae (built 1843) is now a Sikh temple and the focal point of Leith's large Sikh community.

Although Leith Sands (once the venue for Edinburgh's notoriously violent horse-races) have long been claimed by industry, **Leith Links** remain. Now a pleasant tree-edged park, Leith Links was probably the home of world golf.

No one seems quite sure whether it was the Dutch or the Scots who first came up with the idea of knocking a small ball into small holes for fun, but Leith Links was certainly one of the world's first golf courses. It is older by at least 13 years than anything St Andrews can claim. The "Gentlemen Golf-

Newhaven: architects try, not always successfully, to blend old and new.

ers of Leith" did, however, have to share the links with linen-bleachers, horse-riders and grazing cattle (although after a cow attacked a woman in 1862 grazing was stopped). The prestigious and high-toned Honourable Company of Edinburgh Golfers began their playing days on Leith Links, before quitting for the quieter pastures of Musselburgh and then Muirfield (where they still are).

At the northeast corner of the Links is the **Seafield Baths**, a neo-classical bath-house built in 1813 as one of Edinburgh's most fashionable venues and now a fairly nondescript pub. However, **Leith Waterworld** is one of the most exciting leisure facilities built in Edinburgh in recent years.

The new Newhaven: While Leith – especially the centre of Leith – has suffered grievously from the planners of the l960s, the adjacent fishing village of **Newhaven** has been practically killed by conservation. Known since medieval times as "Our Lady's Port of Grace", Newhaven in the 1960s was a brisk if grubby little community, with a useful fishing harbour (pier by Robert Stevenson) and a busy fishmarket. There was a High Street and Main Street, both of which were lined with shops, pubs and small businesses through which tram-cars and later buses used to trundle.

For some obscure reason Newhaveners were known as "bow-tows", had the reputation of being close-knit to the point of clannishness and used to speak a Scots dialect all of their own. They also disliked Leithers, and the boundary between Leith and Newhaven was the scene of many a scuffle. A familiar sight on the streets of Edinburgh was the Newhaven "fishwife" who went from door to door selling fish from a *creel* (basket) on her back, and who would gut and fillet her wares on the doorstep or in the kitchen if asked.

But all that has gone. Now that the picturesque fisherfolk's houses have been "restored" by the City of Edinburgh there is hardly a shop left in the place, the once-crowded Main Street is **Tall tales by the seafront.**

174

a ghostly dead end, and the harbour is occupied by a few pleasure boats. The Ancient Society of Free Fishermen, a trade guild founded in 1572 still exists, but it lists precious few fishermen among its members. There is still a Newhaven "fishwives' choir" in which respectable ladies get tricked out in fishwives' costume and regale audiences with traditional songs like "Caller Herring". The opening in 1994 of a Harry Ramsden harbourside restaurant – an unrivalled name when it comes to fish and chips – and an adjacent local museum have infused some new life into the area.

Newhaven is one of Edinburgh's most interesting corners. The village was (probably) founded in the late 1400s by James IV to build the *Great Michael*, then the biggest warship on earth, and designed to be the flagship of the Scottish navy. It is said that James IV cut down most of the oaks in Fife and Lothian to build the monster. But, like many such grandiose schemes, the *Great Michael* was never a success. After the ruin of the Scots army and the death of James IV at Flodden in 1513, the great ship was sold to the French who left her to rot in Brest harbour.

Newhaven never became much of a ship-building centre but did well enough from cod, haddock and whiting, and the shoals of herring which found their way into the Firth of Forth. But the famous Newhaven oyster-fishery was almost wiped out in the 19th century when the Edinburgh Town Council (who had the rights over the oyster beds) got greedy and leased the fishery to an Englishman, George Clark, for the huge sum of £600 a year for 10 years. To recoup his cash, he brought in a fleet of 60 oyster-dredgers from England – but they overfished the beds and ruined the fishery.

Newhaven sports little in the way of public buildings, apart from the handsome **Newhaven Parish Church** (built 1836) in Craighall Road, and the **Old Newhaven Free Church** in Pier Place (built in 1855 and now a disco). On the plateau above Newhaven are a number of handsome Victorian/Georgian villas, many built for prosperous sea captains.

A mile to the west is the **Old Chain Pier Bar**, once the site of a pier built in 1820 which became the terminus of the Edinburgh & Trinity Railway. For many years the bar was owned and run by a decidedly eccentric lady called Bet Moss who used to keep order among her seagoing clientele with a naval cutlass.

To the west of Newhaven lies **Granton Harbour**, built by the Duke of Buccleuch to a plan by Robert Stevenson in 1834, and completed in 1844. There used to be a train ferry from Granton across the Firth of Forth to Burntisland in Fife, and until recently the harbour hosted a large fleet of trawlers, the lighthouse tenders "Pharos" and "May", and was used by esparto grass boats, oil tankers and even, on one occasion, the Royal yacht *Britannia*. Today it is the home of the Royal Forth Yacht Club.

Most of the West Harbour has been clumsily reclaimed from the sea and covered in huge "retail warehouses".

Pub sing-along.

THE WATER OF LEITH

Critics of Edinburgh (and there are a few) have said that all great cities should have a river – something which Edinburgh lacks. They don't count the Forth estuary, which belongs more properly to the port of Leith and to the old fishing villages of Granton and Newhaven; and they tend to laugh derisively when the **Water of Leith** is mentioned.

True, Edinburgh's "river" is no mighty flood. It is an often meagre stream which only achieves any decent volume when it debouches into the Forth at Leith, and which has found such a furtive channel through the city's gorges that it sometimes seems to disappear altogether.

Yet this humble waterway, which rises in the peaty moorlands of the Pentland Hills above East Colzium, was critical to the economy of 18th-century Edinburgh. It supplied power and water to bleach works, dye works and tanneries, and became the energy source for paper, snuff, flour and timber mills. By the end of the 18th century, 71 mills lined its banks. One or two remain today (although powered differently) and the residue of many others can be traced.

As the river's industrial role declined, so did the appearance of much of its immediate environment, and until 25 years ago the Water of Leith was casually associated with derelict buildings, choked undergrowth, old car tyres, rusting scrap and all the other sleazy detritus of water-borne litter. But in the 1970s Edinburgh District Council, deciding to make a virtue of the river's industrial past and – in some areas – attractive dells and woodland, began building the Water of Leith Walkway.

Eventually, if funds from the council supplemented by grants from the Scottish Development Agency and the efforts of the Water of Leith Trust are maintained, the leafy, traffic-free walkway will follow the entire channel from the outskirts of the city to Leith.

In the southwest of the city a major section, between Juniper Green and Slateford, employs a former railway line to by-pass the village of **Colinton** (where Robert Louis Stevenson often visited his grandfather, who was minister there) under the old railway tunnel, and links up with the Union Canal towpath.

Here, more than anywhere, can be seen the importance of the river valley as a communication route for people and goods, and the recycled **Balerno Branch Railway** (built in the 19th century) uses the valley for much of its length. Many of its bridges and retaining walls still remain, although passenger services were discontinued in 1943 and goods traffic in 1968.

The romantically named village of **Juniper Green** is believed to take its name from the juniper bushes which once covered the lower slopes of the Pentlands. Like all the "villages" along the Water of Leith, it's now part of Edinburgh, one of the city's more

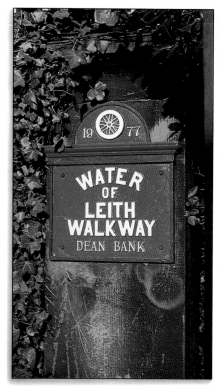

Preceding pages and left: Dean Village in winter. Right, the walkway.

characterful suburbs. Juniper Green is first mentioned in records in 1707 and developed as the industrial use of the river grew.

The prosperous Colinton area was a centre of the milling industries in the 18th and 19th centuries, although Colinton was settled much earlier. The remains of **Colinton Castle**, built in the 16th and 17th centuries, can still be seen in the grounds of Merchiston Castle School, and in 1666 more than 900 Covenanters camped in the village, skirmished with an assault force from the Lothians, then judiciously retreated into the Pentland Hills.

The Water of Leith was for long a tricky crossing at the village of **Slateford**, which takes its name both from the local stone and its function as ford. The crossing was actually a mill dam – "and consequently was extremely difficult and dangerous and thereby occasioned several unlucky accidents and even some melancholy instances of persons who have lost their lives". But such tragedies were avoided after the building of a road bridge, which now converges with the Union Canal Viaduct and the Caledonian Railway Viaduct at Slateford.

The **Union Canal** was opened in 1822 and had its own port, Stoneyport, at Slateford where rags and coal for the mills were offloaded and stone from local quarries taken on board. When the railways took over, traffic on the canal dwindled to nothing, although cruises departing from the Bridge Inn may still be enjoyed. It's now a semi-natural habitat for birds, beasts, fish, walkers, anglers and boatmen.

From Slateford the river then wanders across the flat beds of two drained lochs – **Gogar** and **Corstorphine** – before reaching the **Dean Village** by way of Roseburn. In fact, the crow-stepped huddle of russet buildings in their leafy gorge below Thomas Telford's Dean Bridge (a few minutes' walk from the West End of Princes Street) was once known as Water of Leith Village. "Dean" itself is an old word for gorge or deep valley, and the original Village of Dean was a small community to the north of the river.

By the 17th century the village in the valley had 11 water mills on its short stretch of river. This was the empire of the Baxters Incorporation, whose flour mills supplied much of Edinburgh's bread. (The word *baxter* used to mean baker). Dean Village has its history carved on its walls – in sheafs of corn, in the two wooden paddles which manoeuvred the bread into hot ovens, and in streets like Miller Row and buildings like the Old Tolbooth, where the Baxters would meet to decide the level of wages and prices.

The short walk from Dean to Stockbridge, below the great, viaduct-style arches of Telford's bridge and the soaring domestic ramparts of the New Town, is probably one of the most unusual in Edinburgh.

It also takes you past the territory of one of the city's more fanciful legends,

The Water of Leith

1 mile / 1,6 km

CRAMOND · PILTON · TRINITY · MUIRHOUSE · LEITH · BLACK HALL · DEAN VILLAGE · St. Bernard's Well · MURRAYFIELD · Water of Leith · CORSTORPHINE · NEWINGTON · COLONIES · Union Canal · MORNINGSIDE · SLATEFORD · Union Canal · JUNIPER GREEN · COLINTON · LIBERTON · FAIRMILEHEAD · Water of Leith · BURDIE-HOUSE

which claims that St Bernard of Clairvaux, the founder of the Cistercian Order, visited Scotland in the 12th century while raising soldiers for the Second Crusade.

He was badly received at court and retreated in a huff to weather an illness in a cave (now covered over) near the Dean Bridge. There he was conducted to the healing waters of a spring by the local birds and before he left for France he publicly declared the outstanding virtues of this well.

This tale was probably invented to add romance to **St Bernard's Well**, which, according to tradition, was discovered by three boys fishing in the Water of Leith in 1760. The mineral spring immediately attracted attention when analysis showed that the water was very similar to the sulphur springs of Harrogate in Yorkshire. In 1788 the startling yet very atmospheric Roman Temple which now contains it was designed by Alexander Nasmyth. At the centre of the pillared temple is a statue of Hygeia, the Greek goddess of health.

The village of **Stockbridge** grew up around an important fording point across the Water of Leith, and the present bridge – called simply Stockbridge – is a widened version of the stone one built in 1785 to replace an earlier wooden one.

An attractive section of walkway has been built between it and the smaller **Falshaw Bridge**, taking you close to the Royal Botanic Garden and the intriguingly named **Colonies**.

These distinctive rows of workmen's houses (now much prized by young professionals who can't afford Georgiana) were built in 1861, and have trade symbols depicted in relief on their gable ends. There are groups of similar Colonies elsewhere in Edinburgh.

Sections of the walkway have now been completed from Stockbridge through Canonmills and Bonnington to Leith, where growing in volume and prestige, Edinburgh's small but resourceful river gives its first intimations of a modest maritime life.

Well on the Water of Leith.

VILLAGES

Every city other than those few which have been purpose-built from scratch has its villages; its mature rural pygmies which have been consumed by the expansive appetite of the urban giant. Some fare better than others in the digestive process, surviving more or less intact in substance and robust in identity; others are overwhelmed by the demands of new developments and new needs.

Edinburgh's villages are particularly persistent, many giving their names to whole areas of the city and to many streets. When people talk today of **Corstorphine** they don't mean the cluster of cottages tucked behind the busy artery which is one of Edinburgh's main exits to the west, but the large modern suburb whose most distinguished feature is the Edinburgh Zoo on Corstorphine Hill.

When they talk, however, of **Newcraighall,** they mean somewhere more specific – the tiny mining community on the eastern boundary of Edinburgh which, for reasons of geography as much as through the deep-rooted traditions of miners and their families, has remained oddly isolated from the city. (Cynics might argue that potential developers were scared off by the bleak, dour image of the village presented in a trilogy of autobiographical feature films by the Scottish director Bill Douglas.)

Glorious past: Agriculture, fishing and traditional industries are all represented by Edinburgh's villages, as well as associations with some of the city's past celebrities and, of course, with some of the major events in Scotland's disputatious history. There is, for example, a house in the cobbled Causeway of **Duddingston Village** which was occupied by Charles Edward Stuart on the eve of his most famous success, the Battle of Prestonpans. While his army camped on the flat ground east of the village, Bonnie Prince Charlie planned the strat-

egy which was to defeat the Hanoverian troops of General John Cope and encourage the Jacobites to believe in the future of their doomed rebellion of 1745.

Today Duddingston is one of Edinburgh's best-preserved villages, given some protection from encroaching development by the southeast bulk of Arthur's Seat and pretty little **Duddingston Loch**, which is now a nature reserve and a Christmas card setting for ice skaters and curlers. And if there is any pub in Edinburgh which still has the weathered character of an old country pub it must be the **Sheep Heid** at Duddingston. It's said that this ancient hostelry was patronised by James VI, who presented it with an embellished ram's head in 1580; while for a long time a speciality of the house was the traditional, if grisly, Scots delicacy of boiled sheep's head.

Duddingston dates from the 12th century and owes its existence to the early church built on an elevation above the loch by the Abbot of Kelso, who had

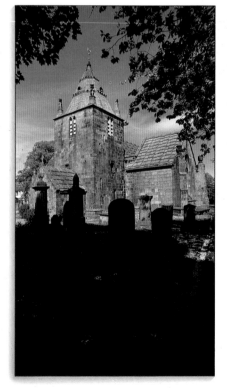

been gifted land by David I. On that same pleasing site today is **Duddingston Kirk**, a characterful Norman building which is one of the oldest churches in Scotland still in use.

To the left of the main entrance is a little two-storey tower now called the **Session House**. But anyone familiar with Edinburgh's history will recognise it for a graveyard watch tower from which elders of the Kirk took turns to repel those body-snatchers whose trade in illegally acquired corpses made infamous the medical schools of 19th-century Edinburgh. To the right of the entrance is a "*loupin-on-stane*" (a mounting block for horse-riding parishioners) and the less charitable "*joug's collar*" – an iron collar and chain used to exhibit and humiliate 17th-century sinners, whose offences might include blasphemy, adultery, drunkenness and failure to attend church regularly.

If Duddingston is the most "rural" village in central Edinburgh (it can be reached pleasantly on foot through Holyrood Park), then **Swanston** is more truly in the country. On the southern boundary of the city, this charming cluster of farmsteads and whitewashed thatched cottages – the thatch alone makes them unusual in Scotland – has been spared the embrace of suburban developers for two reasons: at Swanston's back are the Pentland Hills, with lower slopes already colonised by two golf courses and an artificial ski slope, and at its front, separating farmland from city, is a more recent barrier – the land-gobbling Edinburgh bypass.

There was once a school in Swanston, serving rural children from the hinterland of Edinburgh, but not for 50 years; nor has the village a church, a pub, shops or a bus service. As Malcolm Cant has pointed out in his second volume of *Villages of Edinburgh*, Swanston lacks "many of the traditional essentials of village life" – possibly because the property-owning, car-driving classes who now occupy this prime retreat from the city don't need them.

Peaceful retreat at Duddingston.

Nor does Edinburgh much need Swanston, but there was a time when it did. In 1758, a thirsty and grimy Edinburgh Corporation obtained an Act of Parliament which allowed the city to use Swanston's fine spring water to supplement the public supply from Comiston. The local landowner objected and a famous series of legal disputes followed; but in 1761 a water-house was built and Edinburgh began to drink Swanston water.

The piping of the water would lead indirectly to Robert Louis Stevenson's close association with Swanston. The building of the water-house was followed by a civic decision to build a more general meeting place, or as Stevenson put it, "it occurred to them that the place was suitable for junketing. Once entertained, with jovial magistrates and public funds, the idea led speedily to accomplishment; and Edinburgh could soon boast of a municipal Pleasure House. The dell was turned into a garden; and on the knoll that

shelters it from the plain and the sea winds, they built a cottage looking to the hills."

Swanston Cottage, to which he referred, was enlarged around 1835, and in 1867 Thomas Stevenson, father of Robert Louis, became its tenant. The cottage was their "second home", used only in summer but for 13 years the romantic engine room, off and on, for many of Stevenson's novels and poems.

He has left this evocative description of the little community at the foot of the Pentlands: "The hamlet is one of the least considerable of hamlets, and consists of a few cottages on a green beside a burn. Some of them (a strange thing in Scotland) are models of internal neatness; the beds adorned with patch-work, the shelves arrayed with willow-pattern plates, the floors and tables bright with scrubbing or pipeclay, and the very kettle polished like silver…"

Stevenson is also closely associated with the village of **Colinton**, which was flrst settled round the ancient church of

Halis, or Hailes (a name which has lent itself to one of Edinburgh's newer peripheral housing estates, Wester Hailes) and which now occupies an interesting corner of the southern suburbs.

The village with its wooded dell flourished beside the Water of Leith, which was used to power a variety of mills in the 18th and 19th centuries. Stevenson's grandfather, Dr Lewis Balfour, was minister of the parish between 1823 and 1860, and his dignified manse beside the river was an important and much loved fixture in the writer's boyhood.

Like Swanston, Colinton was then very much in the country and, until his grandfather died in Louis's tenth year, the sickly child was often sent there to play with cousins and recuperate from the debilitating respiratory illnesses which afflicted his childhood.

"Out of my reminiscences of life in that dear place," he wrote in 1873, "all the morbid and painful elements have disappeared. I remember no more nights of storm; no more terror or sickness. I can recall nothing but sunshiny weather. That was my golden age."

Other distinguished sons of Edinburgh found Colinton an amiable alternative to city life. In the old village, tucked into a leafy shelf below the modern roadway, is **Henry Mackenzie's Cottage**, birthplace of the man of letters who is chiefly distinguished for one book, *The Man of Feeling*. Mackenzie, as a plaque informs you, was born in 1745 (the year of the Jacobite Rebellion) and died in 1831.

A ruin in the grounds of another school – **Merchiston Castle** – is all that remains of Colinton Castle. Nearby, in Redford Road, stands the **Covenanters' Monument**.

Under the arches of the viaduct of the station (opened in 1881, now disused) is a flight of steps leading to **Spylaw Park** and **Spylaw House**, which was built in 1773 for Edinburgh's great benefactor James Gillespie. James and his brother John, bachelors both, had a snuff factory and retail shop which made them very rich. Frugal and industrious to the last, James left his fortune for the endowment of a hospital for old people (geriatric patients, we would call them today) and a school for poor boys. His hospital was built in 1802 and his eponymous school, no longer for poor boys, is one of Edinburgh's semi-private schools.

In the 19th century, a branch line of the Caledonian Railway brought the village of Colinton within commuting distance of Edinburgh and many handsome villas, some from the drawing board of Sir Robert Lorimer, appeared.

Like most cities with an interesting history, Edinburgh inspires fierce territorial loyalties in its citizens. Like Glasgow, the city is broadly divided into two camps, North side and South side; but where Glasgow's demarcation line is the Clyde, Edinburgh's is Princes Street. Once they have settled in central Edinburgh to the north or south of Princes Street, few householders would voluntarily change camps. And within these camps there are communities which are particularly binding. One of them is Stockbridge.

Stockbridge begins where the steep downward slope of Edinburgh's Georgian New Town meets the Water of Leith, and is often called the New Town village. This gives it an immediate cachet, but until some 15 years ago it was essentially a working-class community, with much of its modest Georgian property run down.

Now, thanks to a conservation programme of restoration and stone-cleaning, its central position and its own intrinsic character, Stockbridge has become upwardly mobile, infiltrated by the wholefood and designer knitwear classes. But the social mix is still sufficiently rich to make it one of the least artificial yuppiedoms in the country. If many of its original shops have been replaced by retail outlets for herbal preparations, party accessories and (for some reason) charity clothes, it also supports some of the best food shops in

Edinburgh and a scattering of small tradesmen and craftsmen.

Its history is not long by the capital's standards. Its neighbours to the west and east, Dean and Canonmills, are much older, and until 200 years ago Stockbridge was little more than the bridge which gives it its name and which crosses the Water of Leith at a point which was first a ford and then a wooden bridge for the movement of stock. A stone bridge was built around 1785, and widened about 1830. By then, Stockbridge was developing a strong identity.

That identity was given distinction by the portrait painter Sir Henry Raeburn, who was born humbly in Stockbridge in 1756 and who, after his talent had brought him fame, fortune and a knighthood, bought an estate and mansion house in his native village. St Bernard's House, now no more, was its principal residence and Raeburn took an interest in developing housing on his estate.

The exquisite Ann Street, with its cottage gardens and ornamental lamps (where property is now the most expensive in central Edinburgh) was named for his wife, Ann Leslie, and probably designed by the architect James Milne. The main thoroughfare through the community, bustling Raeburn Place, is also a reminder of Scotland's greatest portrait painter.

Stockbridge has had a crop of other notable residents throughout its two centuries. The artist David Roberts was born in one of its oldest houses, the vernacular building Duncan's Land, which was constructed from stones from demolished houses in the Lawnmarket. (It's now a restaurant). Professor Sir James Young Simpson, pioneer of anaesthetics, lived there for a time, as did the eccentric academic and journalist Christopher North, the publisher Robert Chambers (of the dynasty which still publishes dictionaries and reference books in Edinburgh) and George Meikle Kemp, architect of the Scott Monument.

Ann Street was the home, for a time,

The Water of Leith at Colinton.

of an unrelated Kemp – the late Robert Kemp, journalist, playwright, man of letters and author of a contemporary version of the 16th-century Scots classic *The Three Estates*; while 21 Comely Bank – in a pretty little Georgian terrace on the western edge of Stockbridge – was the first married home of Thomas and Jane Carlyle.

The area was particularly dense in churches, church schools and other institutions. Its oldest existing church is **Stockbridge Parish Church** (on Saxe-Coburg Terrace), which was built in 1823 and has a classical facade by James Milne. But the most distinctive is William Playfair's **St Stephen's Church** on the street of that name, an imposing pile built between 1827 and 1828 for just under £19,000.

These days it's also a useful pointer to more secular affairs, being a prominent landmark by which to direct visitors to St Stephen Street – the narrow, atmospheric passage which, of all others, is quintessential Stockbridge today. Fa-

mous for its antique, junk and second-hand clothes shops, St Stephen Street is the mutually beneficial haunt of self-conscious individualists and alternative entrepreneurs.

Nearby, in **Hamilton Place** and its continuation, **Henderson Row**, are two buildings which speak of very different styles of 19th-century philanthropy. The old Dean Bank Institution (now Stockbridge Primary School) was founded in 1832 for the "Reformation of Juvenile Female Delinquents", and was aimed specifically at those "who have no home, or worse than no home to go to, and who manifest a wish to return to better ways." Some of the crimes of these sad girls were pathetically paltry. Case histories tell of one who was "well educated but wholly ignorant of religion – had never received religious instruction – her fault was selling a book which had been stolen by her brother"; and another who was "seemingly friendless" and stole from her mistress.

For over 150 years an attractive build-

Antiques for sale in Stockbridge.

ing in its own arboreal grounds in Henderson Row was a school for deaf and dumb children. In 1977 Donaldson's School for the Deaf, reorganising its other premises in Edinburgh, sold the Henderson Row building to neighbouring Edinburgh Academy. But before that happened Donaldson's had a brief spell of glamour in another role: during the summer of 1968 it became the "Marcia Blane School for Girls" in the film version of Muriel Spark's famous Edinburgh novel, *The Prime of Miss Jean Brodie*. Now it's a school for boys – and traditionally the ethos of the highly conservative Edinburgh Academy has not been dissimilar to that of the fictional establishment of Marcia Blane.

On both sides of Stockbridge – the bridge itself – there are characterful sections of the **Water of Leith Walkway**, the recreational route which will eventually follow the course of Edinburgh's modest little river from the southwest outskirts of the city to the port of Leith. The path to the east of the Bridge gives a splendid view of **the Colonies**, which were low-priced houses built for working people from 1861 by the Edinburgh Co-operative Building Company Limited. One of the leading members of the original company was Hugh Miller, the polymath from Cromarty, in the northeast of Scotland, who was stonemason, writer, journalist and geologist and whose genius eventually became too much for him. He shot himself on Christmas Eve, 1856, not knowing that a Stockbridge street would soon be named after him.

To the west of Stockbridge, in a leafy valley which is almost a gorge, is **Dean Village**, probably Edinburgh's best known and certainly its most quaint. Most visitors to the city get their first astonished glimpse of this Christmas-card community from Thomas Telford's **Dean Bridge**, whose four arches magnificently straddle the Dean Valley from a height of 106 ft (32 metres). This narrow bridge, still one of Edinburgh's main arteries from the city centre, is

Stockbridge keeps up with the news.

only a few minutes walk from the West End of Princes Street.

> *The Dean Bridge is terribly tall,*
> *Please take care that you do not fall*
> *Down into the Water of Leith*
> *Far below, as it flows beneath.*

So many people *did* fall by design from the Dean Bridge that this doggerel was followed by a more sombre poem written by Robert McCandless in 1887, 55 years after the bridge was completed. By then Telford's masterpiece had acquired a gloomy reputation as the place

> *Where many a man*
> *Alas has ran*
> *There in an evil hour*
> *And cast away*
> *His life that day*
> *Beyond all human pow'r*

To discourage the impulses of suicides, the stone parapet was eventually heightened. That slowed the rate but didn't – and doesn't – deter the most determined. Passers-by must now crane their necks to look down into the valley, where they see a huddle of cobbled streets and courtyards, red pantiles and turreted mews, and old mill buildings which now have the huffed and tidied look of desirably converted apartment blocks.

The Water of Leith rushes through them all with unusual energy and the great, overhanging cliffs of New Town tenements add their dimensions to the valley, making this ancient settlement seem more than ever a secluded, secretive place which time has by-passed.

In fact, present times have been very busy down in Dean, restoring, renovating and even building harmonious new housing developments. In one sense, however, the village is flying under false colours. The real village of Dean was a now defunct community on the western lip of the valley. Its inhabitants worked either at Craigleith Quarry or Dean Farm; but when this village surrendered to redevelopment about 1880 its name somehow became transferred to the village beside the river which, until then, had been happy enough to be called Water of Leith Village.

The Water of Leith was its *raison d'être*. There were mills and granaries beside the river as early as the 12th century, although the commercial and industrial heyday of the village was the 18th and 19th centuries, when it was dominated by the Ancient Incorporation of Baxters (or bakers) and the Incorporation of Weavers. There were 11 mills on the short stretch of water which flows through the valley, but towards the end of the 19th century other industries, including distilleries and tanneries, began to replace the dwindling activities of the Baxters and Weavers.

However, it's the influence and memory of the flour millers which persists most strongly today. The Baxters's Arms, sculptured on a stone panel salvaged from the ruins of mill buildings, can now be seen on the facade of an old house at the top of Bell's Brae. It includes this Biblical injunction "In the sweat of thy face shalt thou eat bread." Other emblems of the bakers are recorded on stone elsewhere in the village.

Cramond: a formidable history.

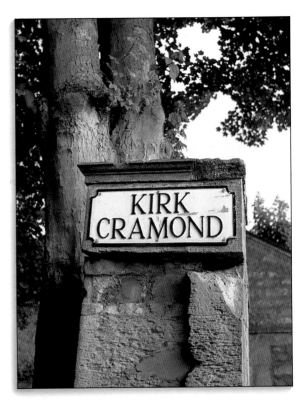

Among the largely vernacular architecture is a bust of designer Victoriana at **Well Court**, an experiment in model housing for working people conceived by John Ritchie Findlay, the philanthropic owner of *The Scotsman*.

If the old economy of Dean Village can still be traced in many of its buildings, the industrial revolution mounted by the village of **Cramond** in the 18th century has all but vanished. Most informed citizens of Edinburgh could tell you that Cramond's history is formidable; that its harbour was used by the Romans and the Roman Fort whose foundations have been exposed was built in the 2nd century AD.

Few now remember that this pretty, whitewashed village at the mouth of the **River Almond** was once a centre of the iron industry. It produced in the 1770s some 300 tons of rod iron a year and exported barrel hoops to the wine-growing areas of Spain, Portugal and Madeira and the rum and sugar producers of the West Indies.

There is now a calm riverside walk from the little marina where the Almond debouches into the Forth estuary, past the stone-lined cuttings which are all that remain of the quarry wharves, beside the shell of a forge which once contained two furnaces and the scanty residue of other iron and grain mills.

These days, people come to this picturesque enclave in the northwest suburbs of Edinburgh for other reasons: to visit its crow-stepped, white-washed 17th-century inn overlooking the Forth; to take the little rowing boat ferry across the River Almond and to walk in the Rosebery estate; or just to admire the views across to Fife and the postcard comeliness of the village.

The Romans came for other reasons, too. About AD 142 a garrison of almost 500 set about building a harbour and fort by order of Emperor Antoninus Pius, who established the frontier line across Scotland from the Forth to the Clyde. Eventually the Romans pulled back to the line of Hadrian's Wall be-

The River Almond: popular with fishermen.

tween the Tyne and the Solway, but were back in Cramond under Septimius Severus, who launched a punitive assault on northeast Scotland a century later. The fort was discovered in 1954.

Cramond's 17th-century parish church (it has a 15th-century tower) is built on a site probably used by the early Christian communities who succeeded the Romans. The churchyard is fertile ground for those with an interest in old tombstones, while some few hundred yards to the north is **Cramond Tower**, a medieval defensive tower of obscure history which is now a private home.

Between tower and churchyard is **Cramond House,** which dates from about 1680 and now belongs to the church. (It's the beadle's residence.) It was once the seat of the Inglis family, and was passed to an Inglis daughter called Lady Torphichen in 1817. Lady Torphichen completed Cramond's industrial decline by demolishing the oldest part of the village to extend the policies of Cramond's House.

Ancient places: Edinburgh has many other villages, each with its claim to distinction. There are the two communities of **Longstone** and **Slateford** in the southwest, with their long commercial dependence on the Water of Leith and their more recent association with the Union Canal. There is ancient **Restalrig** in the east, now surrounded by housing estates, once a place of pilgrimage for people afflicted with eye diseases, who came to bathe their eyes in an early 15th-century well presided over by a legendary saint called St Triduana.

Davidson's Mains, with ghost-ridden Craigcrook Castle; **Liberton**, which may be a corruption of Lepertown and take its name from a hospital for lepers which stood on a ridge outside Edinburgh; **Morningside**, which once served the farms of Oxgangs, Braid and Comiston and which has enduringly given its name to a style of genteel suburban manners… Edinburgh has many other villages. It would take even a local a lifetime to get to know them all.

Summer blooms in Cramond.

194

PORTOBELLO

Portobello was once as sprightly – if never quite as beautiful – as its name. This seaside suburb of Edinburgh has suffered mixed fortunes since its heyday as a major 19th-century resort when it had "an animation and gaiety superior to those of any other sea-bathing station in Scotland." Although plans for the regeneration of its considerable promenade are in the civic pipeline and its sands still attract hosts of local sunbathers and infant engineers, Portobello's present is a forlorn ghost of its past.

Its seafront, however, has curiosity value for those who cultivate a perverse taste for recreational tat. Its seedy amusement arcades and half-hearted funfair have never recovered the vitality they enjoyed before the resort's huge open-air pool was demolished in the 1970s.

Down, too, came Portobello's massive red-brick electricity power station – an eyesore peculiarly loved by locals. Those sites are now being filled with smart new housing and other developments, but for a time the heart went out of the place.

There's another side to Portobello, however: a dignified main street and terraces of handsome Georgian houses which testify to its prosperous past. The suburb owes its fanciful name to a retired seafarer who fought the Spanish in Panama in 1739 and took part in the capture of the town of Puerto Bello. George Hamilton built the first house on this stretch of the Forth estuary and called his home "Portobello". The community thereafter became established through its brick-making and ceramics industry.

When sea-bathing became popular in the early 19th century, Portobello was quick to exploit its extensive sandy strand and soon offered all the essential amenities: promenade, pier, donkey rides and steamer trips across the Forth to Fife. It flourished into the 20th century, but in 1917 its pier was demolished and, after World War I, its appeal as a resort began to dwindle.

The town became part of Edinburgh by Act of Parliament in 1896, but it has robustly defended its special place in Scotland's recreational history, and is particularly proud of its most famous son, Harry Lauder, who was born in humble Bridge Street in 1870. Son of a potter, the music-hall artist became an international celebrity through his comic caricatures of the boozy, "pawky", sentimental Scot. ■

PARKS

"There's a mountain!" exclaimed an excited metropolitan visitor to Edinburgh. "A mountain in the middle of the city – with sheep on it!"

Sheep no longer safely graze on Edinburgh's "mountain", the 822-ft (250-metre) volcanic plug which is the singular centrepiece of the city. But Arthur's Seat and the great, semi-circular rampart of **Salisbury Crags** still bring a mood of wilderness to Edinburgh's largest park, the Royal estate of **Holyrood** which (depending on the gender of the reigning monarch) is also known as Queen's or King's Park.

Once a hunting reserve, now some 4 miles (6.4 km) in circumference, with two small lochs, a scattering of antiquities and a Royal palace at its main entrance, Holyrood Park continues to startle visitors with its craggy style and spectacular scale; while annual events as diverse as the Scottish Miners' Gala, the Orange Walk and Fringe Sunday (when performers from the Edinburgh Festival Fringe hold a jamboree in the park) turn it into a huge, breezy, open-air theatre for locals.

The climb to the summit of **Arthur's Seat** is a favourite hike, although idle mountaineers can reduce the effort by driving half way up Queen's Drive, the one-way road which circuits the park, leaving their cars at **Dunsapie Loch**. There is also parking at the foot of the hill at **St Margaret's Loch** which, like Dunsapie, has a complement of swans, ducks and often greylag geese.

Nearby is **St Margaret's Well** and, a little farther up the hill, perched on a crag, the ruins of **St Anthony's Chapel**, both rather vaguely associated with people suffering from eye afflictions. The well is a late medieval conduit thought to have been established during the reign of James IV and moved to its present site from Restalrig in 1859; the chapel is believed to date from the 15th century and may be connected with a hospital founded by James I at Leith and committed to the care of victims of "St Anthony's Fire", the medieval name for erysipelas, a febrile disease.

Holyrood Park is an uncomfortable place for wives. One of Edinburgh's most notorious murders took place there on an October night in 1720, and those of morbid bent might take a passing interest in **Muschat's Cairn**, near the Willowbrae entrance to the park, which marks the spot where the victims died. As a local rhyme describes the event:

Nicol Muschat had a wife,
But soon grew tired of her;
A surgeon trained, he used a knife
As records do aver.

Nicol Muschat was indeed a young surgeon and apothecary's assistant who married a woman called Margaret Hall in 1719. When he quickly grew tired of her, he launched a bizarre series of attempts to kill her. First he tried to poison her with mercury; after spending weeks in agony, she recovered. Next he hired a

Preceding pages: the Meadows. **Left**, an encounter in Princes Street Gardens. **Right**, Royal Botanic Garden.

gang of incompetent footpads who made several unsuccessful bids to waylay her. Then he decided to do the deed himself.

He persuaded the ingenuous girl to accompany him into the park late at night on a jaunt to Duddingston village on the other side of Arthur's Seat. Then he cut her throat and left her body behind a wall, on the spot now marked by Muschat's Cairn. However, he was just as much a bungler as his predecessors and left so many clues behind that he was soon arrested, convicted and hanged in the Grassmarket.

More than two centuries later, another young husband devised a more calculating plan. In 1973 a 21-year-old Dutch visitor called Ernst Dumoulin celebrated his wedding day in Edinburgh by pushing his bride of a few hours over Salisbury Crags. There were no witnesses and he claimed her death was an accident. But the existence of a large insurance policy which he had taken out on her life a few days before aroused suspicions and he was duly tried and convicted of murder in Edinburgh's High Court.

Despite this disagreeable association, the **Radical Road** where the bride's body was found is one of Edinburgh's favourite walks and viewpoints. In his novel *The Heart of Midlothian* Sir Walter Scott advocates a notion that the best views of the city are to be had from the foot of Salisbury Crags, "marking the verge of the steep descent which slopes down into the glen on the southeastern side of Edinburgh."

He goes on: "The prospect, in its general outline, commands a close-built, high-piled city, stretching itself out beneath in a form which, to a romantic imagination, may be supposed to represent that of a dragon; now, a noble arm of the sea, with its rocks, isles, distant shores, and boundary of mountains; and now, a fair and fertile champaign country, varied with hill, dale, and rock, and skirted by the picturesque ridge of the Pentland mountains."

This heart-stirring passage was pub-

Holyrood Park.

lished in 1818, two years before the Radical Road was built round the base of Salisbury Crags to give work to the unemployed, and describes an Edinburgh of even earlier times. (*The Heart of Midlothian* is set in 1736, the year of the Porteous Riots.)

But although there is perhaps rather less of the "fair and fertile champaign country" to be seen these days, the essence of the city remains true to Scott's imagery. The spiky ridge of the Royal Mile still looks like a dragon's spine – presenting its best profile, perhaps, to the elevations in two of Edinburgh's other major parks, the Royal Botanic Garden and Inverleith Park, both to be found side by side about a mile north of Princes Street.

Action-packed park: Both parks were once part of the Inverleith estate which gave the district its name, and their respective characters make them major crowd-pullers on fine Edinburgh days. Despite their proximity to each other, they not only represent two very differ-ent aspects of the recreational spectrum, but two contrasting moods. **Inverleith Park** is breezy, energetic, expansive, action-packed. It has football, rugby and cricket pitches, tennis courts and a large boating pond, and a well-stocked children's playground. Laid out by the city in 1890, it still contains at its east end the old Inverleith farmhouse which dates from the 18th century, but which was updated around 1900. Its one oasis of tranquillity is a small formal rose garden, whose arboreal wall provides some shelter from hurtling dogs, gasp-ing joggers and rogue cricket balls.

All three, along with other nuisances, are officially excluded from the **Royal Botanic Garden**, which is a sumptu-ous, velvety, sheltered place where even the hillock which supports Inverleith House, and which offers a spectacular panorama of the Edinburgh skyline's most striking landmarks, is well pro-vided with mellow walls and opulent foliage to trap the sun.

The Botanics pre-date Inverleith Park.

Royal Botanic Garden.

The scientific interest in botany goes back a long way. Edinburgh's Royal Botanic Garden was founded in 1670 on a site now obliterated by Waverley Station and between 1822 and 1824 moved to Inverleith, making it among the oldest in Britain.

Enthusiasts identify as its star attractions the magnificent collection of rhododendrons, its heath and rock gardens and the landscaping of exotic plants. Students of greenhouse architecture admire the contrast between the Victorian New Palm House and the adventurous superstructure of the New Glass Houses, designed in the 1960s. Local habituees of the gardens simply relish their heart-lifting beauty and voluptuous calm, despite still lamenting the loss from Inverleith House of the National Gallery of Modern Art, which moved to new premises in 1984, leaving desolate the spacious, grassy, open-air "podium" which once so wonderfully displayed the gallery's collection of Henry Moores and Barbara Hepworths.

Gardens and galleries: Not all visitors find their way to these delightful parks, but few avoid being willingly swept into the great green abyss of **Princes Street Gardens**, that gorgeous gulf between bustling thoroughfare and Castle Rock which helps make Princes Street one of the most celebrated commercial arteries in Europe.

The gardens, separated into East and West by the handsome "bridge" of the Royal Scottish Academy and the National Gallery on the Mound, have their beginnings in Lord Provost George Drummond's visionary plan to extend Edinburgh from the Royal Mile to the North. This scheme, which eventually produced James Craig's neo-classical New Town, began with the draining of the Nor'Loch below the Castle in 1759 and the building of the North Bridge, although neither East nor West Princes Street Gardens was laid out until the 19th century was well under way.

They do, however, pre-date the construction of the railway and the exten-

Princes Street Gardens.

sion of Waverley Station, and have accordingly been tinkered with since – although any attempt to interfere with the view from Princes Street of the Castle Rock and Royal Mile has been vigorously shouted down by the citizens of Edinburgh.

The only permitted interruptions to that view have been commemorative and – with one exception – unobtrusive. The upper edge of the gardens, backing onto Princes Street, is ornamented with statues and memorials, including the Royal Scots Greys Memorial, the David Livingstone Monument and statues of the poet Allen Ramsay, wearing a silk nightcap, the "excellent likeness" of Sir James Simpson, pioneer of anaesthetic, and Thomas Guthrie, who started the "Ragged Schools" for poor children.

The one exception, of course, is the blackened Gothic spire of the **Scott Monument**, whose crumbling, elaborate stonework has so far discouraged any proposal to clean it up. A more discreet attraction, tucked into the angle

Evening in the Royal Botanic Garden.

of Princes Street and the Mound in the West Gardens, is the **Floral Clock**, which dates from 1903 and is believed to be one of the oldest of its kind in the world. A ritual for Edinburgh children is a visit to the clock to watch breathlessly for the moment when its bedding-planted big hand ticks another minute away and a cuckoo darts out of a little house on the quarter of each hour.

A clock o' flowers—a braw conceit,
Lying at Allan Ramsay's feet!
Wi' mony a hue frae mony a flower,
An' cuckoo bird tae tell each hour!

The **West Gardens**, which once extended right round the Castle Rock to the back of the Grassmarket, now end with the west end of Princes Street and two churches. (The graveyard of St Cuthbert's contains the tombs of the writer Thomas De Quincey, who died in Edinburgh; George Kemp, self-taught architect – and some might say it shows – of the Scott Monument; and the painter Alexander Nasmyth.)

Its central feature is the **Ross Open Air Theatre**, venue of everything from old-time dancing to children's talent contests and neighbour to the massive Ross Fountain. But there are one or two more simple curiosities to be found in the West Gardens: a large boulder to the Norwegian Brigade "raised and trained in Scotland", and a rune stone beside the walk beneath the Castle Esplanade – an enigmatic memorial from 11th-century Sweden which was presented to the gardens by the Society of Antiquaries of Scotland.

Princes Street Gardens, Holyrood Park, the Botanics and Inverleith Park are its major organs, but Edinburgh has other green "lungs", many of them smaller, local parks. This review of its open spaces would be incomplete without a mention of the **Meadows**, the common land of informal turf and leafy avenues to the south of the Old Town, behind the Royal Infirmary, and neighbouring Bruntsfield Links; while **Leith Links**, down at the city's port, was one of the earliest golf courses in the world.

THE SEVEN HILLS OF EDINBURGH

It must have been a 20th-century marketing man who claimed for Edinburgh the topographical distinction of Rome, adding Scotland's capital to that mysteriously expanding list of European cities built on seven hills. (Prague is another which makes the same boast, as if some mystical urban virtue were endowed by such specific hilliness.)

Even by the late 19th century there was little of Edinburgh beyond the spreading verges of three hills, as Robert Louis Stevenson reported in 1878: "The ancient and famous metropolis of the North sits overlooking a windy estuary from the slope and summit of three hills. No situation could be more commanding for the head city of a kingdom; none better chosen for noble prospect. From her tall precipice and terraced gardens she looks far and wide on the sea and broad champaigns."

Thrilling crags: In those days, the three hills of Stevenson's "precipitous city" were the three which remain its most dramatic and alluring today: Arthur's Seat, Castle Hill and Calton Hill. But over the years, as the metropolis of the North found its metroland (despite the absence of underground railway), Edinburgh has acquired four more hills. Yet, for all the airy comeliness of the hills of Braid, Craiglockart, Blackford and Corstorphine they seem bland, undistinguished suburban hummocks alongside the thrilling crags and aggressive profiles of the ancient three.

If, at 822 ft (250 metres), Arthur's Seat is the highest and the most oddly-shaped – a "couchant rag-lion," Charlotte Brontë called it – then Calton Hill is the most eccentric and **Castle Hill** the most formidable. The volcanic bastion which supports Edinburgh Castle is 443 ft (133 metres) above the sea (although its sheer black rock makes it look higher) and has been a stronghold from at least AD 600.

According to Sir William Brereton, Parliamentary Commander in the Civil War, when he visited Scotland in 1636 there were those who still called the castle Castrum Puellarum, "because the kings of the Picts kept their virgins therein." To stand at the base of Castle Hill and look upwards is to find your imagination falter before its forbidding basalt, and the sanguinary adventures of history and pre-history which it has witnessed.

But nothing can diminish it. Its stature keeps it secure from any lunatic scheme of architect or developer and it remains, as Stevenson put it, "one of the most satisfactory crags in nature – a Bass Rock on dry land rooted in a garden shaken by passing trains, carrying a crown of battlements and turrets, and describing its warlike shadow over the liveliest and brightest thoroughfare of the new town."

The history of Castle Hill is the history of **Edinburgh Castle** – which means that legion are its stories of siege,

Preceding pages: Arthur's Seat. Left, winter fun on Arthur's Seat. Right, the Nelson Monument on Calton Hill.

subterfuge, heroism, treachery, noble and ignoble acts. The cliffs have had their own unique part to play in Scotland's history. When the saintly Queen Margaret died in the castle in 1093, while it was under siege from Donald Bane, her body was secretly lowered down the rock and taken to her priory in Dunfermline. And in 1313, when the castle had been in English hands for 17 years during Scotland's Wars of Independence, it was re-taken by the Earl of Murray and a handful of men who climbed stealthily up the cliffs.

The broad, battlemented **Esplanade** is the lofty stage above the city where the Festival's Military Tattoo is held. Its history is less festive. Between 1479 and 1722 it was the favoured site for the burning of witches. Scotland's record in the persecution of old, eccentric women – and often young women who had merely made some local enemies – is a shameful one. More than 300 "witches" were burned on the Esplanade alone, on a spot marked by an art nouveau Witches' Well on a wall to the right of the entrance to the Esplanade.

Probably no one has misunderstood the nature of Edinburgh's hills more than the essayist William Hazlitt, who wrote in 1826: "Edinburgh alone is as splendid in its situation and buildings, and would have even a more imposing and delightful effect if Arthur's Seat were crowned with thick woods, and if the Pentland-hills could be converted into green pastures, if the Scotch people were French, and Leith-walk planted with vineyards."

Perfect emblems: The somewhat leaden satire of Hazlitt's observation doesn't diminish the crime of misrepresentation. Edinburgh's hills are, naturally and unalterably, the perfect emblems of Scotland's prevailing topography. The **Pentlands** are a shapely outpost of the Border hills and Arthur's Seat is a Highland peak in miniature. Dorothy Wordsworth recognised this: "We sate down on a stone not far from the chapel, overlooking a pastoral hollow as wild

Edinburgh's dominant feature, the Castle.

and solitary as any in the heart of the Highland mountains: there, instead of the roaring of the torrents, we listened to the noises of the city…"

Nearly 200 years later, the noises of the city are very different, but now the thunder of traffic in the near-distance sounds like the roaring of torrents, and it's just as possible, on winter mornings on **Arthur's Seat**, to believe yourself in the heart of the Highland mountains.

No one really knows which Arthur claimed the eminence for his seat. Some argue for the legendary king of the Round Table, and there is evidence that the Lothians was one of the British (Welsh) kingdoms before they were occupied by the Angles and Scots. But it may have been a sixth-century Prince Arthur of Strathclyde who gave the hill its name; then again – and more probably – the name may simply be a corruption of the Gaelic *Ard na Saigheid,* "height of the arrows."

Earliest times: Whatever its christening, Arthur's Seat was certainly defen-

sively colonised in pre-history. The remains of four prehistoric forts can be traced with perseverance and difficulty on the hill and in the Dunsapie Loch and Salisbury Crags areas, suggesting that it was a major centre in the first millennium and in the early centuries of this one. More easily visible are the groups of cultivated terraces on the east flank of the hill, above and below Queen's Drive. They were once narrow ploughed fields, dating from the Dark Ages.

The view from the top is simply magical. On clear days it embraces the narrow waist of Scotland, from the Firth of Forth to the Firth of Clyde, as well as the mountains of the Trossachs, those comely outriders of the great Highland massif, and, to the southeast, the romantic Lammermuirs and the Border hills.

It was not always thus. The name of Auld Reekie (Old Smokey) was acquired by Edinburgh in the 19th century when the peat and coal smoke from the multiplicity of chimneys in the Royal Mile produced a permanent pall over

the city. The Clean Air Act has changed all that, but the grimy cloud hanging over Arthur's Seat is remembered in this piece of doggerel:

Arthur's Seat, ye're high and humpy,
But whit gars ye look sae grumpy?
Perhaips the smeuch o' Auld Reeike
Maks ye smairt, an' feel richt weerie?

Naturally, this extraordinary urban mountain has not been ignored by writers and film-makers, but few have used it more dramatically than James Hogg in his classic allegory of the duality of human nature *Private Memoirs and Confessions of a Justified Sinner*. A key episode in the book is set on the summit of Arthur's Seat, where the tormented George Colwan is confronted by a giant apparition of his brother – "its dark eyes gleamed through the mist, while every furrow of its hideous brow frowned deep as the ravines on the brow of the hill" – and is later murdered by him and his satanic doppelganger Gil-martin.

In the realm of fact, the hill was the scene of a macabre discovery in 1836, when five Edinburgh boys out hunting rabbits stumbled upon a cache of tiny coffins. There were 17 of them, each four inches (10 cm) long with lids secured by brass pins and sides ornamented with designs in tin. Inside, fashioned in meticulous detail, were 17 diminutive figures. Their origin was never traced but, naturally, witchcraft was suspected. Some of those miniature coffins are now displayed in the National Museum of Antiquities in Queen Street.

Pompous the boast, and yet a
truth it speaks
A "modern Athens" – fit for
modern Greeks.

This waspish comment on both Edinburgh and the Greeks was made by James Hannay in an edition of The Edinburgh Courant in 1860. By then, Edinburgh had lived for nearly 30 years with the "folly" which turned **Calton Hill** into a hand-me-down Acropolis. The two hills can't really be compared, but there's no doubt echoes of the Athens rock are to be found in the steep

Awaiting the solstice on Arthur's Seat.

crags and incomplete Parthenon of the **National Monument** on Edinburgh's Calton Hill – a monument more sheepishly known as "Scotland's Disgrace".

Golden blocks: Still casting around for a suitable monument to commemorate the end of the Napoleonic Wars in 1815, a public appeal was launched in 1822 by various city luminaries, including Sir Walter Scott, Henry Cockburn and Lord Elgin. They wanted £42,000 "to erect a facsimile of the Parthenon" but barely half was subscribed. Nevertheless, the distinguished architect Sir William Playfair was appointed to the task along with C.R.Cockerell, whose job was to guarantee the accuracy of the reproduction, and great golden blocks of Craigleith stone were hauled from the quarry on the edge of the city to the top of Calton Hill.

Work began in 1826 and came to a halt when funds dried up in 1829, with only part of the stylobate and 12 handsome columns with their architrave completed. Today, Edinburgh's heroic folly

Calton Hill.

looks like a kind of flawless ruin of uncrumbled stone.

It is certainly the oddest building on the summit of Calton Hill but not the most preposterous; that honour must go to the **Nelson Monument**, built to honour the hero of Trafalgar in 1807. This circular tower is over 100 ft (30 metres) high with a flagstaff and a time-ball, which gives a visual signal to ships in the Forth at noon, on the top. The time-ball is "in electric communication with the time-gun at the Castle" and falls exactly when the gun is fired at 1pm.

The battlemented base is composed of small rooms "originally intended to give accommodation to disabled seamen", but leased eventually "to a vendor of soups and sweetmeats".

As James Grant wrote in the 1880s, it is "an edifice in such doubtful taste that its demolition has been more than once advocated." But he added, "with all its defects it makes a magnificent termination to the vista along Princes Street."

As indeed does the whole domed,

towered and pillared mass of Calton Hill, which has a third major building on its summit. The cruciform-shaped **City Observatory**, with its characteristic green dome housing the telescope, was also designed by William Playfair. It was built in 1818 for the recently formed Astronomical Institution. The late 19th-century foretaste of pollution – smoke from the railway lines into Waverley Station – compelled the Astronomer Royal to relocate on Blackford Hill in the southern suburbs.

The building now houses the "Edinburgh Experience", the story of the city through 3-D glasses.

For all its curiosities – and they also include a reproduction of the monument of Lysicrates in Athens, dedicated to a perishable Edinburgh University philosopher called Dugald Stewart, and a Portuguese cannon captured at Mandalay – the most satisfying spectacle of Calton Hill is the glorious view from its grassy plateau. (You can drive most of the way up and park near the northwest edge, above the gully of Greenside where they once burned witches.)

The height and position of the hill makes it perfectly positioned for an all-round, close-up study of the city's central anatomy, as well as its relationship with Edinburgh's other hills and the waters of the Firth of Forth. "Leith camps on the seaside with her forest of masts," wrote Robert Louis Stevenson in 1879, evoking the mood and magic of Calton Hill in a series of stunning vignettes. "Leith roads are full of ships at anchor."

The forest of masts has become a copse, but the maritime life of Edinburgh's port can still be glimpsed in the superstructure of oil rig supply vessels, the occasional cruise ship or assorted visitors from the navies of NATO.

Much of Stevenson's intimacy with Calton Hill was acquired on assignations with prostitutes there, although today its sexual notoriety has been hijacked by gays looking for pick-ups (mainly after dark).

Stevenson was too much of a poet,

Grecian echoes on Calton Hill.

however, to neglect the view, with its opportunities for an exhilarating experience in urban voyeurism. "You turn to the city", he wrote, "and see children dwarfed by distance into pygmies, at play about suburban doorsteps; you have a glimpse upon a thoroughfare where people are densely moving; you note ridge after ridge of chimney stacks running downhill one behind another, and church spires rising bravely from the sea of roofs. At one of the innumerable windows, you watch a figure moving; on one of the multitude of roofs, you watch clambering chimney sweeps."

Monstrous bulk: For anyone who loves Edinburgh with the clear-sightedness of Stevenson (who also loathed it), Calton is the paragon of hills. But since his day, its 328 rocky feet (98 metres) have been almost overwhelmed, to the northwest, by the brutal bulk of the **St James Centre** and **New St Andrews House** – the shopping precinct and government office block which seem to have been built by people who hate Edinburgh.

Amiable browsings above the city, but less intense experiences of it, are to be had on the four suburban hills. The most interesting are **Corstorphine**, home of the Edinburgh Zoo since 1927, modelled on the Stellingen Zoo near Hamburg and famous for its penguins, and **Blackford**, a steep shelf above the southern suburbs where the Royal Observatory stands. It is now a joint research institution of the Science Research Council and the University of Edinburgh.

At the foot of the hill is the public garden containing Blackford Pond, while to the west, topping Blackford's 539 ft (168 metres) by another 36 ft (11 metres) is wooded **West Craiglockhart Hill**. The **Braid Hill** – or the Braids, as this boisterous plateau is locally known – is higher still at 675 ft (203 metres), and lies immediately to the south of Blackford.

All three provide heart-stirring views of Edinburgh's place between the Firth of Forth and the Pentland Hills.

The Braid Hills.

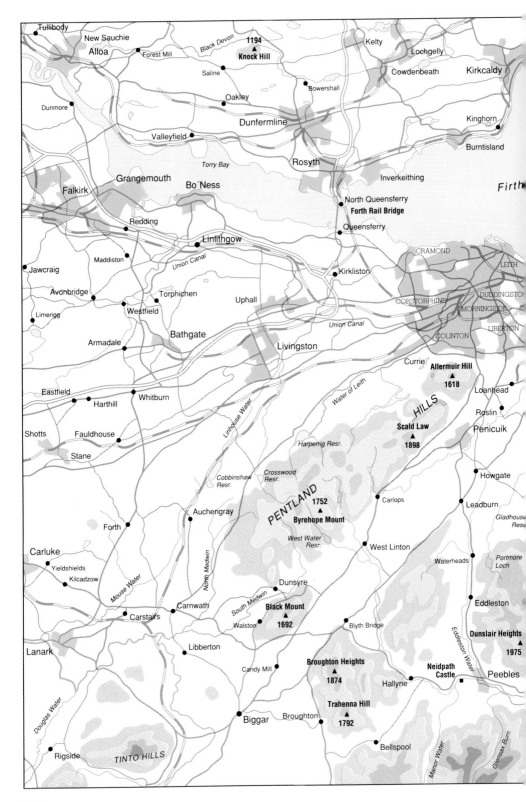

Tullibody
New Sauchie
Alloa
Forest Mill
Black Devon
1194
Knock Hill
Kelty
Lochgelly
Kirkcaldy
Cowdenbeath
Saline
Bowershall
Dunmore
Oakley
Dunfermline
Kinghorn
Valleyfield
Burntisland
Rosyth
Torry Bay
Inverkeithing
Grangemouth
Bo'Ness
Firth
Falkirk
North Queensferry
Forth Rail Bridge
Queensferry
Redding
Linlithgow
CRAMOND
LEITH
Maddiston
Union Canal
Kirkliston
CORSTORPHINE
DUDDINGSTO
Jawcraig
Avonbridge
Torphichen
Uphall
MORNINGSIDE
Westfield
Union Canal
LIBERTON
Limerigg
Bathgate
COLINTON
Armadale
Livingston
Currie
Allermuir Hill
HILLS
1618
Loanhead
Eastfield
Whitburn
Water of Leith
Roslin
Harthill
Scald Law
Penicuik
Shotts
Fauldhouse
Harperrig Resr.
1898
Stane
Crosswood
Resr.
Howgate
Cobbinshaw
Resr.
PENTLAND
1752
Leadburn
Auchengray
Byrehope Mount
Carlops
Gladhouse
Resr
Forth
West Water
Resr.
West Linton
Portmore
Loch
Carluke
Waterheads
Yieldshields
Kilcadzow
Dunsyre
Eddleston
Mouse Water
South Medwin
Black Mount
Blyth Bridge
Carnwath
1692
Eddleston Water
Dunslair Heights
Carstairs
Walston
1975
Libberton
Neidpath
Castle
Peebles
Lanark
Candy Mill
Broughton Heights
Hallyne
Douglas Water
1874
Biggar
Broughton
Trahenna Hill
1792
Rigside
TINTO HILLS
Bellspool
Manor Water
Glensax Burn

North Medwin
Linhouse Water

214

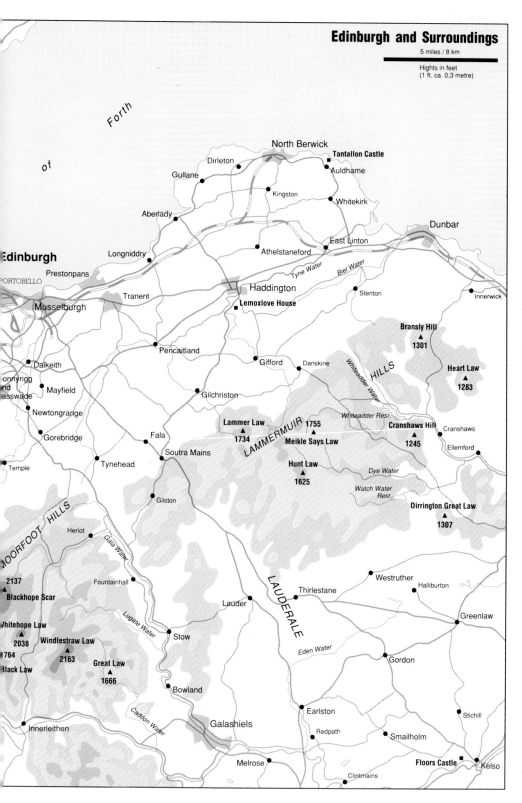

Edinburgh and Surroundings

5 miles / 8 km

Hights in feet
(1 ft. ca. 0,3 metre)

Forth

of

North Berwick

Dirleton
Gullane
Tantallon Castle
Auldhame
Kingston
Whitekirk

Aberlady

Dunbar

Edinburgh
Longniddry
East Linton
Athelstaneford
Prestonpans
PORTOBELLO
Tyne Water
Biel Water
Tranent
Haddington
Stenton
Innerwick
Musselburgh
Lemoxlove House

Bransly Hill
▲
1301

Pencaitland
Dalkeith
Gifford
Danskine
Heart Law
▲
1283
onnyrigg
nd
asswade
Mayfield
Gilchriston
Whiteadder Water
HILLS

Newtongrange
Lammer Law
▲
1734
LAMMERMUIR
Whiteadder Resr.
Cranshaws Hill
▲
1245
Cranshaws
Gorebridge
Fala
1755
Meikle Says Law
Ellemford
Temple
Soutra Mains
Hunt Law
▲
1625
Dye Water
Tynehead

Gilston
Watch Water
Resr.
Dirrington Great Law
▲
1307

MOORFOOT HILLS
Heriot
Gala Water

2137
▲
Blackhope Scar
Fountainhall
Westruther
Halliburton
Thirlestane
Whitehope Law
▲
2038
Lauder
LAUDERDALE
Greenlaw
764
Windlestraw Law
▲
2163
Stow
Black Law
Great Law
▲
1666
Eden Water
Gordon

Lugate Water
Bowland
Caddon Water

Innerleithen
Galashiels
Earlston
Stichill
Redpath
Smailholm

Melrose
Floors Castle
Kelso
Clintmains

DAY TRIPS FROM EDINBURGH

The scale of Scotland allows you to put Edinburgh comfortably in its context. An effortless day's outing from the capital brings you within reach of much of Scotland's past and present and the forces that have shaped the country: its critical topography, its rival clans, its dominant families and ecclesiastical powers and gifted individuals who have left their imprint on the land in castles, great houses, abbeys and museums.

There are plenty of playgrounds, too, within 50 miles (80 km) of the city: the beaches and golf courses of East Lothian, the elegant fishing river of the Tweed, the Lammermuirs, Pentlands and Border hills for riding and hill-walking and the Forth estuary for water sports. It shouldn't be forgotten, either, that Scotland's other great city, Glasgow, is less than an hour away by rail or road. There can be few countries in the world where it is possible to commute so swiftly between competing metropoli, and few neighbouring cities whose characters are so rewardingly different.

East of Edinburgh is the benign and affluent county of **East Lothian**, which many believe to be the most "English" of Scottish counties. Its rolling farmland is ornamented with pretty, prosperous villages and small towns, Scottish in their red pantiles and crowstep gables but English in their village greens. The reason why, for example, the village of **Dirleton** has its cottages and inns organised round a green instead of dispersed in the more typical Scottish way is unclear; although it may have something to do with the expansion of the Anglian kingdom of Northumbria into southeast Scotland in the 7th century.

East Lothian's northern boundary is the **Firth of Forth** with its scattering of precipitous, bird-haunted islands and an attractive littoral of bays, beaches and machair – the sandy links which give it some of the best golf courses in the world. The most famous is **Muirfield**, near the village of Gullane, which takes its turn to host the Open Golf Championship; the oldest is **Musselburgh**, where golf has been played since 1672. (The "Honest Toun" of Musselburgh, now cheek by jowl with Edinburgh's eastern suburbs, also has the oldest racecourse in Scotland).

The main route along the Forth coast is the A198, but it's worth making a detour on the B1348 through the industrial fringe of East Lothian (which has produced coal as well as crops) to the **Scottish Mining Museum** at **Prestongrange**. Sited on a former colliery with 800 years of mining behind it, the museum's relics of mining history include steam locomotives, a steam navvy, a colliery winding engine and a Hoffman Kiln.

Nearby is **Prestonpans**, now one of a string of moribund mining communities but once the scene of Charles Edward Stuart's most famous victory. An undistinguished battle cairn just off the

A198 commemorates the Prince's dawn raid on the government forces of General John Cope, who lost 400 men to the Jacobites' 30 and whose doziness is mischievously recalled in the ballad, "Hey Johnnie Cope are ye waukin' yet".

Soon the drab residue of East Lothian's peripheral industry falls behind and the road continues through a series of picturesque coastal villages to **Aberlady**, which has a cluster of attractions: the Myreton Motor Museum, with a varied collection of vintage road transport, and Gosford Hose, home of the Earl of Wemyss. (It isn't, perhaps, the most interesting of Scottish stately homes but admirers of the Adam dynasty of celebrated Scottish architects will enjoy the central part of the building, which is by Robert Adam.)

Aberlady was once the port of the ancient royal burgh of **Haddington**, five miles (eight km) inland, but there is virtually no trace of that maritime existence. The bay where ships once anchored is now, at low tide, a vast mud flat which is a nature reserve and home to 200 recorded species of bird. The next bay, with fine beaches and massive sand dunes, belongs to the village of **Gullane**, which supports no fewer than five golf courses. When you pass the road-end to Muirfield you will also come close to by-passing Gullane's neighbour **Dirleton**, which you really should visit.

The crowning glory of this exceptionally pretty village is its 13th-century castle, a romantic ruin on a grassy mound within beautiful walled gardens which contain a 17th-century bowling green. The castle was a stronghold of the Ruthven family, who were involved in the murder of Mary Stuart's favourite David Rizzio, and was also attacked by Edward I of England in 1298, during Scotland's Wars of Independence. It survived undiminished until 1650, when Cromwell destroyed it as a Royalist stronghold. The ruins are substantial, however, and from the battlements you can see south to the Lammermuirs, the

Gullane: fine beaches and five golf courses.

setting of Sir Walter Scott's novel *The Bride of Lammermuir*, and north to the hills of Fife.

Prominent, too, are East Lothian's isolated volcanic plugs – the conical Berwick Law and the whaleback of Traprain Law. Less uplifting is the castle's prison pit, where in 1649 a group of men and women accused of witchcraft were contained, before being strangled and burned at the stake.

Berwick Law dominates the handsome, old-fashioned resort of **North Berwick**, 2 miles (3 km) down the coast. The history of this old burgh, given royal status by Robert III, is not as benevolent as its appearance suggests today. On the rocky promontory which divides its two bays of blameless sand is the ruin of the **Auld Kirk**, which has 12th-century foundations and a 16th-century porch. In 1591 the kirk was the scene of an infamous gathering of witches and wizards who were conspiring to encourage the Devil to cause the death of James VI.

In the 19th century North Berwick became known as the Biarritz of the North, when the coming of the railway gave it new status as a resort and inspired the building of the dignified hotels and guest houses which give the town so much of its charming, unspoiled character today. Although it has few artificial attractions, it nevertheless remains the perfect family resort, and an easy day out for the people of Edinburgh who swarm down the coast on summer Sundays.

Its activities are the simple, innocent ones of childhood: picnics on the beach, putting and tennis, scrambles on the rocks (the East Bay has a boundary of exciting cliffs) or boat trips to the islands of **Fidra**, **Craigleith** and the spectacular **Bass Rock**. The sheer cliffs of the Bass Rock – this massive chunk of basalt about one-and-a-half miles (two-and-a-half km) out to sea rises to a height of 350 ft (105 metres) – are home to the country's largest colony of gannets as well as puffins, fulmars, kitti-

Dirleton Castle: a romantic ruin.

wakes and other seabirds. The rock still bears traces of early fortifications, and it was put to its most famous use as a prison for Covenanters after 1671 and, later, for Jacobite prisoners who seized their jailers and held the fort for three years until they were pardoned.

There are vestiges of war, too, on the summit of **Berwick Law**, which is a steep but exhilarating climb some 600 ft (180 metres) above the sea and where, on clear days, you can see north and westwards to the outriders of the Highlands. A ruined watchtower dates from Napoleonic times, when the Law was one of a chain of beacons prepared to warn of a French invasion, and an unseemly concrete bunker was put to similar use during World War II.

The Law's most original endowment, however, is the arch made from the jaws of a whale, like a giant inverted wishbone on its top. The venerable beeches on the east side of this attractive pyramid, incidentally, were planted in 1707 to commemorate the Act of Union, when Scottish and English Parliaments became one – an Act unpopular with a majority of Scots at the time and almost as unpopular today.

Three miles (five km) east of North Berwick is one of Scotland's most dramatic castles: the clifftop **Tantallon**, defended on three sides by vertiginous drops into the sea and on the fourth by a double moat. This gaunt, ruined sandstone fortress was a stronghold of the Douglases, the powerful Border family, and, although it dates from around 1375, it was never taken until 1651, when it fell to Cromwell's General Monk after 12 days of bombardment.

From Tantallon the A198 swings inland to join the A1 at **Dunbar**, a historic fortress port and royal burgh which is now a holiday resort. Today it promotes itself as the birthplace of the pioneer conservationist John Muir, who emigrated to America at the age of 11 and won himself the title of Father of the National Parks by, among other methods, taking Teddy Roosevelt on camp-

Tantallon: it fell to Cromwell's armies.

ing trips. A strip of coastal land, the **John Muir Country Park**, has been dedicated to his memory and the Muir family home in Dunbar's 17th-century High Street is a small museum.

Only fragments remain of **Dunbar Castle**, which was defended by one of Scotland's most heart-stirring heroines, "Black Agnes," Countess of Dunbar. She held the stronghold by the harbour against the English for six weeks in 1339 (during Scotland's Wars of Independence) until it was relieved.

The castle was also associated with Mary Queen of Scots, who fled there with the duplicitous Darnley after the murder of Rizzio, and who later appointed her lover, the Earl of Bothwell, its governor. Her hostile half-brother, the Earl of Murray, razed it to the ground after Mary's defeat by her own nobles at Carberry Hill, and in 1650 Cromwell finished it off by using its stones to improve the harbour.

How Preston Mill got its name.

Dunbar makes a good turning point for a journey back to Edinburgh via the A1, but enthusiasts for the coast could continue via **St Abb's Head Nature Reserve** (accessible only by foot) to the celebrated walled town of **Berwick-upon-Tweed**, which has been wrenched back and forwards so often across the Border that its natives have dual loyalties. Although Berwick has been English since 1482 the Border is only three miles (five km) to the north of the town and many of Berwick's children are born in Scottish hospitals.

A return to Edinburgh by the A1 and its tributaries, however, gives you a chance to visit the quiet rural treasures of East Lothian's interior such as **Tyninghame House Gardens**, near East Linton, where you will find not just the expected charms of a traditional country house garden but the ruins of St Baldred's Chapel. This eighth-century saint is a favourite son of East Lothian, giving his name to roads, pleasure boats and two rocks on the shore. Also near the village of East Linton is **Preston Mill** and the **Phantassie Doocot**, the

first is one of the oldest watermills still working in Scotland, and the second is a beehive building which once gave house-room to 544 doves.

Of the county's inland villages, **Stenton** and **Gifford** are probably the most attractive and interesting. Like so many places of notoriety, Stenton's appearance quite belies the sinister reputation it once had for a particular enthusiasm for the burning of witches. Today it's a conservation area and the village green has a relic of more homely activities; its Wool Stone, or tron, was used for weighing wool at the wool fair.

Gifford was the birth place of the Reverend John Witherspoon, one of the signatories to the American Declaration of Independence and the first president of what is now Princeton University. It has two characterful inns and a pleasant walk beside a stream to the gates of Yestor House, round which the village was neatly assembled in the 17th and 18th centuries.

Yestor House is now the Scottish home of the composer Giancarlo Menotti, but the area's most distinguished grand home is **Lennoxlove House**, the seat of the Duke and Duchess of Hamilton (since 1946). It was named for Frances Stewart, Duchess of Lennox, who in the 17th century was the model for the figure of Britannia used on Britain's coinage. Known as "La Belle Stewart", she was passionately but vainly pursued by Charles II. Lennoxlove is open to the public on selected days throughout the summer. It has a room devoted to Mary Queen of Scots and contains her death mask and a French silver casket given to her by her first husband, Francis II of France.

From Lennoxlove it's a short drive on peaceful minor roads to **Haddington**, fertile hunting ground for antiquarians. Its central streets still contain many of the buildings and still follow the design laid out between the 17th and 19th centuries. However Haddington dates back to at least the 12th century when it was made a royal burgh by David I, and,

although burned and occupied by the English several times since, has long guarded its status as East Lothian's market town and administrative centre. John Knox, great Scottish Protestant reformer and protagonist of Mary Stuart, was born here in 1505 and the Knox Memorial Institute (1879) is the successor to the school where he was educated.

Worth seeing, too, is the 13th-century Church of St Mary, which contains the tomb of another native of Haddington—Jane Welsh, the wife of Thomas Carlyle; and St Mary's Pleasance, the garden of Haddington House, now restored as a 17th-century garden.

Haddington is closely by-passed by the A1, and its fast access to Edinburgh 17 miles (25 km) away has made it a favourite settlement of commuters. But the conservationists of East Lothian have preserved its essential character.

The Borders: This region is a tourist centre in itself. It would be impossible to do justice to all its attractions in a day trip from Edinburgh, but it's easy enough

Jedburgh Abbey.

to visit some of the principal ones: the great abbeys of **Kelso**, **Jedburgh**, **Dryburgh**, and **Melrose**, **Abbotsford** (the home of Sir Walter Scott) and – for compulsive consumers – the woollen and tweed mills of the River Tweed, many of which have shops selling knitwear and cloth at bargain prices.

Rich sheep pasture and soft water from its famous fishing rivers give rise to conditions which once made the Borders prosper as a centre for quality textiles. However, today's economic conditions and overseas competition have not favoured the traditional practices of the mill towns of **Galashiels** and **Hawick**. Tweed, peculiarly, takes its name only accidentally from the River Tweed. The Border weavers called their fabric "tweel", their dialect for twill, and a London merchant jumped to the wrong conclusion.

Scenically, the Borders lack the drama of the Highlands, but has a distinctive beauty which is more pastoral, less challenging. Border hills, some over 2,000 ft (610 metres), are shapely and rounded, rising from river valleys of natural woodland and increasingly planted with conifers. But there is still plenty of bare, lonely upland in the Borders – moors and hills so desolate that it's difficult to appreciate those territorial imperatives which made this region so furiously contested.

It is saturated – some might say stained – with the history of Scotland's old hostilities with England, and with the blood of its own feuding families. Its shattered castles, dismembered abbeys and spectacular local pageants – the Common Ridings which recall the days of *rievers* (freebooters) and moss-troopers – are today's testament to that savage past.

There are three main routes to the heartland of the Borders from Edinburgh: the A68 through Scott Country to Jedburgh, the A7 to Galashiels, Melrose and Selkirk, and the A703 to the comely town of Peebles and the upper Tweed valley. There is always some argument as to whether **Peebles** is

Jedburgh Jail.

"truly" a Border town (it's only 23 miles/37km from Edinburgh) and it is certainly the region's most westerly outpost. But its substantial charm and striking setting on the Tweed make it a durable favourite with excursionists from Edinburgh.

For travellers with their own cars, it's possible to enjoy a comfortable and picturesque circular day-trip down the A703 to Peebles and along the A72 and the broadening Tweed valley to Scott Country, that area which surrounds Abbotsford and the town of Melrose (by far the prettiest of Border towns), and return either via Galashiels and the A7 or by Lauder and the A68.

This, in the space of a full day, would give you the best possible introduction to the Borders and, although it's not suggested that you would have time to visit all the following places, they lie either on this route or within easy striking distance of it.

As you leave Edinburgh to travel south on the A703 you should look for the signposts to **Rosslyn Chapel**, which lies to the east of the road. Within this small, 15th-century chapel (the burial place of the Sinclair family) is the most elaborate stone carving to be found in Scotland, if not in Britain. The Seven Deadly Sins, the Seven Cardinal Virtues and a dance of death are extravagantly represented in bas-relief, but folk interest tends to focus on the Prentice Pillar with its intricate and abundant flowers and foliage.

The story of the Prentice Pillar has never been authenticated, but it's supposed to have been carved by an apprentice while his master was away. The work was so fine that when the master returned he flew into a jealous rage and killed the apprentice. Three carved heads at the end of the nave are alleged to belong to the unfortunate youth, his grief-stricken mother and his master.

A short and beguiling riverside walk from Peebles town centre takes you to **Neidpath Castle**, a dour but well-preserved fortress on an eminence above **Winter at Neidpath.**

the Tweed. It belonged first to the Frasers and then the Hays and was built between the 13th and 15th centuries. Like almost every other fortress in this region, it was besieged by Cromwell.

More can be seen at **Traquair House**, which claims to have been continuously inhabited since the 10th century. This mellow piece of antiquity lies just across the river from **Innerleithen** (on your A72 route to Galashiels) and was a residence of William the Lion. Another 27 Scottish and English monarchs are said to have paid a visit, and when Bonnie Prince Charlie departed through its Bear Gates it was commanded that they remain closed until a Stuart regained the throne. They are, of course, still closed. Today, Traquair makes ale in its 18th-century brewhouse and welcomes visitors to its maze, craft workshops and summer fair.

The mill town of **Galashiels** is the gateway to Scott Country and, being the least attractive of Border towns, a gateway that is best hurried through. You

Traquair House: dates to the 10th century.

will find **Abbotsford House** in parkland off the A7, some three miles (five km) out of the town, and find, too, that its mock baronial aspirations are everything you might expect from the romantic imagination of the man who invented the historical novel.

Abbotsford was very much Sir Walter Scott's own creation. He bought the farm in 1811 and in 1822 demolished the old farmhouse to build the main block which, today, is a museum to the Wizard of the North and his collection of curiosities. (He somehow acquired Napoleon's cloak-clasp, Rob Roy's purse, Burn's drinking glass and a lock of Bonnie Prince Charlie's hair.)

Within sight of the house are the graceful triple peaks of the **Eildon Hills**, where Scott loved to walk, and where legend claims that King Arthur and his knights lie buried and Thomas the Rhymer was given his powers of prophecy by the Faerie Queen. Below the hills is the little town of **Melrose**, distinguished for its 12-century Cistercian

abbey – ruined, like all the Border abbeys, by a combination of English invasion, religious reform and plunderers of building materials. But much remains, including parts of the nave and choir which incorporate some of the best stone carving of their period, and the abbey is popularly believed to be the burial place of Robert the Bruce's heart.

From Melrose the ambitious collector of stones can strike out for all the Border abbeys, which lie within a few miles drive of each other: **Dryburgh**, with its remarkably complete cloister buildings, the impressive **Jedburgh**, founded by David I, and **Kelso**, one of the earliest completed by David I. Kelso was garrisoned as a fortress and, when the English Earl of Hertford entered the town in 1545, its garrison of 100 men (including 12 monks) was put to the sword and the abbey destroyed.

Kelso, with its large and lovely Georgian square, is a market town and, like Melrose, the better for having no mills. It stands at the confluence of the Teviot and Tweed and has long been associated with the Dukes of Roxburgh, whose family seat, **Floors Castle**, is just outside the town on the A6089 and open to the public on selected days. Students of architecture will appreciate the building, which was begun by William Adam around 1721 and given most of its present aspect by William Playfair in 1849. James II was killed in the grounds in 1460, when a cannon exploded.

The great architectural glory of the Borders, however, is **Mellerstain House**, which you can also reach by the A6089 from Kelso. Mellerstain is one of the finest achievements of Scotland's celebrated dynasty of architects, the Adam family. It was begun in 1725 by William Adam, who built both wings, and completed by his son, Robert in 1778. Between them they created what many believe to be the loveliest 18th-century mansion in Scotland, and today it contains work by other distinguished names from the 18th and 19th centuries: furniture by Chippendale, Sheraton and

Floors Castle: James II was killed here.

Hepplewhite and paintings by Gainsborough, Constable and Veronese. (The Border home of the Scotts of Buccleuch, **Bowhill**, 3 miles (5 km) west of Selkirk, is another of the region's finest "art galleries", with paintings by Van Dyck, Reynolds, Gainsborough, Canaletto and Raeburn.)

From Mellerstain you can thread your way back on minor roads to join the A68 for your return to Edinburgh. Those with remaining appetite might stop off at **Thirlestane Castle**, near Lauder, home of the Maitlands, and view its sumptuous state rooms; the weary will enjoy, instead, the moment when the A68 breasts Soutra Hill on the western slopes of the Lammermuirs to open up a panorama of Edinburgh and the Firth of Forth.

For citizens of Edinburgh there is some peculiar, psychological imperative to go east or south, rather that west or north, on days out from the city. Perhaps they feel the hinterland to the east and south is more truly theirs; whereas to the west, another city (Glasgow) begins to impose its identity on the land, and to the north there is the barrier of the Forth estuary. Crossing the Forth Road Bridge, on which tolls are payable, tends to represent a necessary journey rather than a carefree jaunt. Yet among the most popular coach tours from Edinburgh are day trips along the M9 to Stirling and beyond – the **Trossachs** and **Loch Lomond** – to give people a taste of the Highlands; or across the Forth to the Fife coast following it as far as **St Andrews**. We shall not be so ambitious.

Lower Forth Valley: There is plenty of interest and appeal in the lower Forth valley and enough to preoccupy the visitor to Fife without driving more than an hour from Edinburgh city centre (there are also good train services to some of these places). Begin with the bridges themselves, and the ancient ferry crossing of **South Queensferry**. With its Hawes Inn, scene of David Balfour's abduction in Robert Louis Stevenson's classic novel *Kidnapped*, South Queens-

Sunday strollers at St Andrews.

ferry now huddles beneath the giant bridges which provide such spectacular contrast in engineering design: the massive humped girders of the rail bridge, opened in 1890, and the delicate arch of the suspension bridge, opened in 1964. During the summer months there are boat trips from the village to the island of **Inchcolm** with its ruin of St Colm's Abbey, which gets a mention in Shakespeare's *Macbeth*. The abbey was first a priory founded for Augustinians in 1123 by a grateful Alexander I, who was shipwrecked on the island and helped by the resident hermit.

On the south shores of the Forth, on either side of the bridges, are the homes of two of Scotland's noble families. To the east is **Dalmeny House**, built in 1815 and home to the Earls of Rosebery. The fifth earl married the richest heiress in England, became prime minister in 1894 and saddled three Derby winners. He was an expert on Napoleon, and memorabilia of the dictator fill the Napoleon Room. Also of note are tapes-tries from Goya cartoons, portraits by Reynolds, Gainsborough and Raeburn, and 18th-century furniture.

To the west is **Hopetoun House**, home to the earls of that name. This glorious Adam building was begun by William Bruce in 1699 and completed by William Adam and his sons, and contains paintings by Gainsborough, Canaletto and Raeburn. Magnificent views of the Forth bridges can be enjoyed from the rooftop. The large, delightful grounds are full of rare specimen trees.

Other pockets of prettiness in West Lothian exist but require perseverance. Unlike its counterpart in the east this Lothian becomes more industrial the farther you travel from Edinburgh, and only a few miles upriver from the Rosebery and Hopetoun estates is the oil terminal and petro-chemical plant of **Grangemouth**. The plant's flare stacks punctuate views across the flat basin of the Forth like fiery exclamation marks.

Between Edinburgh and Grange-

Hopetoun House: 16th-century splendour.

mouth, speedily reached by the M9, is one of Scotland's oldest towns, home to the well-preserved ruins of its most magnificent palace. **Linlithgow** received its charter from David I and the town was probably a significant royal residence from then on. The palace was built by James I in the 15th century and was the scene of some key events in Scottish history. In 1513 Queen Margaret, unknowingly a widow, waited for the return of her husband James IV from the disastrous Battle of Flodden, in which the king and most of the Scottish nobility were killed by the English.

Mary Queen of Scots was born here in 1542, while her father, James V, lay dying across the Forth in Falkland Palace, and a few years later Linlithgow was host to Edinburgh University, whose scholars had fled the city for fear of the plague. Charles I was the last monarch to sleep in the palace while he contemplated making Linlithgow his Scottish capital, and between 1651 and 1659 the town was garrisoned by Cromwell.

Neglect and fire – the building was gutted when it was occupied by soldiers of the Duke of Cumberland in the aftermath of the 1745 Jacobite rebellion – have destroyed the roof and interiors but the shell of the palace is intact. Together with its large inner courtyard, containing an elaborate fountain, it gives an impressive idea of the scale and elegance of this fortified palace and the considerable style in which even monarchs of a poor, embattled country like Scotland lived. (The fountain was a wedding present from James V to Mary of Guise and was said to have overflowed with wine on their wedding day.)

Alongside the palace and topped with a controversial "crown of thorns" spire, which was lowered by helicopter in 1964, is the ancient, mainly 15th-century **St Michael's church**, the largest pre-Reformation church in Scotland. Spare a thought for James IV, who saw an apparition in the south transept which warned of his doom at Flodden. The church and the palace on its little lake

Linlithgow: inseparable from Mary Queen of Scots.

are distractions for motorists on the M9, which gives inviting glimpses of both.

From the M9, too, you can thread your way down to the river again and the promontory which supports **Blackness Castle** – a 15th-century fortress which juts out into the Forth like the bow of a great stone ship and which, for a while, was one of Scotland's most dramatic youth hostels. Blackness was one of the four important Scottish castles which, under the terms of the Act of Union in 1707, was permitted to maintain its fortifications. It was used as a state prison in Covenanting times, a powder magazine in the 1870s and today is simply yet another public monument.

The nearby **House of the Binns**, however, is still occupied by the Dalyell family, whose most famous ancestor was "General Tam" Dalyell. (The name is pronounced *Dee-ell*). During the Civil War General Tam was a staunch Royalist, and although captured at Worcester he escaped from the Tower of London to serve the Tzar in Russia until summoned home by Charles II. He then became a scourge of the Covenanters, who were doubtless responsible for the story that, on his death, his body was carried off by the Devil. Some have probably wished the same fate on the present Tam Dalyell, the eccentric and engaging Labour MP is almost as much trouble to his own party as he is to the opposing Conservatives.

The Kingdom of Fife: To venture across the great bridges into **Fife** is indeed to enter a new kingdom. (The stubborn, prickly Fifers fought a successful action to hang on to their region's ancient title when the rest of Scotland's old shires were re-organised into new administrative units.) Fife deserves a chapter to itself: its meandering coast and pastoral interior, clasped between the estuaries of Forth and Tay, not only contain some of Scotland's most attractive fishing villages but also some of its oldest mining communities. The elegant and venerable university town of St Andrews, with its famous golf courses, is in Fife,

Crail: built around fishing.

and so – by way of contrast – is Kirkcaldy, which to Scots will always be associated with making linoleum.

Two or three destinations in Fife are readily reached from Edinburgh by the M90, which cuts through the region on its way to Perth. Each gives some idea of the versatility of this highly individual region and its significance in Scotland's history.

The town of **Dunfermline** has been a royal burgh since at least the 11th century, and, although Fife's more recent industrial history has put its imprint on it, Dunfermline's abbey, monastery and palace ruins have close links with the nation's monarchs. Robert the Bruce is buried below the pulpit of the Abbey Church. (The choir of this 12th-century church was re-built in 1818, when Bruce's body was found wrapped in a shroud of embroidered gold and encased in lead. It was re-buried.)

Little is left of the Palace of Dunfermline, but it was occupied by Mary Queen of Scots in 1561 and was the birthplace of a succession of monarchs, including Alexander I, David I and David II, James I and the children of James VI of Scotland and I of England, including the future Queen of Bohemia and Charles I.

Dunfermline is also celebrated as the birthplace of Andrew Carnegie, the industrial tycoon who made his fortune in the steel and iron mills of Pennsylvania and then gave much of it away in philanthropic gifts. Dunfermline wasn't forgotten (it owes its swimming pool, library and public park to Carnegie, as well as an annual festival of music and drama) and Dunfermline has not forgotten the boy who spent his youth there before his family emigrated to America. Their modest house is now a museum.

Two places in Fife are irrevocably associated with the Stuart dynasty: **Loch Leven Castle**, from which Mary Queen of Scots made a romantic escape, only to be defeated at the Battle of Langside and forced to seek the inhospitable protection of her English cousin Elizabeth I; and the favourite Royal residence of **Falkland Palace**, built by James IV and embellished by James V, Mary's father, who died there as his daughter was born with the resigned words: "God's will be done. It cam' wi' a lass and it'll gang (*go*) wi' a lass."

The dying king feared for the Stuart line, which was established through marriage to the daughter of Robert the Bruce, and in one sense he was right to predict that it would end with Mary. Through her own incompetence she lost first her crown and then her head, although her son, James VI of Scotland and I of England, would become the first king to rule over both countries.

Loch Leven, by the town of Kinross, and Falkland, in the shadow of the Lomond Hills, lie within a few miles of each other. The grim little island fortress where Mary suffered and the pretty Renaissance palace which she loved as much as her father represent extremes of fortune for the Stuarts. They make a fitting "double" for pilgrims fascinated by their story.

Falkland Palace. Following page: swans at Leith.

INSIGHT GUIDES

Travel Tips

Insight Guides portray destinations in depth, providing the complete picture and the top photography

Insight Pocket Guides focus on the best choices for places to see and things to do and include large fold-out maps

Insight Compact Guides' portability makes them the perfect books to carry with you for on-the-spot reference

Three types of guide for all types of travel

INSIGHT GUIDES Different people need different kinds of information. Some want *background information* to help them prepare for the trip. Others seek *personal recommendations* from someone who knows the destination well. And others look for *compactly presented data* for on-the-spot reference. With three carefully designed series, Insight Guides offer readers the perfect choice. Insight Guides will turn your visit into an experience.

The world's largest collection of visual travel guides

CONTENTS

Getting Acquainted

The Place

"Although Edinburgh is Scottish in itself, one cannot feel that the people who live in it are Scottish in any radical sense, or have any essential connection with it... the present, which is made up of the thoughts and feelings and prejudices of the inhabitants, their way of life in general, is as cosmopolitan as the cinema," observed the Scottish poet Edwin Muir in 1935.

The people of Edinburgh at the start of a new millennium have perhaps an even more tenuous link with their national past. Life in the city is different in few quantifiable ways from life in Munich or Boston. Yet a survey by Glasgow University found life in Edinburgh more pleasant than in any other British city. Natives fear a mass invasion by London yuppies, whose presence is already felt in the city.

Location: Situated between the Pentland Hills (1,898 ft/578 m) and the south coast of the Firth of Forth, Edinburgh is at 55°57N 3°13W.

Geography: Notable for its hills and bridges, the city can count five extinct volcanoes within its limits. The most commanding is Arthur's Seat (824 ft/251 m) which, surrounded by Holyrood Park, creates an unexpected sense of open country within the city.

The port of Leith, which lies to the East, was united with Edinburgh in the 1920s. The Boundary Bar on Leith Walk still marks the dividing line, and the story goes that, before the towns were joined and their bylaws standardised, one half of the bar would close and the

clientele would move through to continue drinking under the more lenient administration.

The burghs of Canongate, Portobello and Granton have been part of the city since 1856, 1896 and 1900 respectively.

Population: Approximately 450,000.

Time zone: Greenwich Mean Time (GMT) and British Summer Time.

Currency: Scotland has the same currency, the pound sterling (£), as the rest of the UK.

Climate

Who dares generalise about Edinburgh weather? In late May and June there may be a spell of glorious sunshine so that everyone forecasts a marvelous summer. In July it then rains, especially at weekends. In August God tosses a coin to decide whether to drown the Festival. In September and October blue skies and biting winds confuse everyone. The rest of the year it is cold.

For those who trust figures, the coldest months are January and February with average daily temperatures ranging from 1°C (34°F) to 6°C (42°F). August is the warmest month, reaching an average high of 18°C (64°F).

Keen winds and rain make warm clothing and sturdy umbrellas a must at any time of year. Formal dress is seldom de rigueur, even in swanky hotels or the dress circle of the theatre.

Weights and measures: Britain is only half way to accepting the metric system: packaged goods cite weights in grammes; beer comes in pints and half pints; shop assistants will sell you "a quarter" of sweets or "half a pound" of cheese, but will look amazed at requests for 500 grammes of potatoes. Road signs give distances in miles, but petrol is sold in litres.

Electricity: 240 volts is standard. Hotels will usually have dual 110/240 volts sockets for razors.

International dialling code: To call Edinburgh from overseas, dial the local number for an international line, followed by 44 for the UK, 131 for Edinburgh, followed by the seven digit telephone number. From Edinburgh, dial 00 for an international line.

Government

Scotland has been an integral part of the United Kingdom since the 1707 Act of Union with England, but in a referendum in 1997 the Scots voted in their own parliament, which will have its inaugural session in Edinburgh, the new (and old) capital of Scotland, in summer 1999. A new parliament building is under construction at the foot of the Royal Mile.

Scotland will continue to be governed from Westminster, London, in matters such as defence, and will continue to be represented in the British Parliament by members from the Labour and Scottish Nationalist parties.

Having gained the first Scottish parliament for 300 years, many nationalists are talking confidently of eventual independence. The Scottish National Party (SNP), which increased its representation in the 1997 election, wants "an independent Scotland which is part of the European Union".

Local government of Edinburgh is by two elected councils: Lothian Regional Council and Edinburgh District Council. Local elections are held every four years. Both the City Chambers and the Regional Chambers are on the Royal Mile. The Region is responsible for education, planning, transport, the police and fire services, throughout Lothian Region; the District for housing, recreational facilities and sanitation, within the city itself.

Economy

Traditionally, Edinburgh's economy was based on beer, biscuits and books. Brewing on a large scale continues, but takeovers have brought closures and redundancies. Printing and publishing still exist, but the biscuit manufacturers have moved out of town. The city was once surrounded by coal mines, but only two remain and their future is far from certain. The new big employers are finance and tourism.

Within the UK, Edinburgh's financial centre is now second in importance only to London. The financial institutions deal mainly in investment and unit trusts.

Tourism in Edinburgh grows too slowly for the Tourist Board, which enviously watches Glasgow's emergence as a successful tourist centre, but too quickly for those who consider jobs in tourism to be badly-paid and seasonal.

As the Scottish centre of medicine, law and banking, Edinburgh boasts a prominent professional class, its most picturesque manifestation being the robed and wigged advocates who emerge at lunchtime from the courts on the High Street.

Business Hours

Most offices are open Monday–Friday 9am–5 or 5.30pm, and may well be closed between 1 and 2pm. Banks stay open lunchtimes but tend to close slightly earlier in the evening. Building societies, but not normally banks, also open Saturday mornings. See also *Shopping Hours* in the *Shopping* section, page 256.

Public Holidays

In addition to the major British public holidays, which are 1 and 2 January, Good Friday, and 25 and 26 December, **Scottish national holidays** are: May Day (first Monday in May); Spring Holiday (Monday in late May); and Summer Holiday (first Monday in August).

In Edinburgh, there are additional **local holidays** (not universally taken): Edinburgh Spring Holiday (third Monday in April) and Edinburgh Autumn Holiday (third Monday in September).

Planning the Trip

When to Go

Summer is the generally preferred time to visit to coincide with milder weather. See also *Festivals in the Scottish Capital* under *Culture*, page 250. During Festival time in August the city centre gets very crowded.

Entry Regulations

Enquiries about passports and visas should be made to the relevant embassy – see *Practical Tips*, page 238. Visitors to the UK may only bring in the Customs Allowances of alcoholic drinks, tobacco and perfume. Any queries should be addressed to HM Customs and Excise, 44 York Place, Edinburgh EH1, tel: 0131-469 2000. The General Enquiry Office is open Monday–Friday 9.30am–4pm.

Animal Quarantine

Birds and mammals will normally be quarantined for six months. Details of the regulations about bringing animals into and out of the UK and a full list of quarantine kennels are available from The Ministry of Agriculture, Fisheries and Food, Lasswade Veterinary Laboratory, Bush Estate, Penicuik EH26. The average cost of keeping a dog in kennels is £100 a month.

Health

Ezra Pound is reported to have said of Edinburgh: "Most of the denizens wheeze, sniffle, and exude a sort of snozzling whnoff whnoff, apparently through a hydrophile sponge." Apart from the common cold, the only unpleasant contagious disease prevalent in Edinburgh is Aids. European Union countries have a reciprocal agreement for free medical care, but medical insurance is advisable. Everyone will receive free emergency treatment at a hospital casualty department.

Money Matters

The British pound is divided into 100 pence. The coins used are 1p, 2p, 5p, 10p, 20p, 50p, and £1. However, although the £1 coin is widely used, £1 notes issued by the (Royal Bank of Scotland) still circulate along with notes of £5, £10, £20, £50 and £100. (Technically, Scottish notes are not legal tender in England and Wales, but many shops will accept them and English banks will readily change them for you.)

Tourist Information

Edinburgh and Scotland Information Centre, 3 Princes Street (on top of Waverley Shopping Centre), tel: 0131-473 3800. Extensive information on Edinburgh. Also incorporates the Scottish Travel Shop, Accommodation Services, transport and events ticket sales, and an exchange bureau. A useful shop sells maps and guidebooks. Open 9am–7pm Monday–Saturday, 10am–7pm Sunday.
Scottish Tourist Board, Ravelston Terrace, tel: 0131-332 2433. General postal enquiries.

Eurocheques and Eurocard can be used at banks and traveller's cheques can be cashed at banks, *bureaux de change* and many hotels, though the best rates are normally available at banks.

Access (or MasterCard) and Visa are the most commonly acceptable credit cards, followed by American Express and Diners Club. Small guest houses and bed-and-breakfast places may not take credit cards.

Special Needs

Children: An excellent publication, *Edinburgh for the Under-Fives* (£4.95), published by the National Childbirth Trust, provides a lot of ideas for desperate parents.

Lesbian & Gay: Lothian Gay and Lesbian Switchboard, tel: 0131-556 4049 (7.30–10pm daily); Edinburgh Lesbian Line, tel: 0131-557 0751 (7.30–10pm Monday and Thursday).

Disabled: Disability Scotland, Princes House, 5 Shandwick Place, tel: 0131-229 8632; Disability Helpline, tel: (01506) 433468.

Getting There

BY AIR

Edinburgh Airport lies 8 miles (13 km) west of the city centre. Scheduled flights run to and from the Highlands and Islands, various English and Irish airports, and several European cities including Amsterdam, Brussels and Paris. British Airways and British Midland both run comprehensive services to and from London Heathrow, and KLM Air UK flies regularly to and from London Gatwick. EasyJet operates low-cost flights from London (Luton) to Edinburgh, while Aer Lingus flies from Dublin. During the summer there are also various charter flights from Europe and North America.

Scheduled transatlantic flights arrive in Glasgow and Prestwick, from where Scottish Citylink (0990 50 50 50) runs regular bus services into Edinburgh. The bus journey takes about two hours.

There are plenty of porters at Edinburgh Airport. If you have difficulty finding one, ask at the Information Desk. Payment is at your discretion, but £1 is a reasonable tip.

Edinburgh Airport: general flight enquiries: 333 1000
KLM Air UK: 0131-344 3325
British Airways: 0131-334 3180, (0345) 222111
British Midland: 0131-334 3302/3
Servisair: (for other airlines flying to Edinburgh) 0131-344 3111

BY RAIL

The main line to Edinburgh runs up the east coast from London Kings Cross. Journey times from London are between four and a half and five hours (but up to seven hours on a Sunday) and north of Berwick the line passes along the impressive coastline. The journey on the west coast line from Euston takes over six hours. The overnight trains also travel this line. Edinburgh has two railway stations, Waverley and Haymarket at, respectively, the east and west ends of the city centre. Waverley is the main station, but Haymarket is nearer the airport. For all rail passenger enquiries, tel: (0345) 48 49 50.

There are porters Waverley and Haymarket stations. To make sure of help for disabled or infirm travellers phone 0131-556 2477. Railway porter services are free, but tipping is usual.

BY ROAD

From London take the M1 and then link up to the M6. This motorway runs along England's west coast, and is the best road for the main part of the journey. After Carlisle, the motorist can take either the A7, a rather slow tourist route through the Borders; the A701 from Moffat, which is a high, winding, remote road, yet probably the fastest; or the A702 through Biggar, the main trunk road, skirting the Pentland Hills. Motorway addicts can follow the A74 to the outskirts of Glasgow and join the M8 into Edinburgh. The 400-mile (650-km) journey from London takes about eight hours.

The east coast road from London to Edinburgh is the scenic but slow A1. Stretches of the A1 have been converted to motorway A1(M).

BY BUS

National Express (0990 80 80 80) runs daily coaches between London's Victoria Coach Station and Edinburgh's St Andrew's Square Bus Station. The journey takes eight hours. Traditionally very inexpensive, the coach companies now offer a "deluxe" option.

Practical Tips

Media

NEWSPAPERS

The Scotsman, published in Edinburgh since 1817, is the city's – and ostensibly the nation's – quality daily paper. It is rivalled on the national level by the more dynamic Glasgow paper *The Herald*. *The Scotsman* gives sound coverage of national and international news, and is strong on the arts. The *Evening News*, its sister paper, covers local Edinburgh news and interest. The *Daily Record* is the most widely-read Scottish tabloid.

Scotsman Publications ventured into the quality Sunday paper market in 1988 with *Scotland On Sunday*. The English Sunday papers responded with a rash of Scottish sections, covering Scottish concerns with varying degrees of accuracy.

The celebrated *Sunday Post*, last bastion of small-town conservatism, is still a source of amused national pride. Edinburgh also has a number of small, council-supported "community newspapers" serving semi-autonomous areas of the city and providing a platform for local wrangling.

MAGAZINES

Scottish magazines are thin on the ground. There is nothing to compare with London's *Spectator* or (hope springs eternal) the *New Yorker*. The *Edinburgh Review*, published quarterly by the University Press, is a wide-ranging, heavyweight cultural journal. *Radical Scotland* provides a welcome alternative view on Scottish affairs, and sundry literary magazines (*Lines Review, Cencrastus, Chapman*) publish poetry, prose and criticism. *The List* provides watertight coverage of the arts in Edinburgh and Glasgow and invaluable listings of events.

RADIO AND TV

BBC Radio Scotland (FM 92.4-94.7 MW 810kHz/370m) is a national network with news and talk programmes. Radio Forth (FM 97.3 MW 1548kHz) is the local commercial station. BBC Scotland and Scottish Television (STV) are the Glasgow-based television stations which add Scottish news, features and drama to the national network.

Post and Telecoms

POST

The Central Post Office is in St. James Shopping Centre (Kings Mall), at the east end of Princes Street, tel: 556 0478 (Monday 9am–5.30pm, Tuesday to Friday 8.30am–5.30pm, Saturday 8.30am–6pm). Other city centre post offices are at 40 Frederick Street, tel: 226 6937; 7 Hope Street (west end of Princes Street), tel: 226 6823; and 33 Forrest Road (near the university), tel: 225 3957.

Banks

Scottish banks with branches throughout Edinburgh are the Bank of Scotland, Royal Bank of Scotland and Clydesdale. City centre branches of most banks (and building societies) can be found in George Street or Shandwick Place. Opening hours are:
Bank of Scotland: 9am–5pm Monday, Tuesday, Thursday and Friday, from 10am Wednesday.
Royal Bank of Scotland: 9.15am–4.45pm Monday, Tuesday, Thursday and Friday, from 10am Wednesday. The West End branch at 142–144 Princes Street also opens 10am–1pm Saturday.
Clydesdale: 9.15am–4pm Monday–Friday, to 5.30pm Thursday.
Lloyds, 115 George Street. Open

They are open Monday to Friday 9am–5.30pm and Saturday 9am–12.30pm (not Frederick Street).

Some post offices are housed within newsagents and are open slightly different hours. Some close for lunch and most take a half day on Wednesday. The central sorting office at 10 Brunswick Road (off Leith Walk) will deliver next day to London, letters posted up to 9pm on a weekday, and even later for local mail. Tel: 550 8145. For advice on mail services phone 550 8232; counter services (0345) 223344.

TELEPHONE

Area code 0131 should be dialled before an Edinburgh telephone number when calling from anywhere else in the UK.

The traditional red telephone box has been replaced by modern glass booths. Some of these are operated by coins (£1, 50p, 20p, 10p), others by phonecards which can be purchased from newsagents and post offices. Phone boxes are scattered throughout the city, and there is a bank of them at the central post office.

9.15–5pm Monday, Tuesday, Thursday and Friday, from 9.30am Wednesday.
National Westminster, 80 George Street. Open 9.15–5pm Monday, Tuesday, Thursday and Friday, from 9.30am Wednesday.
Barclays, 18–20 St Andrew Square. Open 9.30am–5pm Monday, Tuesday, Thursday and Friday, from 10am Wednesday.
Midland, 76 Hanover Street. Open 9.30am–4.30pm Monday–Friday.
TSB: 9.30am–4pm Monday and Tuesday, 10am–4pm Wednesday, 9.30am–5.30pm Thursday and Friday. The Cameron Toll Shopping Centre branch also opens 9am–5pm Saturday.

Cashpoint machines are open at other times. See *Planning the Trip: Money Matters,* page 235.

To make enquiries about British Telecom services call 0800 309409. To call the Operator, dial 100; International Operator, dial 155; Directory Enquiries, dial 192; International Directory Enquiries, dial 153; the Talking Clock, dial 123; telemessage/telegrams, dial 0800 190190.

FAX

St James Shopping Centre Post Office Shop (556 9546) has a fax machine for inland faxes. It costs £1.50 for the first page and £1 for subsequent pages. There are several other fax bureaux in the city centre.

Tipping

Most restaurants do not add a service charge to the bill. In this case, it is normal (but not compulsory) to give a 10–15 percent tip. Check the bill carefully; if a charge for service is included, there is no need to pay extra unless you wish to reward exceptional service. If the service has been very poor, the service charge can in theory be subtracted from the bill.

A similar percentage tip should be paid to hairdressers and taxi drivers. A tip of about £1 minimum is appropriate for porters at transport terminals or in your hotel. It is not necessary to tip in self-service establishments or pubs.

Religious Services

The main Sunday services are at 11am. Many churches also hold a Sunday evening service.
Albany Church for the Deaf, Albany Street, tel: 556 3128.
Associated Presbyterian Church, Gilmore Place, tel: 445 3673.
The Central Mosque, 50 Potterrow, tel: 667 1777.
Charlotte Chapel (Baptist) Church, West Rose Street, tel: 225 4812.
Church of Jesus Christ of Latter Day Saints, Dalkeith Chapel, Newbattle Road, Dalkeith, tel: 654 0630.
Methodist Church, Central Hall, Home Street, Tollcross, tel: 229 7937.

Emergencies

In emergencies, phone 999. No money is needed to make a 999 call from a public call-box: just dial, and ask for the Fire, Police or Ambulance service.

For non-urgent enquiries contact a local police station. All these stations are continuously staffed:
Dalkeith Police Station, Newbattle Road, Dalkeith, tel: 663 2855.
Gayfield Square Police Station, Gayfield Square (off Leith Walk), tel: 556 9270.
West End Police Station, Torphichen Place, Haymarket, tel: 229 2323.
Leith Police Station, Queen Charlotte Street, tel: 554 9350.

Pentecostal Church, 26 George IV Bridge, tel: 225 3076.
St Andrew's Orthodox (Greek Russian) Church, 23a George Square, tel: 667 0372.
St Columba Free Church of Scotland, Lawnmarket, tel: 225 5996.
St Giles Cathedral (Church of Scotland), High Street, tel: 225 4363.
St Mary's (Catholic) Cathedral, Broughton Street, tel: 556 1798.
St Mary's (Episcopalian) Cathedral, Palmerston Place, tel: 225 6293.
Synagogue Chambers, Edinburgh Hebrew Congregation, 4 Salisbury Road, tel: 667 3144.
Ukranian Catholic Church of St Andrews, Dalmeny Street, tel: 667 5993.

Embassies and Consulates

American Consulate General, 3 Regent Terrace, Edinburgh EH7, tel: 556 8315.
Australian Consulate, tel: 555 4500 (telephone service only).
Belgian Trade Office, 13 Charlotte Square, tel: 220 1490.
Canadian Consulate, 3 George Street, tel: 220 4333.
The Royal Danish Consulate

Lost Property & Left Luggage

Lost Property Department, Police Headquarters, Fettes Avenue, tel: 311 3141. There are Left Luggage lockers at Waverley Station.

Medical Services

There are two 24-hour Accident and Emergency departments in Edinburgh, one at the Royal Infirmary, 1 Lauriston Place, tel: 536 1000. The other is at the Western General, Crewe Road, tel: 537 1000.

There is an emergency dental clinic at the Dental Hospital, 31 Chambers Street, tel: 536 4900. It is open Monday to Friday 9–10.15am and 2–3.15pm.

General, 4 Royal Terrace, tel: 556 4263.
Finnish Consulate and Trade Office, 22 Hanover Street, tel: 225 1295.
French Consulate General, 11 Randolph Crescent, tel: 225 7954.
German Consulate, 16 Eglinton Crescent, tel: 337 2323.
Icelandic Consulate, 24 Jane Street, tel: 555 3532.
Italian Consulate General, 32 Melville Street, tel: 226 3631.
Japanese Consulate General, 2 Melville Crescent, tel: 225 4777.
Netherlands Consulate, 53 George Street, tel: 220 3226.
Royal Norwegian Consulate General, 86 George Street, tel: 226 5701.
The Polish Consulate, 2 Kinnear Road, tel: 552 0301.
Consulate of Portugal, 25 Bernard Street, tel: 555 2080.
Consulate General of the Russian Federation, 58 Melville Street, tel: 225 7098.
Spanish Consulate General, 63 North Castle Street, tel: 220 1843.
Swiss Consular Agency, 66 Hanover Street, tel: 226 5660.

Getting Around

On Arrival

A coach service runs between Waverley Bridge and the airport. At peak times, the coaches run at 30-minute intervals. The journey takes approximately 25 minutes.

Taxis are available outside the airport. The journey into town takes about 20 minutes and should cost around £12.

On Foot

There is a wooden bench at the top of Dublin Street's steep climb which bears the legend, "Remembering JCH who was often tired." Edinburgh is a city of hills and steps, but walking is the best way to see it. There is no more dismaying sight than the huge, air-conditioned coaches inching their way down the narrow Royal Mile, while through a seal of tinted glass, the occupants strain to glimpse the city they have travelled miles to experience.

The narrow closes, arches and stairs which lead off the Royal Mile can only be explored on foot and the elegant New Town squares and crescents are best appreciated from the pavement (although a helicopter also offers a rewarding perspective). Walking tours are organised in summer (see *Attractions* section, page 246) but an unstructured wander through both Old and New Towns is worthwhile. Every newsagent and bookshop stocks a range of maps, both in the unwieldy, accordian-folded variety and the useful book format.

By Bus

The deregulation of the region's bus services meant a free-for-all, with all sorts of bus companies vying for passengers and routes, and Princes Street crammed with vehicles of all hues. The dust settled and two main companies now ply the routes: Lothian Region Transport (LRT), whose maroon and white buses run a comprehensive web of routes through the city and out to the suburbs, and Eastern Scottish (green and white) who also run City Sprinters, small mini-buses which do tend to get you there faster, but are very cramped inside.

The different companies use the same bus stops, and cover more or less every part of the city. Buses run at between 10 and 20-minute intervals until about 11pm, when the LRT Night Service operates. For information on all bus services in the region, call Traveline on 225 3858 or 0800 232323. For information on LRT bus services, ring 555 6363/554 4494 or alternatively call into the sales office on Waverley Bridge. For Eastern Scottish information call 665 2202/663 1945.

Taxis

The big black taxi cab is fairly easy to flag down in the street unless it's a wet Friday evening. They run at all times, and during the day can be picked up from the taxi ranks in Hanover Street, North St Andrew Street, Lauriston Place, Rutland Street (west end of Princes Street), Waverley Station and Haymarket Station.

The fare will be displayed in the front of the cab. There are extra charges late at night and for destinations outside the city limits. There is also a charge if you phone for a cab.
City Cabs: 228 1211.
Central Radio Taxis: 229 2468.
Capital Castle Taxis: 228 2555.
Radiocabs: 225 9000/225 6736.

Self Drive Car Hire

At the Airport
Alamo Rent-a-Car, tel: 333 5100.
Avis Rent-a-Car, tel: 333 1866.
Europcar Inter Rent, tel: 333 2588.
Hertz, tel: 333 1019.

At Waverley Railway Station
Hertz, tel: 557 5272.

City Rentals
Arnold Clark, 1/13 Lochrin Place, Tollcross, tel: 228 4747.
Avis Rent-a-Car, 100 Dalry Road, tel: 337 6363.
Europcar, 24 East London Street, tel: 557 3456.
Hertz, 10 Picardy Place, tel: 556 8311.
Lo-Cost Hire, 1a Wardlaw Terrace, tel: 313 2220.
Mitchell's, 32 Torphichen Street, tel: 229 5384.
Thrifty Car Rental, 42 Haymarket Terrace, tel: 337 1319.
Turner Hire Drive, 47 Annandale Street, tel: 557 0304.
Woods Car Rental, Unit 16 Tartraven Place, East Mains Industrial Estate, Broxburn, tel: (01506) 858660.

Chauffeur Driven Car Hire

Little's Chauffeur Drive, 5 St Ninians Drive, tel: 334 2177.
Majestic Chauffeur Drive, 60 Montrose Terrace, tel: 659 6482.
W.L. Sleigh, 6 Devon Place, tel: 337 3171.

Bicycle Hire

Edinburgh Cycle Hire, 29 Blackfriars Street, tel: 556 5560. Daily 9am–7pm. Deposit required.
Bike Trax, 13 Lochrin Place, tel: 228 6633. Daily 10am–5.30pm. Deposit required.

Where to Stay

Choosing a Place

A wide range of accommodation is available in Edinburgh, from hotels of international standard to simple bed-and-breakfast (B&B) accommodation. Prices vary as well, from under £10 a night for bed-and-breakfast to over £100 at the most expensive hotel. You can book the accommodation of your choice through the Central Reservation Office, tel: (0131) 473 3855.

How does one select a suitable place at which to stay? The Scottish Tourist Board has changed its system of grading accommodation so that quality only is now assessed. Although the Board's symbols still indicate what facilities and services are available, establishments are no longer awarded "crowns" according to these criteria. Star gradings range from one star (fair and acceptable) to five stars (exceptional/world class). These are applied to all types of accommodation including hotels, bed-and-breakfasts and self-catering.

Staying in bed-and-breakfast accommodation is not only economical: with luck you may find the proprietor friendly and a mine of local information with suggestions about what to do and see. Many bed-and-breakfast establishments serve dinner, which is usually excellent and modestly priced, on request.

Particularly good value are Campus Hotels, the name given to bed-and-breakfast or self-catering facilities offered by Edinburgh, Napier and Heriot-Watt universities. Accommodation at the first two is only available during vacations. In addition to accommodation, they offer the use of university facilities such as tennis courts and swimming pools.

Information on all types of accommodation is available from the Scottish Tourist Board and the Edinburgh Tourist Board offices. Please note: accommodation during Festival time is at a premium. Book very early.

Except for the more expensive city hotels, prices quoted include breakfast. Guest houses and private hotels are commercial establishments, normally with a minimum of four guest rooms, whereas B&Bs are private homes with perhaps just one or two guest rooms. On occasion, the distinction between them becomes blurred, especially when the latter have en suite facilities and serve dinner. Below they are listed under a single heading.

Hotels

Albany Hotel, 39 Albany Street, tel: 556 0397, fax: 657 6633. Refurbished listed Georgian building on quiet New Town street just north of Princes Street. Variety of bedrooms, some small. 21 rooms. £££

Apex International Hotel, 31–35 Grassmarket, tel: 300 3456, fax: 220 5345. A new five-storey property in a lively part of the city (pubs and antique shops feature) and facing the back of the castle. 99 rooms. £–££

Balmoral Hotel, Princes Street, tel: 556 2414, fax: 557 3747. Edinburgh's premier hotel reopened in 1991 after a £23 million facelift. Many rooms with castle view. Health club with swimming pool. 189 rooms. ££££

Bank Hotel, 1 South Bridge Road, tel: 556 9043, fax: 558 1362. Former bank in the midst of Royal Mile converted into café-bar with bedrooms above. 9 rooms. ££

Bruntsfield Hotel, 69–74 Bruntsfield Place, tel: 229 1393, fax: 229 5634. Well-established hotel 1 mile (2 km) south of city centre. 50 rooms. £££

Caledonian Hotel, Princes Street, tel: 459 9988, fax: 225 6632. This vast, turn-of-the-century red sandstone building, the "Grande Dame" of Edinburgh hotels is constantly being upgraded. Many rooms with view of castle. 236 rooms. ££££

Carlton Highland Hotel, 19 North Bridge, tel: 472 3102/3000, fax: 556 2691. Splendidly situated in the heart of the city, this imposing Victorian mass has long been a favourite Edinburgh hotel. 197 rooms. ££–£££

Channings, South Learmont Gardens, tel: 315 2226, fax: 332 9631. A series of five adjoining Edwardian houses facing a cobbled, quiet street a few minutes away from the city centre. Country house public rooms; individually furnished bedrooms, a tad on the small side. Pleasant patio. 48 rooms. ££££

Edinburgh City Travel Inn, 1 Morrison Link, tel: 228 9819, fax: 228 9836. This property in the city centre is part of an unpretentious, functional modern chain. 128 rooms of which 80 are family rooms. ££

George Inter-Continental Hotel, 19–21 George Street, tel: 225 1251, fax: 226 5644. A distinguished, well established property in the heart of the city. Rooms at rear of top two floors have superb views of Fife. 195 rooms. ££££

Hilton National, 69 Belford Road, tel: 332 2545, fax: 332 3805. Located on the leafy banks of the Water of Leith yet within minutes of the city centre on the bus route. 144 rooms. ££–££££

Holiday Inn Crowne Plaza, 80 High Street, tel: 557 9797, fax: 557 9789. This modern hotel sits comfortably on the Royal Mile. Leisure centre; on-site parking. 238 rooms. ££££

Holiday Inn Garden Court, 107 Queensferry Road, tel: 332 2442, fax: 332 3408. A typical Holiday Inn property with grand panoramic views. Two miles (3 km) north of town but on main bus route. 119 rooms. ££

Howard Hotel, 36 Great King Street, tel: 557 3500, fax: 557

6515. Three inter-connected 18th-century town houses in the New Town result in a magnificent classical hotel. All bedrooms different and all made the more comfortable by contemporary bathrooms. Splendid breakfast. 16 rooms. ££££

Hotel Prices

- **£** = below £30
- **££** = £30–£50
- **£££** = £50–£70
- **££££** = above £70

Prices are per person in a double room.

Inner Sanctum and **Old Rectory**, 351 Castlehill, Royal Mile, tel: 225 5613, fax: 220 4392. Two suites adjacent to Witchery restaurant. The place – completely over the top – for that once-in-a-lifetime occasion. £££

Jarvis Ellersly Country House Hotel, Ellersly Road, tel: 337 6888, fax: 313 2543. Edwardian country house retaining its original charm and tranquility. Two miles (3 km) from city centre. 57 rooms. ££–£££

Jarvis Learmonth Hotel, 18–20 Learmonth Terrace, tel: 343 2671, fax: 315 2232. Terraced houses converted into a quiet, elegant hotel, a short distance from Princes Street. 62 rooms. ££

Jarvis Mount Royal Hotel, 53 Princes Street, tel: 225 7161, fax: 220 4671. Superly located in the heart of Princes Street with splendid views of the castle. 158 rooms. £££

Marriott Dalmahoy Hotel & Country Club, Long Dalmahoy, Kirknewton, tel: 333 1845, fax: 333 1433. A grand mansion to the west of the city and 3 miles (5 km) from the airport. Leisure facilities include two championship golf coures. 151 rooms. ££–£££.

Prestonfield House Hotel, Priestfield Road, tel: 668 3346, fax: 668 3976. Surrounded by formal gardens and a golf course, yet a mere 5 minutes drive from city centre. Stay here and you are following in the footsteps of Bonnie

Prince Charlie, Benjamin Franklin and Dr Johnson: for those looking for that "something special". 31 rooms of which 26 are in a modern extension which in no way interferes with the ambience of the original distinguished 16th century baronial mansion. ££££+

Roxburghe Hotel, 38 Charlotte Square, tel: 225 3921, fax: 220 2518. Situated on Edinburgh's grandest square, just off Princes Street, this refurbished "county" hotel has some grand bedrooms as well as smaller rooms. 75 rooms. ££££

Royal British Hotel, 20 Princes Street, tel: 556 4901, fax: 557 6510. A comfortable landmark property immediately opposite the main railway station. 72 rooms. ££

Royal Circus Hotel, 19–21 Royal Circus, tel: 220 5000, fax: 220 2020. Linked town houses in the city centre overlooking gardens. Close to city centre. 29 rooms. ££

Royal Terrace Hotel, 18 Royal Terrace, tel: 557 3222, fax: 557 5334. Georgian terrace buildings on a cobbled street, minutes from the east end of Princes Street, constitute this handsome chintzy hotel. Complete leisure club and large private garden. 94 rooms. £££–££££

Sheraton Grand Hotel, 1 Festival Square, tel: 229 9131, fax: 229 6254. Refurbished hotel within stone's throw of new exhibition centre and several major theatres. Many rooms with superb views of castle. Leisure centre; on-site parking. 261 rooms. ££££

Stakis Edinburgh Airport Hotel, Edinburgh International Airport, tel: 519 4400, fax: 519 4466. Built in 1995, 20–30 minutes from city centre. 134 rooms. £–£££

Stakis Edinburgh Grosvenor Hotel, Grosvenor Street, tel: 226 6001, fax: 220 2387. Situated at the west end of town across from Haymarket railway station. 188 rooms. ££–£££

Thrums Private Hotel, 14–15 Minto Street, Newington, tel; 667 5545, fax: 667 8707. Detached Georgian house with garden, 3 miles (5 km) south of city centre. 14 rooms. £££

Guest Houses

A-Haven Town House, 180 Ferry Road, tel: 554 6559. Situated in Leith, 20 minutes from city centre and on main bus routes. Private parking. Dinner served; licensed for sale of alcohol. 12 en-suite rooms. £££.

Abcorn Guest House, 4 Mayfield Gardens, tel: 667 6548. A detached Victorian villa with private parking on the main bus route, 2 miles (3 km) to south-east of city centre. 7 en-suite rooms. ££

Ashlyn Guest House, 42 Inverleith Row, tel: 552 2954. Listed Georgian house close to Botanic Garden and 2 miles (3 km) from city centre. Dinner served. 8 rooms (5 en suite). ££

Guest House Prices

- **£** = below £20
- **££** = £20–£30
- **£££** = above £30

Prices are per person in a double room.

Bonnington Guest House, 202 Ferry Road, tel: 554 7610. Townhouse built in 1840 situated in Leith, 20 minutes from city centre and on main bus route. Private parking. Bedrooms non-smoking. 6 rooms (3 en suite). ££

Cameron Toll Guest House, 299 Dalkeith Road, tel: 667 2950. Be entertained by the sound of bagpipes while you enjoy your eveing meal (table licence) in an imposing 3-storey guest house about 2 miles (3 km) south-east of city centre. Parking available. 11 rooms (10 en suite). ££

Classic House, 50 Mayfield Road, tel: 667 5847. Elegant Victorian guest house, on main bus routes, about 2 miles (3 km) south-east of city centre. 4 rooms (3 en suite). £

Dukes of Windsor Street, 17 Windsor Street, tel: 556 6046. Centrally situated restored Georgian town house. Continental, rather than customary hearty Scottish, breakfast. On-street parking. 10 en-suite rooms. ££–£££

Galloway Guest House, 22 Dean Park Crescent, tel: 332 3672. In lively Stockbridge district, popular with bright young things, 1 mile (2 km) north of Princes Street. 10 rooms (6 en suite). ££

International Guest House, 37 Mayfield Gardens, tel: 667 2511. Victorian guest house on main bus route, about 2 miles (3 km) south-east of city centre. Private parking. 9 en-suite rooms, 4 of which are singles. ££

Joppa Turrets, 1 Lower Joppa, tel: 669 5806. For those who must be by the seaside. On the beach at Joppa but close to bus routes and 5 miles (8 km) from city centre. Parking no problem. 5 rooms (3 en suite). £–££

Kirklands Guest House, 128 Old Dalkeith Road, tel: 664 2755. Near Holyrood Palace and on main bus route. Large car park. 9 rooms (7 en- suite). £–££

Meadows Guest House, 17 Glengyle Terrace, tel: 229 9559, fax: 229 2226. Quietly situated terraced house overlooking the green space of Bruntsfield links 2 miles (3 km) south of city. 7 rooms (5 en suite). ££

Ravensneuk Guest House, 11 Blacket Avenue, tel: 667 5347. This elegant Victorian guest house is close to Holyrood Park. Private parking. Non-smoking. 7 rooms (3 en suite). ££.

St Bernard's Guest House, 22 St Bernard's Crescent, tel: 332 2339. Elegant Georgian town house within walking distance of city centre. 8 rooms (4 en suite). ££

Salisbury Guest House, 45 Salisbury Road, tel/fax: 667 1264. Georgian listed building near Holyrood Palace and Royal Mile. 12 rooms (9 en suite). ££

Six Mary's Place Guest House, 6 Mary's Place, off Raeburn Place, tel: 322 8965, fax: 624 7060. Georgian town house near city centre. Dining conservatory and gardens. Home cooked vegetarian cuisine. Non-smoking. 8 rooms (2 en-suite). £££

Stuart House, 12 East Claremont Street, tel: 557 9030. Refurbished Georgian house 3 miles (5 km) north of city centre. Non-smoking. Dinner served. 7 rooms (6 en suite). ££

The Thirty-Nine Steps, 62 South Trinity Road, tel: 552 1349. Victorian house situated close to Botanic Gardens and to the city centre. Parking available. 7 rooms (6 en suite). £–££

Campgrounds

Edinburgh Caravan Club, Marine Drive, tel: 312 6874. Caravans and 2-man tents. All facilities including disabled units and children's playground.

Mortonhall Caravan Park, Frogston Road East, off the A720, tel: 664 1533. Tents and caravans.

Pentland Park Marine Ltd, Pentland Park, Loanhead, off the A701, tel: 440 0697. Residential and touring caravans.

Hostels

The Scottish Youth Hostel Association (161 Warrender Park Road tel: 229 8660. Information only) runs two Grade 1 hostels in Edinburgh, at 7 Bruntsfield Crescent (447 2994) and 18 Eglinton Crescent (337 1120). Accommodation, in comfortable dormitories, ranges from (for adults) £8.60 per night low season to £9.60 high season at Bruntsfield hostel, with cooking facilities; £11.50 to £12.50 at Eglinton hostel, meals provided. Advance booking is usually necessary in the summer months.

University Accommodation

Heriot-Watt University, Riccarton, tel: 451 3669. At extreme western fringe of city but open all year round. ££

Napier University, 219 Colinton Road, tel: 445 4427. Located about 3 miles (5 km) south of city. Summer holidays only. ££

Queen Margaret College, 36 Clerwood Terrace, tel: 317 3310. Residential area, west of city

centre on main bus route. Excellent sports facilities. Car parking available. Summer holidays only. £

University of Edinburgh: Pollock Halls, 18 Holyrood Park Road, tel: 667 1971. Conveniently situated close to the Commonwealth Pool and Holyrood Park and near Royal Mile. Easter and summer holidays only. ££

Belford Hostel, Belford Church, 6–8 Douglas Gardens, tel: 225 6209. Hostel within historic church offers both dormitory accommodation (£9–£15) and double rooms (£30–£35 per person). Barbecues and licensed bar.

Castle Rock Hostel, 15 Johnston Terrace, tel: 225 9666. Dormitory accommodation at £10 per night per person. Free tea and coffee. Smoking and non-smoking lounge.

Edinburgh Backpackers Hostel, 65 Cockburn Street, tel: 220 1717. Dormitory accommodation from £9.50–£15 per night per person or double rooms (£15–£17.50 per person).

High Street Hostel, 8 Blackfriars Street, tel: 557 3984. Dormitory accommodation £9 per night.

Kinnaird Christian Hostel, 13–14 Coates Crescent, tel: 225 3608. For women, married couples and families. Dormitory accommodation (£12–£14), single rooms (£18–£20), double rooms (£15–£17 per person), includes breakfast.

Royal Mile Backpackers, 105 High Street, tel: 557 6120. Dormitory accommodation at £10 per night per person.

Where to Eat

Eating Out

Edinburgh, as befits any capital city, is choc-a-bloc with restaurants and most world cuisines can be savoured here. However, many visitors, aware of the renown of Scottish produce – seafood, beef and game – will opt for Scottish fare, frequently cooked in the French manner whether or not the chef follows Escoffier. An annual publication, which grows thicker by the year, is *Taste of Scotland* (33 Melville Street, tel: 220 1900) which lists those restaurants specialising in Scottish cuisine.

"Scottish" restaurants tend to be at the upper end of the market and those on a budget may prefer to dine in one of the many Italian, Indian or Chinese restaurants in the city. Bistros also abound – a legacy of the Auld Alliance? – and are very popular. Vegetarian restaurants are, as everywhere, on the increase. Some restaurants have a BYO (bring your own bottle) policy and impose a modest corkage charge (usually about £2).

Leith, the port for Edinburgh and formerly a municipality in its own right, but now merely a suburb, is enjoying gentrification and has many excellent eateries and watering-holes. Among these are a row of smart restaurants in a new development close to the Scottish Office and the berth of the Royal Yacht Britannia.

A rough guide: for a two-course evening meal excluding wine, **£** = under £10, **££** = £10–£20; **£££** = over £20. When a fixed-price dinner – usually three courses – is offered the symbol shown is for that meal.

CHINESE

Chinese Home Cooking, 34 West Preston Street, tel: 668 4946. Straightforward Cantonese cooking. Bring your own bottle. £

Kweilin, 19 Dundas Street, tel: 557 1875. Large space serving authentic Cantonese dishes, especially strong on seafood. Many swear this is the best Chinese in town. £

Restaurant Prices

- £ = under £10
- ££ = £10–£20
- £££ = over £20

Prices are per person for a two-course evening meal excluding wine.

Szechuan House, 12 Leamington Terrace, tel: 229 4655. For those who like it hot and spicy. Basic surroundings, near the King's Theatre, serving authentic Szechuan dishes. £

CONTEMPORARY AND INTERNATIONAL

The Atrium, 10 Cambridge Street, tel: 228 8882. Located in the foyer of the Traverse Theatre, this is one of the most stylish place in town. Sophisticated, imaginative menu served in mellow, contemporary ambience with excellent service. £££

(Fitz)henry: a brasserie, 19 Shore Place, Leith, tel: 555 6625. A beautifully restored old warehouse is one of only two Edinburgh restaurants to boast a Michelin Red M. Dining is theatre and presentation here is all, which is not to say that the food is not superb. £££

Martin's, 70 Rose St North Lane, tel: 225 3016. Difficult to find this small, well established restaurant but well worth the trouble. Limited but confident menu with best cheeseboard in town. Excellent discreet service. £££

Vintner's Rooms, The Vaults, 87 Giles Street, Leith, tel: 554 6767. Dine either in a unique candelit restaurant in old wine merchants' auction room or in a high functional space with a fire at one end and a bar down one side. In either case, the creative cooking of fresh produce, especially fish, is robust. Everything from the bread to the fudge with coffee is home-made. Single dishes from menu available in wine bar. Naturally, wine list is excellent and not too pricey. £££

The Witchery, 352 Castlehill, Royal Mile, tel: 225 5613. New-wave cooking served in two restaurants, each with unusual atmosphere. Upstairs is dark and atmospheric – beams and oil lamps – while downstairs is bright with lots of greenery and small outdoor terrace. Wine list with 300 bin numbers including many halves make excellent reading. £££

FRENCH

Chez Jules, 1 Craig's Close, 29 Cockburn Street, tel: 225 7007. A simple, pleasant restaurant serving authentic French food at reasonable prices. ££

Duck's at Le Marché Noir, 2–4 Eyre Place, tel: 558 1608. An elegant two-roomed restaurant offering informal yet sophisticated dining. The cuisine combines Scottish and French elements. Extensive, interesting wine list. £££

Howies, 75 St Leonard's Street, tel: 668 2917: 208 Bruntsfield Place, tel: 221 1777: 63 Dalry Road, Tel: 313 3334. Long established favourite serving Scottish/French cuisine in informal, somewhat spartan, setting. Venison, pigeon and salmon dishes feature. BYOB. ££

L'Auberge, 56-58 St Mary's Street, tel: 556 5888. Successful marriage of Scottish produce and French culinary skills. excellent fish dishes and wide selection of desserts. 600 wines, almost exclusively French, with numerous half-bottles. £££

Le Café Saint-Honoré, 34 N.W. Thistle Street Lane, tel: 226 2211. Step into this pleasant bistro, leave Scotland behind and enter France. Good value lunch. Some very imaginative dishes and a decent wine list. ££

La Cuisine l'Odile, 13 Randolph Crescent, tel: 225 5685. Monday–Saturday noon–2pm. Simple bistro (no alcohol) in the basement of L'Institut Français d'Écosse. Serves a limited menu of delightful, inexpensive dishes. £

Pierre Victoire, 38 Grassmarket, tel: 226 2442. Also at 8 Union Street, tel: 557 8451, 10 Victoria Street, tel: 225 1721, 5 Dock Place, Leith, tel: 555 6178 and 17 Queensferry Street, tel: 226 1890. Closed Sunday or Monday. All five restaurants have limited menus yet serve excellent dishes. Decent, moderately priced wines. Train yourself to breath in unison. £

Pompadour, Caledonian Hotel, Princes Street, tel: 459 9988. Possibly Edinburgh's most elegant and formal dining room. Lunchtime features Legends of the Scottish Table while in the evening the other member of the Auld Alliance (France) holds sway. Classic wines, impeccable service and soothing piano music. £££+

A simpler menu with, nevertheless, a good range of classic and some international dishes is served in **Carriages**, the Caledonian's second restaurant – see under *Scottish*.

INDIAN

Indian Cavalry Club, 3 Atholl Place, tel: 228 3282. The paramilitary uniforms – some ill-fitting – of the staff should not be off-putting. This up-market Indian restaurant with an emphasis on steaming attempts, with a fair amount of success, to blend brasserie and Indian restaurant. Better than average wine list at reasonable prices. ££

Kalpna, 2 St Patrick Square, tel: 667 9890. Gujerati and southern Indian vegetarian food in a non-smoking restaurant. Decent, moderately priced wine list. £

Lancers, 5 Hamilton Place, tel: 332 3444. Elegant space with three rooms serving Bengali and north Indian cuisine. Renowned for curries. Modest wine list. ££

Shamiana, 14 Brougham Street, tel: 228 2265. Kashmir dishes served in this rather elegant Indian restaurant. Excellent Tandoori and curry. Booking essential. ££

ITALIAN

Ferri's Pizzeria, 1 Antigua Street, Leith Walk, tel: 556 5592. Good food in a cheerful environment. ££

Pizza Express, 32 Queensferry Street, tel: 225 8863, and 1 Deanhaugh Street, tel: 332 7229. Reliable standby with reasonable prices. The Deanhaugh Street branch is in an old clock tower by the Water of Leith. £

Raffaelli's, 10 Randolph Place, tel: 225 6060. North Italian cuisine for the gourmet. Elegant surroundings. Superb wine list – Italian, naturally. £££

Tinelli, 139 Easter Road, tel: 652 1932. Small, unpretentious restaurant with a limited menu of superb North Italian food. Splendid cheese selection. ££

JAPANESE

Daruma-ya, 82 Commercial Street, Leith, tel: 554 7660. A most succesful husband and wife team restaurant serving Japanese food at Scottish prices (the wife is Japanese, the husband a Scot). Housed in a converted warehouse, the decor is minimal and tasteful. Ten different food categories on the menu. ££

MEXICAN

Viva Mexico, 41 Cockburn Street, tel: 226 5145. Cosy restaurant that transfers the diner back to the atmosphere of old Mexico. Food (for some) on the spicy side. Good selection for vegetarians. Great margaritas. ££

Tex Mex, 47 Hanover Street, tel: 225 1796. Exactly as the name suggests: reasonably priced and authentic. ££

SCOTTISH

Carriages, Caledonian Hotel, Princes Stret, tel: 459 9988. Informal dining from a wide selection of dishes displayed on a central buffet. This is the place for

haggis, kangaroo and pigeon. View of courtyard garden. ££

The Dial, 44–46 George IV Bridge, tel: 225 7179. Bold, innovative, sophisticated interior. Select from six main courses which have a Mediterranean bias. When all other eateries have closed their kitchen The Dial still functions. ££

Igg's, 15 Jeffrey Street, tel: 557 8184. Is this small, cheery family run establishment a Scottish restaurant with Spanish influence or vice-versa? Either way the food, featuring game and seafood, is excellent. Full tapas menu at lunchtime. ££

Jackson's, 209–213 High Street, tel: 225 1793. Atmospheric basement restaurant serving imaginative Scottish cooking in somewhat cramped space. Very popular with tourists. Set lunch an excellent bargain. £££

Stac Polly, 29–33 Dublin Street, tel: 556 2231 and 8–10 Grindlay Street, tel: 229 5405. Enter especially the latter which is resplendent in tartan, and you are aware immediately that you are in Scotland. Food, making use of height, is served in three dimensions. The wine list may be modest but more than 70 malts are available. ££

36, 36 Great King Street, tel: 556 3636. A basement restaurant in the New Town with a subdued clublike atmosphere. The decor is contemporary and the dishes are "intrinsically Scottish with worldly influences". Definitely for that special occasion. ££

SEAFOOD

Café Royal Oyster Bar, 17a West Register Street, tel: 556 4124. An Edinburgh institution where the ambience is everything. Stained glass and polished wood Victorian atmosphere which is always bustling and where seafood is preferred. Also in the same chain are Queen Street Oyster Bar, 16a Queen Street, tel: 226 2530, and Leith Oyster Bar, 58 The Shore, tel: 554 6294. £–£££

Creelers, 3 Hunter Square, tel: 220 4447. Sit at this seafood

restaurant and watch buskers in a square just off the Royal Mile. Carnivores are not denied their pleasures. ££–£££

Marinette, 52 Coburg Street, Leith, tel: 555 0922. Fish and chips as they should be but rarely are: cooked with Gallic flair: simply the best. ££

Skippers, 1a Dock Place, Leith, tel: 554 1018. "Very fishy, very quayside, very French" with a somewhat nautical atmosphere. £££

The Shore, 3 The Shore, Leith, tel: 553 5080. Naturally on the waterfront where, in non-smoking dining room and bar (smoking alright) seafood with a Scottish flair is served. ££. The menu in the bar, where prices are less than in the main restaurant, is posted on the blackboard. £–££

SWISS

Denzler's, 121 Constitution Street, Leith, tel: 554 3268. Swiss specialities graciously served in a clean-cut, pastel-coloured dining room. Disappointing wine list. Easy parking. ££

THAI

Siam Erawan, 48 Howe Street, tel: 226 3675. The city's top Thai restaurant with authentic Thai food and laid-back waiters. Good wine list. Booking essential. ££

Sukhothai, 23 Brougham Place, tel: 229 1537. Good range of Thai dishes and obliging service. ££

VEGETARIAN

Bann's, 5 Hunter Square, tel: 226 1112. Just off the Royal Mile with outdoor tables where diners can enjoy the buskers in the square. Small smoke- free basement. Large portions served in an efficient, informal and friendly manner, but leave room for the seductive pastries. £

Helios Fountain, 7 Grassmarket, tel: 229 7884. A self-service non-smoking café in a craft shop, serving mostly organic and proper vegan food. Well established; excellent bread. Also a Helios café at the Theatre Workshop, 34 Hamilton Place, tel: 225 8802. £

Henderson's Salad Table, 94 Hanover Street, tel: 225 2131.Basement self-service eatery always busy, especially at lunch, with a mainly young clientele enjoying excellent vegetarian cookery. Real ale and wine. Also Henderson's Bistro in nearby Thistle Street, tel: 225 2605. Table service. Live music in evenings. £

Bistros

Cafe Rougé, 43 Frederick Street, tel: 225 4515. This stylish French bistro is part of a chain which seriously attempts to create the ambience of a French bistro. Patio dining. £

The Dome Bar & Grill, 14 George Street, tel: 624 8624. A modest menu of international dishes and a modest wine line served in a stunning (especially when the sun shines) domed 18th century building, once headquarters of a bank. Two bars. The setting is everything. Downstairs an upmarket nightclub for over-25s. ££–£££

The Doric Tavern, 15 Market Street, tel: 225 1084. A brash upstairs bistro, a long term favourite, with reasonable wine. Strong on vegetarian dishes. Pleasant at lunch and trendy in the evenings. £

Passepartout, 24 Deanhaugh Street, tel: 332 4476. Intimate restaurant just north of the city centre, with colonial era travel themed decor. Small changing menu, cosmopolitan cuisine and friendly service. ££

Waterfront Wine Bar & Bistro, 1c Dock Place, Leith, tel: 554 7427. Moderately priced fish dishes and good choice of vegetarian dishes

served in a conservatory on the dock. Excellent wine selection on blackboards. ££

Granary, 42 Queensferry Street, tel: 220 0550. Large, lively space at the west end of Princes Street with views onto the street. Good for breakfast and all-day dining. £

Ryan's, 2-4 Hope Street, tel: 226 7005. A pleasant, relatively small space below a pub at the west end of Princes Street. Small but imaginative menu and courteous staff. £

Cafés

Bewley's, 4 South Charlotte Street, tel: 220 1969. This renowned Irish institution, now in Edinburgh, continues its Dublin approach to dining – self-service at several counters and the dining area divided into several spaces. Open 8am–6pm. £

Blue Bar Café, Cambridge Street, tel: 221 1222. Upstairs in the Traverse Theatre, managed by Andrew Radford who also runs the highly successful downstairs Atrium. Modern, light dishes served in a minimalist blue ambience. £

Buffalo Grill, 14 Chapel Street, tel: 667 7427. A hamburger joint serving great inexpensive food. Vegetarians are not ignored. No licence. £

City Art Centre Café, 2 Market Street, tel: 220 3359. This attractive, mural-painted cafe emphasises vegetarian food. Seductive sweets. Open 8.30am–5.30pm. £

Clarinda's, 69 Canongate, Royal Mile, tel: 557 1888. A small crowded old-fashioned tea-room at the bottom of the Royal Mile which serves delightful home cooked snacks. Great cakes. £

Fruitmarket Café, Fruitmarket Gallery, 29 Market Street, tel: 226 1843. A contemporary bright stylish space, fronted by sliding floor to ceiling plate-glass windows and housing an art gallery. Light meals served 10.30am–5.30pm. £

Laigh Coffee House, 117a Hanover Street, tel: 225 1552. An old world stone-flagged basement kitchen

which serves glorious salads and cakes to die for. Self-service; very popular. £

Queen Street Café, Scottish National Portrait Gallery, Queen Street, tel: 557 2844. Delightful home-cooked food and excellent cakes offered (self-service) in a somewhat cramped space. Strong on vegetarian dishes. £

Scottish National Gallery of Modern Art, Belford Road, tel: 332 8600. Delightful self-service café with garden, serves delicious home-cooked lunches. Attracts many locals. Licensed. £

Valvona & Crolla Caffe Bar, 19 Elm Row, tel. 556 6066. A handsome, bright, airy conservatory recently built at the rear of what has been the city's finest deli for nearly 70 years. Freshly prepared light Italian cuisine – including breakfast dishes, and sumptuous pastries – is served from 8am–5pm. Any of the 600 Italian wines sold in the store may be purchased (prices range from £4–£500 a bottle) and brought into the cafe where it will be served (whites can be chilled in four minutes); corkage charge £2 a bottle. £–££

Attractions

Guided Tours

Auld Reekie Tours, 45 Niddry Street, tel: 557 4700. Underground city horror tours daily every hour from 12.30–3.30pm and 7–10pm. Start at Tron Kirk.
The Edinburgh Literary Pub Tour, tel: 226 6665. Daily in July and August at 6pm and 8.30pm; Thursday to Sunday at other times (Friday only November to March) at 7.30pm. Starts at Beehive Inn, Grassmarket.
Geowalks Volcano Tours, 24 Argyle Place, tel: 228 2410. Guided walks of Arthur's Seat and Holyrood Park April to September. Meet at Holyrood Palace car park 2pm Wednesday, Friday and Sunday. Booking advised.
Lothian Region Transport, 27 Hanover Street, tel: 544 4494/555 6363. Tours of Edinburgh. Day and half-day tours to other parts of Scotland. Evening "Taste of Scotland" and "Murder & Mystery" tours. Book at the Waverley Centre tourist office or one of the Ticket Centres in Hanover Street or on Waverley Bridge.
Mercat Ghost and History Walks, 47 Willowbrae Avenue, tel: 661 4541. Tours: Royal Mile Walk daily all year at 2pm (plus 11am April to September). Ghosts and Ghouls Tour all year at 7pm and 8pm. Ghosthunter Trail all year at 9.30pm (plus 10.30pm April to October). Day-time historical walks and haunting evening walks reveal the city's ancient past – optional pub visit in evening. Start at Mercat Cross outside St Giles, Royal Mile.
Robin's Ghost and History Tours, City Chambers, tel: 661 0125. Royal Mile Walk daily 10am, 11am.

Ghost Walks nightly at 7pm (plus 9pm April to November). Start outside the Tourist Information Centre on Princes Street (east end).
Scotline Tours, 87 High Street, tel: 557 0162. Tours of the city and surrounding areas, the Borders, St Andrews etc. Book at the Waverley Centre tourist office.
Witchery Tours, 352 Castlehill, Royal Mile, tel: 225 6745. Costumed walking tours start at the Witchery Restaurant. Book in advance for the Murder and Mystery Tour (every evening, all year) or the Ghosts and Gore Tour (every evening May to August).

Churches

The city has many fine churches, the grandest being the 15th-century High Kirk of St Giles on the High Street. Canongate Kirk can be visited, on application to the manse in Reid's Court. In the churchyard can be found the graves of famous people such as Robert Fergusson, Adam Smith and Burns's friend Clarinda.

Other impressive churches are St John's and St Cuthbert's at the west end of Princes Street. The former has a splendid collection of Victorian stained glass and its One World shop and restaurant in the crypt are both very popular. St Cuthbert's, an ancient church, was rebuilt by Hippolyte Blanc in 1894. Thomas de Quincey is buried in the churchyard and there is a

Viewpoints

At the east end of Princes Street, a 350ft (100 m) climb (or drive) is rewarded with views over the city and the Forth. The hill is topped by the Nelson monument, the old Observatory and "Edinburgh's folly", the reproduction of the Parthenon, begun in 1824 to commemorate the Scots who died in the Napoleonic Wars, and left unfinished when the money ran out. Even better views can be obtained if you climb to the top of

monument to Napier of Merchiston, inventor of logarithm. Nearby, in York Place, St Mary's Episcopalean Cathedral with its three spires is one of the largest Gothic churches built in Britain since the Reformation.

Greyfriar's Kirk, Candlemaker Row, a charming church, was the scene in 1638 of the adoption and signing of the National Covenant. In 1679, 1,400 covenanters were imprisoned in the kirkyard where there is a Martyrs' monument. Opposite stands the statue of Greyfriar's Bobby which, when it hasn't been covered in paint by irreverent students, fondly commemorates a Skye terrier which visited his master's grave daily for 14 years.

The Calton Burial Ground, off Waterloo Place, contains the graves of many luminaries, including David Hume.

Other Attractions

See also the box *Out and About with Children*, page 248.
Camera Obscura, Outlook Tower, Castlehill, Royal Mile, tel: 226 3709. Open April to October daily 10am–6pm (later in July and August); rest of year 10am–5pm. Camera presentations during daylight hours only. Enthralling 19th-century version of TV projects a moving picture onto a screen. Great views of Edinburgh.
Craigmillar Castle, Craigmillar Castle Road, tel: 661 4445. Open

the Nelson Monument (tel: 556 2716). Open April to September, Monday 1–6pm, Tuesday to Saturday 10am–6pm; rest of year Monday to Saturday 10am–3pm.

Good views can also be had from the tops of the other hills within the city, notably Arthur's Seat above Holyrood Park. An easier climb is up to the castle, either from Princes Street Gardens or up the gentler gradient of the Royal Mile.

April to September, Monday to Saturday 9.30am–6.30pm, Sunday 2–6.30pm; rest of year Monday to Saturday 9.30am–4.30pm (closed Thursday pm and all day Friday), Sunday 2–4.30pm. Delightful 15th-century castle. Mary Queen of Scots came here after the murder of Rizzio.

Dynamic Earth, opposite Palace of Holyrood House, tel: 550 7800. Open April to October, daily 10am–6pm; November to March, Wednesday to Sunday 10am–5pm. The formation and evolution of the planet are recreated in a series of galleries at this new attraction (opening May 1999) with lots of sophisticated interactive features.

Edinburgh Castle, Castlehill, tel: 225 9846. Open April to September daily 9.30am–6pm; rest of the year daily 9.30am–5pm. A magnificent Royal Fortress housing the crown jewels of Scotland, the Scottish National War Memorial, the Military Museum, the 12th-century St Margaret's chapel and the 15th-century palace apartments.

Edinburgh Experience, Old Observatory, Calton Hill, tel: 337 8530. Open April to October daily 10.30am–5pm. A 20-minute slide show explores the city in three-dimensional colour photography.

Lauriston Castle, Cramond Road South, tel: 336 2060/1921. Open April to October, daily except Friday 11am–5pm; rest of year Saturday and Sunday 2–4pm. Tower house originally built for Napier, father of logarithms. Completely refurbished in 1903 and Edwardian interior with 18th-century Italian furniture and oriental rugs well preserved.

National Library of Scotland, George IV Bridge, tel: 226 4531. Open all year Monday to Saturday, 10am–5pm, Sunday 2–5pm. Telephone for times and details of frequent exhibitions. Treasure-house of 5 million books and manuscripts. Currently closed for refurbishment.

Nelson Monument, Calton Hill, tel: 556 2716. April to September, Tuesday to Saturday 10am–6pm, Monday 1–6pm; October to March, Monday to Saturday 10am–3pm.

Clans and Ancestors

Edinburgh offers rich opportunities to the ancestor-hunter. In New Register House at the east end of Princes Street are records of every birth, marriage and death in Scotland since 1855, the national censuses since 1841, and parish records from even earlier. For a fee of about £6 a day you can inspect the records and should be able to trace several generations.

Information may be found in New Register House, tel: 334 0380, and in the Central Library on George IV Bridge, tel: 225 5584. The serious ancestor-hunter should read *Scottish Roots* by Alwyn James, which explains the various records in great detail.

Those keen to belong to a clan even though their name is Hui Bing, Watanabe or Berkovitch should visit the Scottish Tartans Museum, 39–41 Princes Street, tel: 556 1252; Clan Tartan Centre, 70–74 Bangor Road, Leith, tel: 553 5161; Kinloch Anderson, Commercial Street/Dock Street, Leith, tel: 555 1390; Edinburgh Old Town Weaving Co., 555 Castlehill, tel: 226 1555; Scots Ancestry Research Society, 29b Albany Street, tel: 556 4220 and/or Scottish Roots Ancestral Research Service, 16 Forth Street, tel: 477 8214. There, with the assistance of computers, they may find that they are Stuarts, Macduffs or McGregors.

Climb the 143 steps of this 106 foot (30 metre) high upturned telescope for stunning views of Edinburgh and its surroundings.

Palace of Holyroodhouse, foot of Royal Mile, tel: 556 7371/1096. Open April to October, daily 9.30am–5.15pm; rest of year, daily 9.30am–3.45pm. Palace may occasionally close for state visits; telephone for details. The Queen's official residence in Scotland. State apartments and portraits of 100 Scottish kings.

Royal Botanic Garden, Inverleith Row, tel: 552 7171. Open daily from 9.30am; closes around dusk in winter, at 7pm April to September. Rare and exotic plants from around the world. Extensive rhododendron collection. The Glasshouse Experience comprises 10 interconnected areas for climatic zones and different plant types.

Royal Observatory, Blackford Hill, tel: 668 8100. Open Monday to Saturday 10am–5pm, Sunday noon–5pm. Historical exhibition, discovery room and Scotland's largest telescope.

Royal Yacht Britannia, Ocean Drive, Leith Docks, tel: 555 5566. Open daily all year, 10.30am–6pm (last entry 4.30pm).The Queen's recently decommissioned luxury yacht has come to rest at Leith, where some of the quarters are now open to the public, supported by an on-shore visitor centre.

Scott Monument, Princes Street. This Edinburgh landmark is currently fenced off while restoration and development work is carried out. It is scheduled to reopen in late 2000 or 2001, when visitors will again be able to ascend to the top and to view a new historical exhibition.

Outside Edinburgh

Abbotsford House, Melrose, tel: (01896) 752916. Open mid-March to October, Monday to Saturday 10am–5pm, Sunday 2–5pm (from 10am in summer). This 19th-century mansion built by Sir Walter Scott contains relics associated with famous Scots history as well as Scott's library.

Blackness Castle, 4 miles (6 km) north of Linlithgow on B903, tel: (01506) 834807. Open April to September, daily 9.30am–6pm; rest of the year Monday to Saturday (except Thursday pm and Friday) 9.30am–4pm, Sunday 2–4pm. Once a 15th-century stronghold, then a state prison in Covenanting times and then a powder magazine. **Dalmeny House**, by South Queensferry, tel: (0131) 331 1888. Open July and August, Monday and Tuesday noon–5.30pm, Sunday 1–5.30pm. Stately home housing the Napoleon collection.

Dirleton Castle, 8 miles (13 km) west of North Berwick on A198, tel: (01620) 850330. Open April to September, Monday to Saturday 9.30am–6pm, Sunday 2–6pm; rest of the year Monday to Saturday 9.30am–4pm, Sunday 2–4pm. Ruins dating back to 1225 with 15th–17th-century additions. Garden encloses a 17th-century bowling green surrounded by yews.

Dunfermline Abbey and Palace, Monastery Street, Dunfermline, tel: (01383) 739026. Open in summer daily 9.30am–6.30pm; winter Monday to Saturday (except Thursday pm and Friday) 9.30am–4pm, Sunday 2–4pm. Robert the Bruce was buried beneath this great Norman church and Charles I was born in the guest house which was made into a royal palace.

Falkland Palace and Gardens, Falkland, tel: (01337) 857397. Open April to September, Monday to Saturday 11am–5.30pm, Sunday 1.30–5.30pm; October, Monday to Saturday 10am–5pm, Sunday 2–5pm. A Renaissance-style Royal palace in a picturesque small town. Delightful small gardens and the oldest real tennis court in Britain.

Floors Castle, Kelso, tel: (01573) 223333. Open April to October, daily 10am–4.30pm. Impressive mansion built in 1721. Holly tree in ground said to mark spot where James II was killed.

Gosford House, Longniddry, tel: (01875) 870201. Open June and July, Wednesday, Saturday and Sunday 2–5pm. This part-Robert Adam House with famous marble hall has splendid setting on Firth of Forth. Ornamental waters with wildlife including nesting wild geese.

Hopetoun House, west of South Queensferry, tel: (031) 331 2451. Open Easter to September, daily 10am–5.30pm. Home of the Hope family since 1703 this glorious Adam House is set in magnificent parkland. Superb place to visit.

House of the Binns, Linlithgow, tel: (01506) 834255. House open May to September, daily (except Friday), 1.30–5.30pm. Park open daily, April to October 10am–7pm; rest of the year 10am–4pm. Earliest part of the house dates from 1478 with major 17th-century additions.

John Muir Country Park, Dunbar, tel: (01368) 63886. Open at all times. Country park established in 1976 and named after Muir who was in the forefront of the movement to establish national parks such as Yosemite in the United States.

Lennoxlove House, 1 mile south of Haddington on B6369, tel: (01620) 823720. Open Easter to October, Wednesday, most Saturdays and Sunday 2–4.30pm. Romantic ancient house with associations with the Stewarts. Excellent collection of portraits and porcelain.

Linlithgow Palace, Linlithgow, tel: (01506) 842896. Open April to September, daily 9.30am–6.30pm; rest of year Monday to Saturday 9.30am–4.30pm, Sunday 2–4pm. The ruined palace where Mary Queen of Scots was born. Later housed Bonnie Prince Charlie.

Loch Leven Castle, on an island on Loch Leven, Kinross, tel: 0131-668 8800. Open April to September, Monday to Saturday 9.30am–6pm, Sunday 2–6pm. Mary Queen of Scots was imprisoned here in 1567 and escaped 11 months later.

"Maid of the Forth", Hawes Pier, South Queensferry, tel: 0131-331 4857. Open Easter to October daily. Ring for up-to-date details. Cruise under the Forth Bridge to lovely Inchcolm Island, medieval abbey, seal colony and bird sanctuary. Takes about two hours.

Mellerstain House, 7 miles (11 km)

Out and About with Children

Attractions recommended for the whole family in and near Edinburgh include:

Brass Rubbing Centre, Trinity Apse, Chalmers Close, High Street, tel: 556-4364. Open Monday to Saturday 10am–5pm; Sunday 2–4.45pm Easter to September only. Fascinating range of moulds, from Pictish stones to medieval brasses, located in the remains of one of the city's oldest churches. Free entry.

Butterfly and Insect World, Melville Nursery, Lasswade, tel: 663 4932. Open March to October daily 9.30am–5.30pm; November to January 10am–5pm. Tropical environment featuring free-flying butterflies plus insect displays. In the Bugs and Beasties room visitors are invited to handle tarantulas and snakes.

Deep Sea World, North Queensferry, Fife, tel: (01383) 411411/411880. Open July and August daily 10am–6.30pm; end of March to June, September, October 10am–6pm; November to March 11am–5pm (weekends and public holidays 10am–6pm). Europe's first "underwater safari", the largest aquarium of its kind in the world, giving a diver's eye-view of the denizens of the deep.

Edinburgh Zoo, Corstorphine Road, tel: 334 9171. Open April to September, daily 9am–6pm; October and March 9am–5pm; November to February 9am–4.30pm; Sundays from 9.30pm. The world's largest penguin enclosure and Europe's largest colony of penguins. In summer the 2pm penguin parades, when the birds mingle with visitors, are great fun.

Museum of Childhood, 42 High Street, tel: 529 4142. Open Monday to Saturday 10am–5pm, Sundays during the Festival 2–5pm. This was the first museum in the world to specialise in the history of childhood. Toys through the ages and from different countries. Popular with adults and children alike. Free.

northwest of Kelso, tel: (01573) 410225. Open Easter and May to September, Sunday to Friday 12.30–5pm. Glorious house, especially inside, begun by William Adam and completed by his son Robert. Attractive terraced gardens. **Neidpath Castle**, Peebles, tel: (01721) 720333. Open Easter to September, Monday to Saturday 11am–5pm, Sunday 1–5pm. Medieval castle. Superb views. **Preston Mill and Phantassie Doocot**, East Linton, 6 miles (10 km) west of Dunbar, tel: (01620) 860426. Open Easter and May to September, daily 11am–1pm and 2–5pm; October, Saturday and Sunday only 11am–1pm and 2–5pm. Picturesque water-mill, possibly the only one of its kind still in working condition in Scotland. **Rosslyn Chapel**, Roslin, 7 miles (11 km) south of Edinburgh on A703, tel: 0131-440 2159. Open Monday to Saturday 10am–5pm, Sunday noon–4.45pm (to 4pm in winter). Fifteenth-century chapel renowned for magnificent sculpture. **Tantallon Castle**, 3 miles (5km) east of North Berwick on A198, tel: (01620) 892727. Open April to September, Monday to Saturday 9.30am–6pm, Sunday 2–6pm; rest of year Monday to Saturday (except Thursday pm and Friday) 9.30am–4pm, Sunday 2–4pm. Extensive ruins of 14th-century stronghold in magnificent clifftop setting. **Thirlestane Castle**, Lauder, tel: (01578) 722430. Open Easter week 11am–4.15pm (last admission); May to October, daily except Saturday 11am–4.15pm (last admission). Castle steeped in Scottish history housing huge toy collection and Border Life Exhibition. **Traquair House**, Innerleithen, tel: (01896) 830323. Open April to September, daily 12.30–5.30pm (in June, July and August 10.30am–5.30pm); October Friday to Sunday 12.30–5.30pm. House rich in associations with Mary Queen of Scots, the Jacobites and Catholic persecution. Ale is still brewed in and sold from the 18th-century brewhouse.

Culture

Museums

Edinburgh Old Town Weaving Company, Castlehill, tel: 226 1555. Open Monday to Saturday 9am–5.30pm, Sunday 10am–5pm. This is no twee exhibition but a new functional factory which, with the aid of a water wheel, produces large quantities of tartan cloth. Visitors are offered the opportunity to try their hand at weaving. There's also a display of Highland costumes, a tartan shop and a bureau to determine whether the visitor has a family clan and tartan. **Georgian House**, 7 Charlotte Square, tel: 225 2160. Open April to October, Monday to Saturday 10am–5pm, Sunday 2–5pm. Town house furnished as a New Town house would have been in the period 1760–1820. **Gladstone's Land**, 477b Lawnmarket, tel: 226 5856. Open April to October, Monday to Saturday 10am–5pm, Sunday 2–5pm. A 17th-century tenement with one floor furnished as the home of a merchant and the ground floor reconstructed as a 17th-century shop. **Huntly House Museum**, 142 Canongate, tel: 529 4143. Open Monday to Saturday 10am–5pm, Sunday (during the Festival only) 2–5pm. The history of Edinburgh displayed in a 16th-century house. Free entry. **John Knox House**, 43-45 High Street, tel: 556 9579/556 2647. Open Monday to Saturday 10am–5pm. Medieval house that features religious reformer Knox's library and his meeting with Mary, Queen of Scots. **Museum of Scotland**, Chambers Street, tel: 225 7534. Open

Monday to Saturday 10am–5pm (late night Tuesday until 8pm), Sunday noon–5pm. National history museum in a new building adjoining the Royal Museum, opened at the end of 1998 to mark Scotland's transition to self-government. Contains ancient Scottish treasures including St Fillan's Crozier, a holy staff said to have given luck to Robert the Bruce. **Myreton Motor Museum**, Aberlady, 6 miles (10 km) southwest of North Berwick, tel: (01875) 870288. Open daily 10am–6pm. Varied collection of road transport from 1897 including World War II military vehicles. **The People's Story**, Canongate Tolbooth, Royal Mile, tel: 529 4057. Open Monday to Saturday 10am–5pm, Sunday (during Festival only) 2–5pm. The museum tells of the lives, work and leisure of the ordinary people from the 18th century to the present. Free entry. **Royal Museum of Scotland**, Chambers Street, tel: 225 7534. Open Monday to Saturday 10am–5pm (late night Tuesday till 8pm), Sunday noon–5pm. National collection of decorative arts, ethnography, natural sciences and technology. Often has special exhibitions and lectures. **Scotch Whisky Heritage Centre**, 354 Castlehill, Royal Mile, tel: 220 0441. Open June to September 9am–6pm; rest of the year 10am–5pm. Travel in whisky barrel through history of the "guid stuff": audio-visual show and tasting. **Scottish Agricultural Museum**, Ingliston, near Edinburgh, tel: 333 2674. Open April to September daily 10am–5pm; October to March Monday to Friday 10am–5pm. Life and work of Scotland's countryside over the past two centuries. Audio-visual presentations. **Scottish Mining Museum**, Lady Victoria Colliery, Newtongrange, tel: 663 7519. Open April to November 10am–5pm. Mining comes alive at this excellent museum. Guided tours with former miners and hands-on exhibits. Ten miles (16 kms) south of Edinburgh.

Festivals in the Scottish Capital

For 50 years, during the month of August, Edinburgh has been aglitter with the **Edinburgh International Festival** (last three weeks; general info: tel: 473 2001; bookings: 473 2000) and its associated **Fringe** (general: tel: 226 5257; bookings: 226 5138), which commences and finishes (officially) one week before the International Festival. Together they provide a feast of entertainment for young and old, high and low brow.

Other festivals held during August are the spectacular **Edinburgh Military Tattoo** (tel: 225

1188), the **Edinburgh International Film Festival** (tel: 228 4051), the **International Jazz Festival** (tel: 557 1642), and the **Edinburgh Book Festival** (tel: 228 5444).

In March there's a week-long annual **Folk Festival** (tel: 557 1050) and a two-week annual **International Science Festival** (tel: 473 2070) which extends into the month of April.

In October, those who want to know about the "guid stuff" will wish to attend the **Edinburgh and Speyside Whisky Festival** (tel: 473 3800), whose features have

included blend-your-own-whisky, a whisky nosing competition, "illicit still walks" and whisky master classes.

Then for four days, commencing 29 December, Edinburgh's **Hogmanay Festival** (tel: 473 1999) is held, culminating on New Year's Eve (Hogmanay) in what may well be Britain's biggest street party complete with fireworks. A Scottish food fare, ceilidhs, a torch-lit procession and fire festival are some of the activities during the Hogmanay bash. The Millennium celebrations promise to be the biggest yet.

Scottish Tartans Museum, The Scotch House, 39–41 Princes Street, tel: 556 1252. Open Monday to Saturday 9am–5pm (Thursday until 7pm), Sunday noon–4.30pm. Probably the only "real" tartan museum in Edinburgh, if not in Scotland. Glorious displays of costumes and 700 tartans. Explanations in several languages.
The Writers' Museum, Lady Stair's House, off Lawnmarket, Royal Mile, tel: 529 4901. Open 10am–5pm, Sunday (during Festival only) 2–5pm. Built in 1622 and now a museum devoted to Burns, Scott and Stevenson. Free entry.

Art Galleries

The city centre boasts over 50 venues which regularly hold exhibitions of art and crafts. The permanent collections of the National Galleries are balanced by temporary exhibitions of important Scottish and international artists and by the hoard of small, privately-run galleries with frequently changing shows of paintings, prints, sculpture, glassware and jewellery. Entry is free to all the galleries, but for special exhibitions there is a small charge.
Calton Gallery, 10 Royal Terrace, tel: 556 1010. Open Monday to Friday 10am–6pm, Saturday 10am–1pm. Exclusive fine art

dealers in 19th- and 20th-century Scottish paintings and watercolours.
City Art Centre, 2 Market Street, tel: 529 3993. Open June to September, Monday to Saturday 10am–5.30pm, Sunday during Festival 2–5pm; rest of year Monday to Saturday 10am–5pm. Council-run gallery which hosts a wide variety of exhibitions including international scoops like the Emperor's Warriors from China and the Gold of the Pharaohs.
Collective Gallery, 22–28 Cockburn Street, tel: 220 1260. Open Tuesday to Saturday 11am–5.30pm (5pm Friday), or by arrangement. Innovative gallery specializing in Scottish and other young contemporary trailblazers.
Dean Gallery, Belford Road, tel: 624 6200. Monday to Saturday 10am–5pm, Sunday 2–5pm. Recently opened outpost of the National Gallery of Modern Art, housing the collection of Leith-born Sir Eduardo Paolozzi, including Dada and Surrealist works. Also temporary exhibitions.
Demarco European Art Foundation, New Parliament House, Building No. 2, 5–7 Regent Road, tel: 557 0707. Monday to Saturday 10am–6pm. The renowned figure behind this gallery guarantees that there will usually be an interesting, if not extraordinary, exhibition here.

Edinburgh Printmakers Workshop, 23 Union Street, tel: 557 2479. Tuesday to Saturday 10am–6pm. Interesting exhibitions of prints above the workshop where classes are run.
Fruitmarket Gallery, 45 Market Street, tel: 225 2383. Monday to Saturday 10am–6pm, Sunday noon–5pm. The venue for Edinburgh's most striking showings of contemporary international artists.
National Gallery of Scotland, The Mound, tel: 556 8921. Monday to Saturday 10am–5pm, Sunday 2–5pm. There are many delights here, some of the best on loan from the Duke of Sutherland. The collection spans from the Renaissance to Post-Impressionism. Recorded information on the exhibitions in the National, Modern and Portrait Galleries is available on: 332 4939.
Portfolio Gallery, 43 Candlemaker Row, tel: 220 1911. Tuesday to Saturday noon–5.30pm. Photography gallery concentrating on Scottish work.
Royal Scottish Academy, The Mound, tel: 225 6671. Monday to Saturday 10am–5pm, Sunday 2–5pm. Various touring exhibitions and the annual shows of the Scottish artists' organisations.
The Scottish Gallery, 16 Dundas Street, tel: 558 1200. Monday to

Friday 10am–6pm; Saturday 10am–4pm. Regularly changing exhibitions of contemporary artists, occasional past masters and interesting modern jewellery and ceramics.

Scottish National Gallery of Modern Art, Belford Road, tel: 556 8921. Monday to Saturday 10am–5pm; Sunday 2–5pm. Beyond bijou Dean Village, this old school building overlooking a broad lawn has an exciting permanent collection of 20th-century painting, sculpture and graphic art.

Scottish National Portrait Gallery, 1 Queen Street, tel: 556 8921. Monday to Saturday 10am–5pm; Sunday 2pm–5pm. Famous Scots from time immemorial. Also the fascinating Scottish Photography Archive.

Stills Gallery, 23 Cockburn Street, tel: 662 6200. Tuesday to Saturday 10am–6pm. Small but potent photography exhibitions.

Talbot Rice Gallery, Old College, University of Edinburgh, tel: 650 2211. Tuesday to Saturday 10am–5pm (open seven days during the Edinburgh Festival). The University's restful exhibition space has a high standard of temporary shows, often by contemporary artists.

369 Gallery, 223 Cowgate, tel: 225 3013. Tuesday to Saturday noon–6pm. Large, modern gallery which promotes young artists' work.

Scottish Entertainment

At several locations an evening of Scottish entertainment with lots of bagpipe music and tartan may be enjoyed. Dinner is usually included in the admission price. These entertainments are mounted for the visitor rather than for the locals.

Hail Caledonia Scottish Evening, Carlton Highland Hotel, North Bridge, tel: 472 3000. May to September at 7pm.

Jamie's Scottish Evening, King James Thistle Hotel, 107 Leith Street, tel: 556 0111. Tuesday to Sunday from April to October at 7pm.

Scottish Evening, George Inter-Continental Hotel, 19-21 George Street, tel: 225 1251. May to September, Sunday to Thursday at 7pm for 7.15pm. Possibly the best show in town.

A Taste of Scotland, Round Stables, Prestonfield House, Priestfield Road, tel: 668 3346. April to October, Sunday to Friday at 7pm. Festival of food and entertainment in a superb historical setting.

More authentic entertainment in the form of ceilidhs (informal, energetic dances to ceilidh bands playing Scottish folk music) can be enjoyed at:

Assembly Rooms, 54 George Street, tel: 220 4348. Occasional – usually Friday – throughout the year.

Caledonian Brewery, 42 Slateford Road, tel: 337 1286. Usually every other Saturday 8–11.45pm. Top ceilidh bands, food and drink.

Spontaneous entertainment can be found at:

Tron Ceilidh House, 9 Hunter Square, tel: 226 0931. Behind the Tron church at the corner of High Street and "The Bridges". For details see *Nightlife: Pubs with Live Music*, page 252.

Theatre

Outside the theatrical mayhem of the International Festival and Fringe, Edinburgh has a solid core of theatres, each with its own style of production and habitual audience.

Bedlam Theatre, 2 Forrest Road, tel: 225 9873. Slightly seedy, converted church which is home to the University Theatre Company. Productions can be brilliant or awful.

Brunton Theatre, High Street Musselburgh, tel: 665 2240. Located outside the city centre, the theatre is building a reputation for good, family theatre.

Church Hill Theatre, 33 Morningside Road, tel: 447 7597. Mainly amateur productions of varying quality.

Festival Theatre, 13–29 Nicholson Street, tel: 529 6000. Finally, in 1994 Edinburgh opened its grand theatre with the largest stage in

Comedy

Edinburgh has recently acquired a permanent comedy venue: **The Stand**, 5 York Place, tel: 558 7272. Performances throughout the week. Regular slots include a comedy quiz show every Wednesday evening and improvised comedy (free entry) Sunday afternoons.

Britain. Scottish Opera and Scottish ballet now perform here.

Kings Theatre, 2 Leven Street, tel: 220 4349. Beautifully renovated, gilt and velvet theatre where large-scale touring productions tend to pause. On the whole it is middle of the road fare, but it can reach dizzy heights when the National Theatre or some such ventures north.

Netherbow Arts Centre, 43 High Street, tel: 556 9579. Small-scale theatre from various local and touring groups, notably the interesting Oxygen House, who stage a regular lunchtime series.

Playhouse Theatre, 18–22 Greenside Place, tel: 557 2590. Big-name comedians, touring musicals and infrequent plays.

Royal Lyceum, Grindlay Street, tel: 248 4848. Edinburgh's repertory theatre airs the classics and stages the occasional new play. Highly respectable productions, they often fall short of the innovative.

Theatre Workshop, 34 Hamilton Place, tel: 226 5425. Small theatre space hosting exciting touring companies, and the Workshop's own lively pro-am productions.

Traverse Theatre, 10 Cambridge Street, tel: 228 1404. The place to see new Scottish theatre and new translations of foreign plays. The Traverse affords a glimpse of the exciting and controversial and is one of the most important theatres in Britain for performing new work.

Music and Dance

Assembly Rooms, 54 George Street, tel: 220 4348. A variety of events including ethnic music.

Festival Theatre, 13–29 Nicholson

Street, tel: 529 6000. Opened in 1994, with the largest stage in Britain. Scottish Opera and Scottish Ballet companies perform here.
Playhouse Theatre, 18–22 Greenside Place, tel: 557 2590. This massive venue, seating over 3,000, is the city's port of call for rock and pop stars on tour.
Queen's Hall, Clerk Street, tel: 668 2019. A charming concert hall, home of the dynamic Scottish Chamber Orchestra, whose winter season of concerts is performed either here October to May. There is a regular series of jazz concerts on Fridays, and a variety of other concerts during the week.
Reid Hall, Teviot Row, University of Edinburgh, tel: 650 2423. Irregular classical concerts and the annual performance of Bach's St Matthew Passion on or near Good Friday. The

Cinema

Cameo, 38 Home Street, tel: 228 4141. Stylish, independent cinema showing well-selected new releases. Late-night double-bills and Sunday afternoon showings cater for movie buffs.
ABC Film Centre, 120 Lothian Road, tel: 228 1638. Three screens show the latest releases. Licensed bar.
Dominion, 18 Newbattle Terrace, tel: 447 2660 (recorded information), 447 4771 (bookings and enquiries). Cosy, four-screen cinema. Booking is usually necessary for the long-running favourites in the small Cinema 3. Licensed bar and restaurant.
Filmhouse, 88 Lothian Road, tel: 228 2688. Even a passing interest in cinema makes a visit here essential. Three screens show well-constructed special seasons and a basic diet of interesting international movies. The Edinburgh International Film Festival is held here during August. Licensed bar.
Odeon, 7 Clerk Street, tel: 668 2101. Commercial new releases on five screens. Licensed bar.

Reid also houses a collection of historic musical instruments. Open Wednesday 3–5pm, Saturday 10am–1pm (also Monday to Friday 2–5pm during the Festival). Tel: 447 4791.
St Cecilia's Hall, Cowgate, University of Edinburgh, tel: 650 2805. A beautiful little concert hall, the city's earliest, dating from 1763. It houses classical concerts and the university's collection of keyboard instruments.
Scottish Ballet (tel: 0141 331 2931) gives a week of performances in Edinburgh, usually twice a year, at the Festival Theatre. Well-respected company with a wide repertoire of new and classic ballet.

Dance companies from England and abroad also visit the city on a fairly regular basis.
Scottish Opera (tel: 0141 248 4567) have built a reputation for punchy productions of the classics and modern opera. They visit the Festival Theatre for week-long seasons in spring, summer and autumn. Scottish Opera Go Round present reduced versions, for principals and piano, of interesting operas. Their tours of smaller venues often bring them to Portobello Town Hall.

Edinburgh boasts a handful of amateur opera companies who each perform a full-scale opera once a year. Productions run from Gilbert & Sullivan to grand opera.
Usher Hall, Lothian Road, tel: 228 8616. Full-scale concert hall, built by the brewer Andrew Usher at the turn of the century. Currently closed for renovation, but will be open for the Festival period in August 1999.
The Venue, 15–21 Calton Road (behind Waverly Station), tel: 557 3073. Long-established rock and pop music venue. The Venue has hosted big names such as Nirvana and Scottish bands Texas and Primal Scream. Also up-and-coming bands. Live music Sunday to Thursday.

Many pubs have live music in the evenings – see the next section.

Nightlife

Pubs

Most pubs in Edinburgh now sell "real ale", cask-conditioned beer in various strengths (60°, 70° and 80°) made by Scottish brewers, large and small. Ask for 80/- ("eighty shilling"). Connoisseurs should look out for Caledonian 70/- and 80/-, which are made using traditional methods in a Victorian brewery in the city. Most pubs have a reasonable selection of malt whiskies.

Licensing hours in Edinburgh are liberal. If you try hard enough, so they say, you can drink for 22 out of 24 hours. Certainly, there is no shortage of pubs which are "open all day", which usually means from about 11am until midnight or 1am. Sunday afternoons can be more difficult, but the desperate can always try a hotel bar. Most bars are bearable, and some of the traditional drinking haunts shouldn't be missed.
The Abbotsford, 3 Rose Street, tel: 225 5276.
Bennets, 8 Leven Street, tel: 229 5143.
Café Royal Circle Bar, 17 West Register Street, tel: 556 1884.
The Canny Man's (The Volunteer Arms), 237 Morningside Road, tel: 447 1484.
Diggers (The Athletic Arms), 1 Angle Park Terrace, tel: 337 3822.
Leslie's Bar, 45 Ratcliffe Terrace, tel: 667 5957.

PUBS WITH LIVE MUSIC
Drinking is the main evening pursuit in Edinburgh pubs, but many feel duty-bound to provide some sort of music at the weekend. Others are the venue for semi-spontaneous outflowings of traditional music.

Nightclubs

The Cavendish, Coasters, 3 West Tollcross, tel: 228 3252. Open Thursday to Saturday 10pm–3am. Popular disco specialising in 1960s and 1970s music with a smattering of live bands. Friday night is reggae night.
Club Mercado, 36–39 Market Street, tel: 226 4224. Trendy club with state-of-the-art decor.
Dome, 14 George Street, tel: 624 8624. An upmarket nightclub in occupying the basement of an elegant new bar and grill in what was once the headquarters of a bank.
The Liquid Room, 9c Victoria Street, tel: 225 2564. Club nights throughout the week provide music to suit a range of tastes, plus occasional live music.

Minus One, Carlton Highland Hotel, North Bridge, tel: 556 7277. Designed for the more mature, more sedate night-clubber.
Po-Na-Na, 43b Frederick Street, tel: 226 2224. This small, central and not-too-busy club advertises itself as a soul bar. DJs spin nightly everything from dub to disco.
Wilkie House, 207 Cowgate, tel: 225 2935. Very student-, and at times gay-orientated.
The Venue, 15–21 Calton Road (behind Waverly Station), tel: 557 3073. Live music and club venue (club nights Friday and Saturday). Pure was the UK's first techno club; it still runs fortnightly on Friday until late.

The Antiquary, 77–78 St Stephen Street, tel: 225 2858. Cosy cellar bar with an informal celtic folk session every Thursday.
Ensign Ewart, 521 Lawnmarket, the Royal Mile, tel: 225 7440. A great spot near the castle for Scottish folk music at weekends.
Fiddler's Arms, 9/11 Grassmarket, tel: 229 2665. Folk music on Mondays.
Finnegan's Wake, 9b Victoria Street, tel: 226 3816. Spacious pub offers the hottest folk music with live music nightly.
Green Tree, 180–4 Cowgate, tel: 225 1294. Folk sessions on Tuesdays.
Hebrides, 17 Market Street, tel: 220 4213. This small pub is a great venue for folk music on Friday, Saturday and Sunday evenings.
Malt Shovel, 11–15 Cockburn Street, tel: 225 6843. Tuesday is jazz night.
Sandy Bell's, 25 Forrest Road, tel: 225 2751. Long renowned for live folk music.
The Shore, 3 The Shore, tel: 553 5080. Pleasant folk and jazz music in a popular harbour-front bar.
Tron Ceilidh House, 9 Hunter Square, tel: 226 0931. Its music all the way, almost every day, at this

legendary Edinburgh pub. Informal turn-up-and-play session every evening except Sunday, also Saturday afternoon; top folk bands in cellar bar Saturday and some Sunday nights.
Whistle Binkies, 6 Niddry Street, tel: 557 5114. Live folk, jazz or rock music nightly at this intimate bar.

Gay Nightlife

Broughton Street is Edinburgh's mini-Castro.
New Town Bar, 26b Dublin Street, tel: 538 7775. Cruisy, popular with the older civilized crowd. From 10pm–1am Thursday to Sunday there's a disco, **Intense**, downstairs (men only Friday and Saturday).
Blue Moon Café, 60 Broughton Street, tel: 556 2788. Well-established bar and café with three rooms. Breakfast served all day.
Café Kudos, 22 Greenside Place, tel: 558 1270. Smart café in the gay district. Good food.
C.C. Blooms, 23 Greenside Place, tel: 556 9331. Bar with dance floor space. Karaoke. Busy and popular with the young crowd.
French Connection, 89 Rose Street North tel: 225 7651. An intimate bar. Karaoke.

No Eighteen, 18 Albert Place, tel: 553 3222. Sauna club for gay gentlemen. Monday to Saturday, noon–10pm, Sunday 2–10pm.
Planet Out, 6 Baxter's Place, tel: 524 0061. Gay bar. Food served until 9pm (7pm weekends).
Taste at The Honeycomb, 36–38a Blair Street, tel: 220 4381. Clubbers, both gay and straight, make for here on Sunday 11pm–3am.

Casinos

If you want to gamble at a casino, the law requires that you become a member of the club about 48 hours before you play. Membership is free. Men are expected to wear a jacket and tie.
Berkeley Casino Club, 2 Rutland Place, tel: 228 4446.
Casino Martell, 7–11 Newington Road, tel: 667 7763.
Stakis Maybury Casino, 5 South Maybury Road, tel: 338 4444.
Stanley Edinburgh Casino Club, 5b York Place, tel: 624 2121.

Sport

Participant Sports

SPORTS CENTRES

Craiglockhart Sports Centre, 177 Colinton Road, tel: 443 0101. Open Monday to Thursday 9am–11pm, Friday 10am–11pm, Saturday and Sunday 9am–10.30pm. Noted especially for its tennis courts but also has squash, badminton, weights, fitness room and boating pond.

Marco's Leisure Centre, 51–95 Grove Street, tel: 228 2141. A privately-run club with squash courts, gym, pool tables, sauna, sunbeds. Non-members can use the facilities but cannot book them. Avoid lunchtime and evenings.

Meadowbank Sports Centre, 139 London Road, tel: 661 5351. Open daily 9.30am–10.30pm. Scotland's premier athletic arena. More than 60 sports and activities available.

Saughton Sports Complex, Stevenson Drive, tel: 444 0422. Open Monday to Thursday 8am–10.30pm, Friday 11am–10.30pm, Saturday 8am–6.30pm, Sunday 8am–10.30pm. All-weather synthetic track, tennis and more.

SWIMMING

Royal Commonwealth Pool, 21 Dalkeith Road, tel: 667 7211. Open all year 9am–9pm Monday to Friday (Wednesday from 10am) and summer weekends, winter weekends 10am–4pm. Check for extended hours in summer. Has Europe's largest indoor flume.

Ainslie Park, 92 Pilton Drive, tel: 551 2400. Open Monday to Friday 10am–10pm (early morning swim Wednesday 7–8am), Saturday and Sunday 10am–6pm.

Leith Waterworld, 377 Easter Road, Leith, tel: 555 6000. Open Wednesday and Thursday 10am–1pm, Friday to Sunday 10am–5pm. Closed Monday and Tuesday. Calls itself the "ultimate water experience". More than 20 water features and a beach area.

GOLF

Municipal courses are open seven days a week (with the exception of Braid Hills No. 1 course which closes on Sunday) and are unaffected by public holidays except Christmas Day.

Braid Hills, No. 1 and No. 2 courses, Braid Hills, tel: 447 6666.

Carrick Knowe Golf Course, Balgreen Road, tel: 337 1096.

Craigentinny Golf Course, Craigentinny Avenue, tel: 554 7501.

Portobello Golf Course, (9 holes), Stanley Street, tel: 669 4361.

Silverknowes Golf Course, Silverknowes Parkway, tel: 336 3843.

In addition to the above, Edinburgh has a number of private golf clubs, most of which welcome visitors.

Winter Sports

Midlothian Ski Centre, Hillend, Biggar Road, tel: 445 4433. Open 9.30am–9pm Monday to Friday all year; September to April, Saturday 9.30am–9pm, Sunday 9.30am–7pm; May to August Saturday and Sunday 9.30am–7pm. Largest artificial ski slope in Europe.

Murrayfield Ice Rink, 13 Riversdale Crescent, tel: 337 6933. Ice skating. Phone for opening times. Next door is **Murrayfield Curling**, tel: 346 7353.

Spectator Sports

FOOTBALL

Edinburgh has two premier division teams. Heart of Midlothian (Hearts) play at Tynecastle Park, Gorgie Road, tel: 200 7200. Hibernian (Hibs) play at Easter Road Park, tel: 661 2159. Matches are on Saturday afternoons and some weekday evenings.

ATHLETICS

Meadowbank Stadium, 139 London Road, tel: 661 5351.

OTHER SPORTS

Basketball: The Edinburgh Rocks is the only Scottish team in the Budweiser League. Weekend matches are played September to April at Meadowbank Sports Centre, 139 London Road. Tel: 476 7201.

Horse Racing: Musselburgh Racecourse, Linkfield Road, tel: 665 2859.

Ice Hockey: The local team, Murrayfield Racers play at Murrayfield Ice Rink, Riversdale Crescent, tel: 337 6933.

Rugby: Murrayfield Stadium, tel: 346 5000. Hosts international rugby matches throughout the season.

Shopping

Those who enjoy wandering up back streets and stumbling across a treasure of a shop will find plenty in Edinburgh to divert them. Once you get away from Princes Street and the same array of shopfronts which dominates every high street in Britain, there is a host of specialist shops and idiosyncratic traders, where buying can feel like a personal choice rather than a pre-conditioned, subliminal reaction to marketing and muzak.

THE OLD TOWN

The Grassmarket has mostly been taken over by restaurants and bars, but Victoria Street offers an exceptional range of curio shopping with the **Byzantium Market** at the top featuring a range of craft stalls. The Royal Mile is mostly given over to souvenirs and tartan, with a vast but predictable range. But running off this is Cockburn Street for the trendy shopper, with such shop names as **Whiplash Trash** and **Return to Sender.**

THE NEW TOWN

Princes Street remains Edinburgh's main shopping street with the predictable presence of **Marks & Spencer, BhS, Debenhams, Frasers, Boots, Virgin Megastore,** and **Waterstone's. Jenners** is the last of the independently owned Princes Street department stores.

There are two indoor shopping centres at the east end of Princes Street: the large, bland St James Centre (with a big John Lewis) and the more tourist-oriented Waverley Shopping Centre in a light modern building.

Streets parallel to Princes Street, such as pedestrianised Rose Street, the larger, upmarket George Street, and Thistle Street, provide a range of smaller shops. Stockbridge and Broughton Street are good for antique hunters.

Specialist Stores

HAGGIS

Crombies of Edinburgh, 97 Broughton Street.
Macsween of Edinburgh, 118 Bruntsfield Place.

SCOTCH WHISKY

Cadenhead Whisky Shop, 172 Canongate.
Royal Mile Whiskies, 379–381 High Street.
The Whisky Shop, Waverley Shopping Centre, Princes Street.

HIGHLAND DRESS AND TARTAN

Geoffrey (Tailor) Highland Crafts, 57–59 High Street.
Hector Russell Kiltmaker, 95 Princes Street, 137–141 High Street, and 509 Lawnmarket.
Hugh Macpherson (Scotland), 17 West Maitland Street.
John Morrison Kiltmaker, 473 Lawnmarket.
Kinloch Anderson, Commercial Street/Dock Street, Leith. Kiltmakers to the Royal Family.
Murray Brothers, 495 Lawnmarket.
The Scotch House, 39–41 Princes Street.
Stewart Christie, 63 Queen Street.

TRADITIONAL OUTFITTERS

Burberry's and the Scotch House, 39/41 Princes Street.
Crombie, 63 George Street.
Ede & Ravenscroft, 46 Frederick Street.

OUTDOOR PURSUITS

Blacks, 24 Frederick Street.
John Dickson & Son, 21 Frederick Street.
Rohan Designs, 86 George Street.
Tiso, 115–123 Rose Street.

DESIGNER SCOTTISH CASHMERE

Belinda Robertson Cashmere, 22 Palmerston Place.
Cashmere Store, 67 George Street, 1 Princes Street and 555 Castlehill.
Designs on Cashmere, 28 High Street.
Harrisons of Edinburgh, 24 Jane Street.

SCOTTISH WOOLLENS

Bill Baber Knitwear Design, 66 Grassmarket.
Canongate Jerseys, 166 Canongate.
Edinburgh Woollen Mill, 62 & 139 Princes Street, and 543 Lawnmarket.
Gleneagles of Scotland, Unit 27–28, Waverley Shopping Centre.
Judith Glue, 64 High Street.
Mill Shop, 134c Princes Street.
Number Two, 2 St Stephen Street.
Old Town Knitwear, 125 Canongate.
Ragamuffin, 276 Canongate.
Sheeps Clothing for Ewe, 46 High Street.
The Shetland Connection, 491 Lawnmarket.
Simply Scotland, 299 Canongate.
The Woollen Mill, 179 High Street.

SCOTTISH JEWELLERY

Clarksons of Edinburgh, 87 West Bow.
Hamilton & Inches, 87 George Street.
Joseph Bonnar, 72 Thistle Street.

ANTIQUES

Aldric Young, 49 Thistle Street.
Auchinleck, 143 West Port.
Bacchus, 95 West Bow Street.
Bow-well Antiques, 103–105 West Bow.
Carson Clark Gallery, 181–183 Canongate. Antique maps.
James Scott, 43 Dundas Street.
Laurence Black, 60 Thistle Street.
Phillips, 65 George Street.
Sotherby's, 112 George Street.
Unicorn Antiques, 65 Dundas Street.

Antique and Period Jewellery

Laing the Jeweller, 29 Frederick Street.
Mappin & Webb, 88 George Street.
Ortak Jewellery, Unit 29, Waverley Shopping Centre.
Ringmaker, Unit 19, Waverley Shopping Centre.
Royal Mile Curios, 363 High Street.
Scottish Gems, 24 High Street.

ART

Bourne Fine Art, 6 Dundas Street.
Dundas Street Gallery, 6a Dundas Street.
The Edinburgh Gallery, 18 Dundas Street.
Malcolm Innes Gallery, 4 Dundas Street.
The Scottish Gallery, 16 Dundas Street.

CRAFTS

Azteca, 16 West Bow and 5 Grassmarket.
Braveheart Trading Post, 189 Canongate.
Byzantium, 9a Victoria Street.
Clarksons, 87 West Bow.
Celtic Craft Centre, 101 High Street.
Geoffrey (Tailor) Highland Crafts, 555 Castlehill.
Helios Fountain, 7 Grassmarket.
Rana, 88–92 West Bow.
Ware on Earth, 15 Howe Street.

BAGPIPES

Kilberry Bagpipes, 38 Lochrin Buildings, Gilmore Place, Tolcross.

SCOTTISH HERALDRY

Claymore Studios, 173 Canongate.

BOOKSHOPS

Bauermeister, 19 George IV Bridge.
James Thin, 53 South Bridge Road and 57 George Street.
McNaughtan's Bookshop, 3a–4a Haddington Place. Second-hand and antiquarian books.
Waterstones, 83 George Street, 13–14 Princes Street and 128 Princes Street.

Shopping Hours

High Street and Princes Street shops are open 9am–5.30pm Monday to Saturday, and till 7pm or 8pm on a Thursday. Smaller shops may not open until 10am, and may close at 6pm or later. Since Waterstones introduced competition to the bookselling market, the big bookshops open until 10pm during the week, and are open on Sunday afternoons. While Princes Street is mainly closed on a Sunday, a growing number of shops are open. The big out-of-town shopping centres and local grocers also disrespect the Sabbath.

Customer Complaints

Contact Advice Shop at 85–87 South Bridge Street, tel: 225 1255.

Export

Some shops operate a VAT refund scheme for visitors, which allows you to claim back tax on goods you buy and take out of the country. Ask the shopkeeper for details.

Further Reading

General

Black, George P., *A History of Edinburgh's Volcano – Arthur's Seat*, Oliver & Boyd (1966).
Bruce, George, *A Festival in the North*, Hale (1975).
Cant, Malcolm, *Villages of Edinburgh: An Illustrated Guide*, 2 vols, Malcolm Cant Publications (1997).
Chambers, *Traditions of Edinburgh: Anecdotes of People and Places in the Old Town*, first published 1824, Chambers (1996).
Corrance, Douglas, *Edinburgh*, Collins (1979).
Daiches, David (ed.), *Edinburgh: A Travellers' Companion*, Constable (1986).
Dudley Edwards, Owen, *City of a Thousand Words: Edinburgh in Festival*, Mainstream Publishing (1991).
Dudley Edwards, Owen, and Richardson, Graham, *Edinburgh*, Canongate (1983).
Fraser, Duncan, *Edinburgh in Olden Times*, Standard Press (1976).
Harris, Stuart, *The Place Names of Edinburgh*, Gordon Wright Publishing (1996).
Gifford, John, McWilliam, Colin, and Walker, David, *The Buildings of Scotland: Edinburgh*, Penguin Books (1991).
Lochhead, Marion, *Edinburgh: Lore and Legend*, Robert Hale (1986).
Massie, Allan, *Edinburgh*, Sinclair-Stevenson (1994).
McKean, Charles, *Edinburgh: An Illustrated Architectural Guide* (1992). Available from RIAS Bookshops, 15 Rutland Square, Edinburgh EH1 2BE.
Mullay, Sandy, *The Edinburgh Encyclopoedia*, Mainstream Publishing (1996).
Nimmo, Ian, *Portrait of Edinburgh*, Batsford (1975).

Pennycook, Andrew, **Literary and Artistic Landmarks of Edinburgh**, Albyn Press (1973).

Stevenson, R.L., **Edinburgh: Picturesque Notes**, Salamander Press (1983).

Wright, Gordon, **A Guide to the Royal Mile: Edinburgh's Historic Highway**, Gordon Wright Publishing (1979).

Youngson, Alexander J., **The Making of Classical Edinburgh**, Edinburgh University Press (1988).

Other Insight Guides

Apa Publications produces three series of guidebooks to suit the needs of every traveller.

The 190-title **Insight Guides** series places destinations in their total cultural context and features some of the world's top photo-journalism.

The intensely practical **Compact Guides** series (almost 100 titles) structures information for handy on-the-spot reference, with text, pictures and maps all carefully cross-indexed. These are the books to look for when you are exploring particular areas of Great Britain in detail.

The 110-title **Insight Pocket Guides** series provides specific recommendations from a local host, aimed especially at visitors with limited time to spare, and most titles include a full-size fold-out map which can be used separately from the book.

The Compact and Pocket series are not cut-down versions of Insight Guides – they contain original material and are designed to complement the parent series.

• Insight Guides to the British Isles include:
Great Britain, Scotland, Wales, Oxford, Glasgow, Edinburgh, Channel Islands, Ireland and Dublin.

• Insight Pocket Guides cover:
South-East England, London, Scotland and Ireland.

• The Compact Guides series includes:
London, Bath, Cornwall, Devon & Exmoor, The Cotswolds, Oxford, Shakespeare Country, New Forest, South Downs, Lake District, York, North York Moors, Yorkshire Dales, Dublin, Scotland, Scottish Highlands and Edinburgh.

ART & PHOTO CREDITS

Photography by
Douglas Corrance
and
Catherine Karnow, cover
Bill Wassman, 26, 27

Maps Berndtson & Berndtson
Publications

© 1999 Apa Publications GmbH & Co.
Verlag KG (Singapore branch)

Cartographic Editor **Zoë Goodwin**

Production **Stuart A Everitt**

Design Consultants
Carlotta Junger, Vicky Pacey

Picture Research **Hilary Genin**

Index

The World of Insight Guides

400 books in three complementary series cover every major destination in every continent.

66 I was first drawn to the Insight Guides by the excellent "Nepal" volume. I can think of no book which so effectively captures the essence of a country. Out of these pages leaped the Nepal I know – the captivating charm of a people and their culture. I've since discovered and enjoyed the entire Insight Guide series. Each volume deals with a country in the same sensitive depth, which is nowhere more evident than in the superb photography. 99

Sir Edmund Hillary